THE INSIDE LOOK AT RUSSIA THAT HAS OPENED AMERICA'S EYES

"A profile of the Soviet *klass* system that is mind-boggling...analytical and often anecdotal...perceptive and politically astute"
Kansas City Star

"The most vivid and human indictment yet of the superstate's imperfections...captivating in the wealth of gritty detail he and his wife observed...convincing, often poignant"
The Cleveland Plain Dealer

"ONE OF THE MOST SIGNIFICANT REPORTS FROM THE SOVIET UNION TO APPEAR IN RECENT YEARS"
Barkham Reviews

KLASS
HOW RUSSIANS REALLY LIVE

David K. Willis

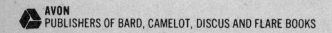

AVON
PUBLISHERS OF BARD, CAMELOT, DISCUS AND FLARE BOOKS

AVON BOOKS
A division of
The Hearst Corporation
105 Madison Avenue
New York, New York 10016

Copyright © 1985 by David K. Willis
Published by arrangement with St. Martin's Press
Library of Congress Catalog Card Number: 85-1740
ISBN: 0-380-70263-0

The St. Martin's Press edition contains the following Library of Congress Cataloging in Publication Data:

Willis, David K.
  Klass: how Russians really live.

  Includes index.
  1. Social classes—Soviet Union. 2. Soviet Union—Social conditions—1970–
1. Title.
HN530.Z9S6465   1985   305.5'0947   85-1740

First Avon Printing: June 1987

Printed in the U.S.A.

K-R 10 9 8 7 6 5 4 3 2 1

*To Margaret
With gratitude and love*

CONTENTS

AUTHOR'S NOTE

My wife and I and our three children, Sarah, Alexandra, and Alastair, lived in a dun-colored, eight-story, foreigners-only apartment block (built, it was said, by German prisoners of war) two floors above twelve lanes of traffic on Moscow's Sadovoye Koltso (Garden Ring Road) from August 1976 to January 1981.

We went with some trepidation but we had tears in our eyes as we left; it was a remarkable time of intensity, emotion, and learning.

We took with us the usual outsiders' preconceptions, hardly diminished for me by the first Russian word I saw after landing at Sheremetyevo airport: OGNEOPASNO, or "inflammable." It was stenciled on the side of a fuel tanker, but as I looked down at the khaki-uniformed, rifle-carrying KGB border guard at the foot of the ramp, thinking of the incredulity with which some of our friends had greeted our decision to take the Moscow assignment, I wondered whether it might be an omen as well.

It was not. We met our share of coldness, official as well as meteorological, but we found much warmth and spirit as well, not only in the close-knit Western community of diplomats, journalists, and businessmen, but also among Russian contacts. It took quite a while before we began even to sense the social nuances, the *klass* privileges, the striving for privilege that mark Soviet society; we offer our thanks and appreciation to all those who helped widen our understanding.

Our four and a half years was a period in which the détente of the early 1970s froze over. The Kremlin took great exception to President Carter's human-rights policies. The SALT talks ended. Soviet troops went into Afghanistan. The United States boycotted the 1980 Summer Olympics in Moscow. Staunch anticommunist Ronald Reagan ran for and won the Presidency. Yet some doors remained open.

To write this book I not only made use of invaluable contacts with American diplomats, including former ambassador Malcolm Toon, but most of all with innumerable conversations and meetings with Soviet citizens across the country. I traveled to more than forty cities in all fifteen Republics. Margaret, my wife, also traveled extensively. I have tried to protect sources wherever possible, for obvious reasons. Everything herein reflects the reality we found as accurately as possible; where I have felt obliged to make some changes, I have tried not to distort meaning or contexts.

To everyone who helped us, but especially to the people of the Soviet Union, my good friend Alexander Levich, and to the thirty or more other émigrés in Europe and the United States who have sat down with me since I left Moscow in 1981 for conversations often lasting many hours, I offer my deepest thanks.

The book could not have been written at all without the counsel and support of Margaret who succeeded triumphantly in turning her Moscow years into a happy, fulfilling time both in and out of her ballet classes. I have leaned heavily on her insights as well as my own, though the responsibility for any errors is wholly mine.

Often in distant, frozen cities like Yakutsk in Siberia, or in blazingly hot ones like Samarkand and Bukhara in Central Asia, we felt like privileged interlopers in societies as unfamiliar and remote as the dark side of the moon. We admire and feel compassion for all those Soviet individuals raising children and leading lives in a system that places Party above individual welfare.

We carry with us many incomparable memories of those four and a half years. Many of those to whom we owe the most must go unnamed, but they know who they are.

—*London, 1984.*

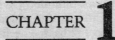

CLASS IN THE
CLASSLESS SOCIETY

"What's it like in Russia—I mean, really?" people ask when they discover I lived there. "How do people live?"

When such questions come, my mind goes back to two of the countless scenes imprinted by five winters and five summers of the most absorbing, most demanding, most intense, and most difficult years I have yet spent on this earth.

The first scene was a glimpse of life without class, privilege, or status almost seven decades after the 1917 Revolution was supposed to have created equality and eliminated class. The second illustrated some of the ways in which possession of class privilege can enrich and smooth the cold, spartan angularities of everyday Soviet life.

The first: on my last full day in Moscow I walked down Herzen Street toward the Kremlin walls to buy a present for Margaret, my wife. It was January, and very cold. Men in rabbitskin caps and women in caps or head-shawls slipped and slid on ice and snow as they trudged along narrow, uneven sidewalks, eyes automatically scanning dreary, uninviting shop fronts. It was as though an invisible hand had turned a spigot and drained all color from the world: no bright advertising signs, no chic shops, no coffee bars, no movie marquees. Gray buses lumbered by under leaden skies.

My eye was caught by a long line of people halfway down

1

the next block. Soldiers in uniform read books behind young mothers with small children and elderly women weighed down by immense shopping bags. The line did not lead to a shop but to a narrow gap between two buildings. In a tiny open space behind a shop, two women were ripping open cases and selling, at prices slightly cheaper than those in state stores, small boxes of commonplace chocolate candy. The candy was rare and expensive in state stores, and much of its appeal came from the bright red boxes, which stood out against the gloom.

Above the clouds circled Soviet space capsules and killer satellites. In their remote bunkers sat ICBM missiles. Down on earth, in the capital city of Communism itself, which is allocated the best food and consumer goods in the country, soldiers and mothers stood in the slush for thirty minutes or more to buy candy available in even the most ordinary shops in most of the rest of the world.

The second glimpse came after I had driven down Kalinin Prospect (Avenue), past the ornate stone bulk of the Lenin Library (where proscribed books are kept in hidden rooms closed to all but a few Party officials), over the Moscow River and onto the broad, prestigious stretch of Lenin Prospect which runs southwest from the Kremlin. Iron-faced, gray-uniformed traffic militia men glared suspiciously from the center of each intersection, ready to blow a whistle and impose fines on the spot on any hapless motorist who committed the smallest offense—while they waved long, black, official limousines into specially reserved center lanes and saluted as they passed. Beyond a tall, shiny metal column commemorating Yuri Gagarin's first space flight stood the Univermag Moskva (Moscow Department Store). Opposite was a plain, worn wooden door in a wall not far from the corner of Gubkin Street.

There were no signs, no indication of what lay behind the unmarked door. I stood on tiptoe to peer into tall windows a little further along. Each glass pane was painted over with white emulsion so that passersby could not see in: at top levels, much *klass* tends to be hidden. By straining, I could see a long, high-ceilinged dining room. Chandeliers hung above individual tables. Yet this was no ordinary restaurant; it was a passport out of the slush, away from the long boring waits in line and rude shop assistants and shoving crowds and disappointing displays. This was the Akademicheskaya Stolovaya, or dining room for the members of the Academy of Sciences. The Academy is the center of the scientific and space research and development upon which the Party leans heavily for the Soviet Union's international reputation. Its members enjoy immense prestige and social *klass*, and the restaurant served to its members food simply unavailable to ordinary shoppers outside: steak, caviar, crab. The room behind the unmarked door is an extra, and virtually priceless, bonus: it is where Academicians and their families could pick up their *payoki*—special rations of quality food ordered in advance by telephone and picked up in person. No lines, no waiting, no freezing, no legs splashed by passing buses.

I had a friend whose whole life had been cushioned by such privileges. "Inside the room sits a woman we all know and who knows all of us," he told me one day. "If I go in, or my mother, or my brothers, the woman smiles: we've been going there for years. But if she sees a strange face, she snaps at it to leave, at once. We order packages of high-class food from the storeroom at the back. The packages are brought in by members of the staff—good vegetables and fruit that you can't find in state stores, and fresh meat, and sausage, as well as *defitsitnyi* (hard to get) items such as sturgeon . . ." In contrast to state stores, where nothing is wrapped, the *payok* food is already packaged and ready to go.

Before I went to Moscow for the first time, I saw the Soviet Union as most outsiders do: a distant abstraction, a giant granite wall topped by guns and rockets, forbidding, closed, austere.

Actually living there revealed the human side of the wall, the individuals who spend their days worrying, not about Marx or Lenin or NATO, but about how to make the granite yield, how to find ways of making their slow-moving, rigidly centralized, state-run system work for them as they go about the basic business of eating, shopping, traveling, studying, working, raising children.

The Soviet system is ponderous, slow, unimaginative. It can brilliantly achieve selected goals: space flight, building tanks, specialized mathematical and medical research, winning international ice-hockey titles. Yet it still cannot provide its people with enough grain, enough meat, enough stylish clothes, or the opportunity for individual dignity and fulfillment.

Some seventy years after Lenin, the USSR is an extraordinary amalgam of modern and ancient, new and old, Europe and Asia. The advanced and the backward rub shoulders at every turn. Alas for the average man, he confronts the worst part of the system as he shops, eats, and works. The consumer, as a rule, comes last.

So how do the people survive?

They start with their jobs, and they try to squeeze every ounce of privilege and status from them. They search for whatever benefits or privileges or social status—*klass*—might be hidden on the factory floor, in military barracks, in Party and government offices. They add every inch of family connection: every friend, every contact who might know where to find fresh oranges or a pair of summer shoes or a doctor willing to give special attention (for a fee) to a daughter needing dental work, or a university official who can get a son into college (and out of the otherwise compulsory military draft at age eighteen).

Without a second thought they accept that the Soviet Union is alive with *klass*—class in a classless society. *Klass* usually means social divisions, as it does in the West, except that the Bolshevik Revolution of 1917 was supposed to have ended them. The Party itself acknowledges only two classes—workers and peasants—though it has begun to recognize a third category which it calls "brain workers"—white-collar workers, computer technicians, planners, administrators, machine supervisors, and many other professionals. Ideological rhetoric, however, is increasingly unable to come to grips with the real world. Soviet workers tend to ignore it or scoff at it, and to take for granted the need for class—*klass*—to achieve privilege, status, style, and comfort.

In theory, the Soviet people are governed by the ideas of Karl Marx and Vladimir Ilyich Lenin. After almost seven decades, the differences between social classes should be growing less and less. True, the Party has explained that Utopia cannot be achieved for the moment: the country has to pass through a stage of "developed socialism." Officials are frequently pleased to announce that this stage has arrived. One day, they say, it will yield to full "communism," though they refrain from saying just when that may be. Some minor differences will remain, the theory runs, but the concept of class will end, along with exploitation and despair. Men will be equal, and rewarded not according to their ability but to their needs.

The truth is that life in the Soviet Union today is the opposite of this theory, and is moving further from it with every passing moment. Privilege is deep in the fabric of Soviet life. The people want it; the Party wants to control it. Ideology is for the dry pages of *Pravda*. Reality is that each social rank, or class, is so tangible, so evident, that the Party recognizes it and awards it specific privileges not available to the class or subclass below.

To the bulk of Soviet citizens, Marx and Lenin are yesterday's theory. *Klass* is today's reality.

Money can buy some of it but by no means all of it. *Klass* connections are needed for access to better-paying jobs as well as to consumer goods and opportunities. In a one-party, semi-Asian state, bribery helps; and in the south, in freewheeling

Azerbaijan on the Iranian border and in the Caucasus, bribery is a way of life. But this underside of *klass* has its limitations. *Klass* can be only partially bought. Money is an adjunct of *klass*, but not *klass* itself.

A Moscow professional woman told me jubilantly that her husband had just constructed a sixteen-foot motor boat in a rented garage. He needed money for the materials—but *klass* to gain access to the plans (and to find a garage to rent: in Moscow garages are as rare as hen's teeth). The woman was even more delighted at the Mercury outboard motor for the boat that he had bought on the black market—another case of *klass* knowing where to buy, and *klass* arising from his privileged job, which brought him into contact with foreigners. She was still more thrilled with an elaborate camping tent he had brought back from West Germany; without *klass* he would never have been able to make such a coveted trip in the first place. The family set off to go boating and camping at a lake north of Moscow in a roseate glow for which money was only partially responsible.

In the United States class is linked to income. In the United Kingdom it is still connected to birth, speech, manners. In the USSR, *klass* is a deadly serious business, bound up with job, connections, initiative, vigilance, and ingenuity.

Without class, Soviet society resembles a vast military camp. Basic services are provided: hot water, a roof, minimum space, free (but overloaded) education and health care, potatoes, cabbage. People certainly live better than their parents did. Yet there is only one Party, one boss, one employer, one arbiter of who gets what. There is enough food, but not enough good food, such as the meat Russians love so much. There are clothes, but few stylish clothes. Television, radio, newspapers, movies—all are censored, and tend to be excruciatingly dull. There is hardly any chance for anyone to leave the camp and see the rest of the world.

With the acquisition of even a small amount of *klass*, however, life begins to change. The camp doesn't seem so drab.

Opportunities open up. Favors are swapped, backs are scratched, goods are bartered, promises are made and kept. If you've got access to something, no matter how small, that someone else wants, you use it to the hilt.

The mother of one woman I knew worked in a theater box office. In the United States such a woman might be able to sell a few tickets to a hit show for some extra money. In Moscow, the woman exchanged tickets all year round for shoes, candies, ballpoint pens, dresses, scarves, vacation passes, and more. Another friend had an acquaintance who worked in a meat store; the man could almost name his own terms for supplying the occasional cut of good-quality meat.

Shopgirls go through new warehouse deliveries before they go on sale. They set aside the best items and trade them for anything they can (another reason why shopping is often disappointing in the USSR). Intellectuals can do very well: one friend in a scientific institute prepared high school graduates for university entrance examinations at five rubles an hour each; so great was the demand to get into higher education, and so few the places, that he earned more on the side than at his regular job: by taking four classes a day of five students each, he earned as much in twenty-four hours as many workers do in a month.

In fact, there exists an elaborate, calibrated, semihidden framework of privileges and benefits at almost every echelon of Party, government, military officers, workers, peasants, intellectuals, sportsmen, scientists, and more. The framework starts on the factory and office floor and broadens and deepens as jobs move from menial to supervisory positions, as Party officials move slowly up from microdistricts to citywide and perhaps provincewide or even national government. The principal echelons carry with them access to new shops, better stocked as an individual keeps rising. Salaries, too, increase, but it's the access to consumer goods and permissions to build dachas (summer cottages) and to go abroad that hold the real attraction.

The framework is largely hidden from outside eyes, and from many Russian eyes as well. It took several years before I became aware of its scope and size.

Klass is the oil that helps keep the cogs of Soviet life from seizing up. *Klass* is a ticket to the Bolshoi (usually reserved for foreign tourists or senior officials or friends of the dancers); *klass* is a place for a child at Moscow State University (the equivalent of Harvard, Yale, Princeton, and Stanford all rolled into one).

Klass is Bolshoi superstar ballet dancer Maris Liepa driving a bright orange Volvo bought in Helsinki amid the lackluster traffic of Moscow . . . *klass* is internationally known artist Ilya Glazunov gingerly but proudly piloting a white Mercedes 230 sedan delivered to him from West Berlin . . . *klass* is a vial of American medicine, a Japanese tape deck, a Scandinavian couch, English lipstick and face cream, even a simple box of Finnish tissues . . . high *klass* is imported from the West; lower *klass* is a Polish ham or a ballpoint pen from Budapest.

Klass is cocooning a son or daughter in Moscow's prestige-laden Fourth School of Physics and Mathematics which guarantees excellent training and a good chance of acceptance into Moscow State University . . . *klass* is avoiding state movie houses showing such stirring Soviet realism as *Traktorisky* (the tale of heroic tractor drivers bringing in the harvest) in favor of a Broadway show flown in on video from New York, or a pornographic video from Finland (because many a Russian believes Westerners watch such videos all the time).

Klass is Bolshoi prima ballerina Maya Plisetskaya's having a Moscow duplex apartment and a live-in maid . . . a retired opera singer and his wife having two servants (a friend of mine was brought up in Moscow by a nanny and a maid).

At elevated political levels, Politburo and top Academy of Sciences officials have red telephones, or *vertushkas* (slang for a talkative, flighty woman) on their desks, able to reach the private numbers of the few dozen men who really govern the Soviet Union.

Klass is a type of second Russian revolution, fought not with guns but with Western jeans, not with armies but with antiques, not with dreadnoughts but with diamonds, not with iron tanks but with bright cotton tank tops. It does not aim for political power: the Party is, for the moment, at least, secure. The Party has survived revolution, civil war, famine, purges, collectivization, Hitler, the cold war and economic stagnation, and the waning of ideological faith; it has long since penetrated the military and the Russian Orthodox Church and all other potential power centers. It is strong and shrewd enough to try to control *klass* by using it to reward both loyalty and achievement and (by withholding it) to punish deviation. It hopes that *klass* is a force for conservatism. It wants Soviet citizens to toe the line for fear of losing *klass* benefits. Most do.

On a deeper level, the Party holds sway because Russia has been ruled from the center for one thousand years; central authority has never been diluted, either under the tsars or the commissars. Russia has been governed from Moscow or St. Petersburg (now Leningrad). It has seen no centuries of kingly power eroded by clergy, nobles, or burghers. There has been no Renaissance, no Reformation, no Luther, no Erasmus.

First there were the city-states of Kiev, Moscow, Novgorod, and others, and then the stunning invasion of the Mongols, who galloped in from the East in 1237 and stayed for almost 250 years. After them came the equally brutal, despotic tsars, who learned from the Mongol model. The tsar held title to all the land; he tolerated the Church in return for designation by the Church as divine. Peter the Great, the astonishing giant who threw open the windows to the West and tried singlehandedly to drag a backward, illiterate, shambling, Asian Russia into Europe, stamped form and shape onto social class with a military-style Table of Ranks in 1722. While bureaucrats usurped much tsarist authority in the nineteenth century, Russia was still ruled from St. Petersburg,[1] and Lenin inherited and continued the tradition, shifting the capital to Moscow. Stalin, the Ivan the Terrible of the Communist Party, ensured that central control did not waver; it is still firmly in place today.

Nonetheless, *klass* is a contemporary revolution of expectations in millions of daily lives, urban and rural. While there has always been a thin layer of intellectuals and nobles at or near the top of Russian society who patterned their lives on Western manners and styles, *klass* today cuts wider and deeper.

It goes further than the "New Class" of Party administrators described by Yugoslav Milovan Djilas. It includes these administrators, of course, but it reaches as low as the man behind the meat counter who swaps the best cuts of meat for theater tickets and passes to a Black Sea resort. It includes an apartment-painter who gives priority to a university director in return for a place at the university for his son. It enfolds a doctor who finds he is suddenly able to buy stationery because he offers to recommend a colleague to perform an abortion for the sister of the salesgirl.

Klass can be as elevated as Foreign Minister Andrei Gromyko's retinue bringing back so many video recorders, cassettes, television sets, tape recorders, and clothes from a United Nations session in New York that it's a wonder his Aeroflot Ilyushin jet leaves the ground. It can be an East Coast American businessman making sure that Victor Louis (self-styled journalist but widely considered by Western experts to work either for the KGB or the Party Central Committee) takes delivery in Bakovka, outside of Moscow, of a late-model U.S. station wagon with New Jersey plates. It can be a swarthy Soviet Georgian flying privately grown oranges to Moscow and selling them at enormous profit at an officially sanctioned farmers' market.

Klass is both a high-water mark and a low-water mark in Soviet life. It is a measure of how far the universal human struggle for individuality, comfort, and self-worth has come in the USSR, and it measures just how far that struggle still has to go.

Who maneuvers for *klass* privilege? Who has it? Who wants it?

We are not talking here of any minuscule social set imitating Tolstoy's elite in *War and Peace.* I have identified five separate social ranks, or classes, of which three contain the bulk of *klass* privilege: a Top Class, a Military Officer Class, and a Rising Class with three distinct sublayers in it; the Rising Class is roughly equivalent to a Western middle class, but without its political power. Below them are an Urban Class and a Rural Class, both aware of *klass* privileges above them, and anxious for at least some of them.[2]

The Top Class is small: perhaps 25,000 Party chiefs, government ministers, military marshals, and senior generals, the elite of the KGB and the police, and a handful of very well known scientists, intellectuals, artists, and entertainers. Together with families this group might add up to 100,000 individuals, separated in turn into layers and subgroups, with Mikhail Gorbachev and the Politburo at the top. Each is allotted its own privileged level of food deliveries, access to clothes, health clinics, vacation resorts, apartments, and official cars.

The Military Officer Class is larger: some 800,000 including families.[3] At the top are generals not senior enough to edge into the Top Class; at the bottom are captains and lieutenants. In a country historically surrounded by enemies, invaded by Mongols, by Napoleon, and by Hitler, and deeply suspicious of all outsiders, officers are showered with privilege throughout their careers, from good-quality food to well-tailored clothes cut from the best of cloth. The privilege is also a kind of warning; any mutiny against the Party will result in its loss.

One Leningrad woman whose father was a colonel told me that she and her mother dressed for many years in clothes cut from bolts of superb materials regularly delivered to her father for his dress uniforms. The colonel needed only a few consignments for his uniforms and turned subsequent ones

over to his family. It is difficult to convey what a difference
this made to my friend and her mother: state stores usually
sell badly made, unattractive garments, and women thirst
after something different, something fresh. Real quality is
rare: my friend had access to it, *klass* access, via her father.

When officers retire, earlier than civilians, they are guaranteed an apartment from the state (which means skipping the
usual long waiting period) wherever they choose to settle.
With their Party clearances (officers must be Party members)
and their KGB clearances, they can select a number of lucrative fields for a second career, from security work to personnel and administration in sensitive military-industrial
plants.

Perhaps most interesting to an outsider is the Rising Class,
which I estimate to contain some 23 million employed people. Including their immediate families and parents, their
klass privileges cover perhaps 40 million individuals, or almost one Soviet citizen in every six.

This is the group that senses the even bigger *klass* privileges above it, and is very conscious of the gap that its own
share of *klass* puts between it and the Urban and Rural
Classes below it. In fact, most of it does not live as well as a
middle-class American or European, but compared to the
classes below, and to the poverty and deprivation of its parents and grandparents, it does very well indeed.[4]

The Rising Class is mainly urban, reflecting something
brand new in Russian history: the transformation of society
from a rural base. Under Stalin, cities grew rapidly as industry
(and especially heavy industry) expanded. Only 18 percent of
Russians lived in cities in 1913, whereas the figure had risen
to 33 percent by 1940. By 1980 it had hit 62 percent, a daz-
zling switch from two-thirds rural to two-thirds urban in four
decades.

From the Baltic to the Pacific, across eleven time zones, the
city is where middle-class ambition thrives. Almost 16 million people fled from primitive villages to growing cities in

the decade of the 1970s alone, according to the official census of 1979. In 1917 Russia had only two cities containing 500,000 people or more; today the figure is forty-five, and twenty number more than one million each.

So the breeding and feeding grounds of the Rising Class are not just Moscow and Leningrad and Kiev, but grimy Kharkov and the Black Sea port of Odessa; the Slav centers of Minsk and Chelyabinsk; Ukrainian Donetsk and Siberian Omsk; Central Asian Tashkent; industrial Volgograd (formerly Stalingrad); Tula, the home of samovars and guns; Voronezh, a center of aircraft manufacture; Russian Sverdlovsk and Smolensk; the three Baltic capitals of Riga, Vilnius, and Tallinn; and more.

The rise of *klass* has also been helped by the greater number of foreigners visible in the major cities since World War II, and especially during the détente with the United States that flowered in the early 1970s. The Rising Class patterns its style and manners on the United States and Western Europe. It eagerly follows trends and fashions as best it can perceive them from glimpses of magazines and foreign tourists and friends who have achieved the ultimate status symbol: the trip abroad. The upper levels listen avidly, it appears, to Russian-language shortwave broadcasts of the British Broadcasting Company, the Voice of America, Deutsche Welle, and Canadian and Swedish radio. The VOA claims that from the time Moscow stopped jamming its broadcasts in 1973 (a gesture toward détente) until it resumed jamming in late 1979 (after the invasion of Afghanistan) some 12 million Russians listened to VOA programs at any one time. Such a figure is impossible to verify, but I know that the 9 P.M. *Panorama* news program on VOA was a highlight for many an intellectual in the late 1970s. A number of Russians (not only dissidents) mentioned that they had heard my *Christian Science Monitor* articles summarized on VOA frequencies. Anatoly Shcharansky told me in late 1978 that he had seen a transcript, in Russian, of the previous night's VOA transmission on the desk of the minister of the interior during a meeting, shortly before Shcharansky's arrest and trial. The VOA and the BBC gave news to the Communist Party in Moscow far faster than its own agency TASS or their own embassies abroad could, and their cultural programs were a prime source for Top and Rising Classes alike.

Who, then, has made it into this Rising Class? Its upper rungs include middle- and lower-level members of the Party Central Committee apparatus . . . *oblast* (provincial) . . . some Party first secretaries in important areas . . . citywide Party men in the bigger cities . . . middle and junior KGB and police officials in the capitals of the fifteen Soviet republics . . . directors and senior engineers in factories in the military-industrial-scientific complex . . . senior-level people in national (all-union) government ministries headquartered in Moscow such as defense, foreign affairs, foreign trade, oil, steel, natural gas, and more . . .

The upper Rising Class also contains directors of scientific institutes and university professors in departments (from mathematics to geology) affiliated with the USSR Academy of Sciences . . . senior Party officials supervising culture from writing to ballet to printing . . . successful (i.e., approved but not necessarily the most talented) writers, dancers, singers, musicians, composers . . . Olympic medal–winning athletes and Soviet chess grandmasters.

The middle of the Rising Class includes *oblast* officials in remoter areas . . . senior Party officials in smaller cities . . . officials in lesser national ministries such as health and light industry, as well as republicwide ministries . . . junior Academy of Sciences and Institute staff . . . lawyers . . . judges (not nearly as senior a job as in the West; in the final analysis, the Party is the law) . . . ice-hockey and soccer players of international caliber . . . foremen in industrial factories . . . leaders of primary Party organizations (formerly called cells) in factories and offices . . . junior ministry staff . . . non-Academy Institute staff . . . intellectuals for whom the Party has no great time or use, such as librarians, philologists, archivists, archaeologists . . . senior blue-collar workers in big factories . . . and more.

I should mention here that a separate subgroup in the Rising Class consists of speculators, black marketeers, and "fixers" who exploit shortages, bottlenecks, and the endless red tape endemic to the Soviet system. These are the expediters who get bricks to a construction site and cement to a factory and vegetables to the railhead—for a price. They are Soviet Georgians, Armenians, Azerbaijanis, and Uzbeks who carry fruit and vegetables and homemade clothes to Russian cities in the north. People such as these earn semicapitalistic fortunes and use the rubles to bribe their way into restaurants; in some Central Asian Republics, they penetrate Party and government offices controlling the flow of permits and licenses and agreements that everyone needs and many are willing to pay for.

The transformation of the United States into a middle-class society after World War II was a sociological phenomenon. A similar one swept Western Europe in the 1950s–60s. Belatedly, a somewhat similar movement—lacking political influence—is under way in the Soviet Union, which has been the last of the major industrial nations of the world to resist the spread of a Rising Class mentality. In theory this is a refutation of Marxist-Leninist doctrine. In fact it is the material, though not political, Westernization of millions of urban Russians begun some three centuries ago by Peter the Great.

The very lack of political power and participation in the USSR intensifies the search for *klass*. The efforts of the Rising Class are not divided between material and political gain. For the Rising Class, *klass* is not just one aspect of daily life; it is the bedrock of ambition, the sine qua non of achievement. It is a tacit rejection of the Party's claim that in all things people must sacrifice so that the nation can prosper.

Beneath the Rising Class lies the Urban Class. It contains some 73 million urban workers, as far as I can tell, many of them husband and wife, since some 95 percent of all Soviet women work. Even further down the scale is the Rural Class, which still contains some 35 million people. Taking into account parents and small children, the two classes add up to about 200 million individuals—a toiling and struggling mass, whose higher levels are aware of at least some of the *klass* privileges above them and who would dearly like to extract some for themselves.

The gap between the social classes, especially between intellectuals and blue-collar, can be wide indeed. Soviet émigré singer Alexander Galich was shocked to discover that one of the daughters of his host in Norway, artist Viktor Sparre, had taken a job in a shoe store. Galich told Sparre that if Russian intellectuals obey the Party they lead an almost aristocratic life: "They never touch such a common thing as a tool; their wives never take a scrubbing brush." Mrs. Sparre was struck by this attitude: "Class differences," she remarked, "are obviously far greater in the USSR than in Norway."[5]

The Rising Class in particular is dissatisfied with the basic level of comfort, style, and color that the Party has allocated to it. It wants better times after decades of sacrifices during civil war, famine, purge, and world war.

One reaction of the Rising Class is to turn away from the grim present into a more romantic past: to patriotism, to Russian roots, to the Russian Orthodox Church, and, in Central Asia, to Islam.[6] However much a Russian might dislike the present, though, he must live in it. This book is an effort to see how he copes with it. It is about the more pragmatic side of the Russian character: its practicalities rather than its backward looks.

About a century and a half ago, Alexis de Tocqueville wrote: "America's conquests are made with the ploughshare, Russia's with the sword. . . . To attain their aim, the former relies on personal interest and gives free scope to the unguided strength and common sense of individuals. The latter in a sense concentrates the whole power of society in one man. One has freedom as the principal means of action; the other has servitude. . . ."[7]

The growth of the Rising Class and its privilege is bringing a sense of de Tocqueville's "personal interest" to the Soviet people for the first time. At the close of his first volume of *Democracy in America*, de Tocqueville also predicted that America and Russia, would be "called by some secret design of Providence one day to hold in [their] hands the destinies of half the world." The accuracy of his crystal ball has made the changing social fabric in the Soviet Union that much more significant.

A Rising Class on the move is an awesome historical phenomenon. In the Soviet Union it moves slowly, almost glacierlike, but it moves nevertheless. The crucial question is whether it can be controlled by the state, or whether it will gather momentum as it enters the recesses of Soviet minds, where even the Party cannot reach.

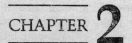
FOOD AS *KLASS*

S hopping for food is no fun in Moscow.

It is even less fun in Leningrad and Smolensk and all the other cold Russian cities that lack the status of the country's capital and must make do with lesser consumer goods. The food that does find its way into even Moscow's grimy, small, ill-lit, unswept food stores is a clear indication that providing food for the people as a whole is an industry that lacks status and prestige. Anyone who must depend on the state stores for most or all of his food lacks social *klass* and position. Russians who know how to wield *klass* use state stores only for milk, bread, and some other staples; otherwise, they plot and scheme to use *klass* connections. *Klass* makes the difference between eating scrag end and eating steak.

Even a quick look around average Moscow stores is enough to see what Russians with *klass* work so hard to avoid. On my second day in Moscow I walked around our block adjoining the Sadovoye Koltso (a misnomer if ever there was one: there is little horticultural about twelve lanes of thundering trucks, buses, taxis, cars, and even, at midnight several times, jet fighter planes being towed from airfield to airfield with spare parts in trucks behind them). The first shop was little more than a sidewalk stall offering wizened apples. Around a corner was a butcher's shop. The sign above it stated simply, MYASO—"meat"—but there wasn't much of it about. I went down two steps into a dark room. Shelves were almost empty. The floor was filthy. The white coats on the sales assistants had not been laundered for some time, if ever. Large bottles containing various pickled parts of unnamed animals stood here and there. A single twenty-watt bulb without a shade provided the only light.

The one place I found that had an array of interesting food was a farmers' market further along a side road. With the permission of the government, several floors and outbuildings allow collective and state farmers to bring in what they grow on the small private plots they are allowed to keep. Sometimes food—fruit, vegetables, meat—is plentiful, sometimes not, but prices are always high: too high for most Russians to buy there all the time.

When I arrived back at our apartment, I talked to a correspondent who had lived in Moscow for two years. "Tell me," I said, "where are the good shops?"

"You've just seen them," she replied. "This is a choice area, not far from the Kremlin . . ."

I tried a large food store, a *universam*, in another area. The meat was tragic: odds and ends, mostly bones. The good cuts had long since been taken by the shop staff, either for their own families or to barter for other valuable goods with friends or neighbors. The very best food, as Russians know full well, never appears in state stores at all: it goes to senior Party and government officials, and the best of all is made available to the Top Class by means of a hidden but efficient delivery network known simply as the "Distribution" (*raspredelitel'*).

Meat came into the *universam* only once a week. The store was open from 9 A.M. to 9 P.M. and aisles were always clogged with lines for this item or that. Since newspapers carry no advertising (neither does radio or TV), no one can tell in advance what will be available, so women visit the same round of stores, maybe a dozen, every single day. In their pockets they keep as many rubles as they can, just in case. The iron rule is that if Russians see something good, they buy it on the spot: he who hesitates may never see the item again.

There was often a shortage of butter and sometimes of

kefir, the cultured buttermilk Russians love to drink (and which is said to be good for hangovers). Vegetables are unwashed: carrots and potatoes are sold as they are pulled from the earth, without being wrapped. Shoppers bring their own bags. In my experience some of the store assistants could smile but most were weary and bored. Dark bread was almost always available. So were eggs, and potatoes, and vodka. The price of vodka keeps going up, and the social costs of alcoholism are incalculable in the USSR, but there never seems to be a shortage. The *universam* carries only the cheapest of brands. Stolichnaya is a quality brand for export only, sold to bring in foreign currency (and to buy Pepsi-Cola concentrate under a two-way deal that sees Moscow swapping vodka for Pepsi). Countless Russians told me their vodka was not for sipping: "We drink it fast, to forget," one man said. "The taste is not good, but—"

The only time the state stores carry better than average food is on or before state holidays such as the November 7 celebration of the 1917 Revolution by Lenin's Bolsheviks, and at New Year's. Even then, the quality and quantity vary.

A common way to bypass these kinds of stores is to order food every week from a factory or an office canteen. The more important the factory—machinery, computers, military trucks, weaponry, space-flight components, oil- or natural-gas-related—the better the food its canteen is able to order in bulk. However, for workers in the courts and legal system, or in ministries dealing with agriculture or light industry, or in any field connected with construction or transportation or, ironically, with retail stores, the Party allows less prestige and thus poorer quality food.

Lyuba was an extremely bright young Moscow woman, lively and quick with dark hair. She had a habit of talking so fast that her words fell over themselves like a waterfall. She worked for several years in a Moscow city institute that designed buildings. After she emigrated to Boston, she spent an evening telling me how the food system worked for her.

The institute staff of 3,000 was divided into groups of between 100 and 150 each. One woman in each group was responsible for taking weekly food orders and relaying them to a building purchasing officer. Moscow is the top city in the country, and the city government there has influence beyond the dreams of a distant metropolis such as, say, Sverdlovsk. The design institute is respectable, and has a definite measure of prestige.

So the purchasing officer had access to bulk orders of food of reasonable quality that never finds its way into the state stores. Each layer of Party and government officialdom has access to separate levels of quality food. The same is true among scientists, creative artists, the military, and so on.

Notices went up at the institute each week listing what food was available. Food was always offered in groups, each containing some *defitsit* or scarce items along with less desirable ones. It's a sales technique widely used by a Party apparatus that is desperate to fulfill sales quotas on which salary bonuses are based and which knows many of the goods on offer are substandard.

"Once," Lyuba recalled, as memories returned to throng her living room, "I wanted canned coffee. You remember that it was almost impossible to find at the end of the 1970s, and it was very expensive besides. Anyway, I found it on one list. One can per order. The rest of the list contained one kilo [about two pounds] of sugar (good), one box of cookies (which turned out to be three years old, I swear), and one box of chocolates. Well, I didn't want the cookies or the chocolates, but I ordered the list anyway to get the coffee."

Alas, by the time the senior workers had been served that week, the coffee had run out and she, as a younger worker, had to order again the following week. "I was fortunate," she said. "I got it then."

Another list included one kilo of fresh beef, two cans of pressed meat (something like Spam), a length of Finnish sausage, one kilo of hamburger meat, and one kilo of frozen vegetables. Lyuba, delighted, placed an immediate order. The beef and the sausage were rare. When the order arrived (she picked it up at the Institute) the vegetables were poorly frozen and virtually uneatable and the hamburger was turning green inside. But the beef and the sausage were both good. Lyuba was happy: she had saved hours of lining up in the snow outside or inside a state shop.

In spring, a typical Institute list might contain fresh apples, a pineapple from Cuba, and some oranges. Lyuba recalled that on one occasion the pineapple turned out to be an unripe dark green, and it doggedly stayed that way. The oranges were small, with thick rinds. Yet the apples were good and she still avoided those awful food shop lines. In recent years, the weekly consignments, or *payoki*, have concentrated on more basic foods—sausage and butter, for instance—than in the past.[1]

The higher the institute or office or factory, the better the food.

The top management of Lyuba's institute would have had access to the distribution network available to the local *raion* (urban microdistrict) Party officials. The director may even have been able to tap the Distribution for Moscow city as a whole: high privilege indeed. That would have meant the right to patronize a special food store reserved exclusively for those of his own rank. I have been told that such shops usually consist of a single room, its shelves stuffed with domestic and imported food—from caviar to sturgeon—rarely seen by lesser beings outside. The higher the level of shop, the cheaper prices become.

On Karl Marx Prospect, most employees at the Gosplan office (the State Planning Agency, which draws up targets and plans for the entire economy) have access to much better weekly *payoki* than Lyuba. Senior staff also eat across the street in the vast, gray Moskva Hotel, which is so prestigious that the Party uses it to house VIP guests from abroad. When I visited the then incoming International Olympic Committee president Juan Antonio Samaranch there in the summer of 1980, each IOC member had his own staff of white-aproned maids on tap. Hotel kitchens are able to bulk-order fine food indeed.

At an even higher level, the senior (and even some of the middle-ranking and junior) staff at the infamous KGB headquarters just up the road in the ocher-colored Lubyanka building on Dzerzhinsky Square ate even better. A Russian who once worked at a meat-processing factory in Moscow told me that KGB officers holding the rank of captain and above (the KGB is run on military lines) can order large weekly boxes of food, which are brought to their desks.

Between 4 and 5 P.M. each working day, the processing factory at which this Russian worked killed only the finest young calves. Carcasses were hung in a special enclosure, forbidden to all but a few workers who had to carry special passes. The meat, my acquaintance learned, went to the KGB and to some other senior Party offices. Some was exported to earn hard currency.

Enormous privilege goes to scientists who belong to the USSR Academy of Sciences. One famous man was able to pick up his telephone and order consignments of meat, vegetables, fruit, and other food brought to his apartment once a week in a small, unmarked van. Food deliveries are commonplace in big European and American cities, but in the USSR they denote the very highest *klass*. The only conditions, I was told, were that each order had to be worth 100 rubles, and that the driver was to receive ten rubles as a tip. There was a ten-ruble delivery fee as well. The scientist was able to afford the money: his monthly salary was well over 1,000 rubles, in a country where the national average is estimated by the Party to be about 160 rubles a month for a blue-collar worker, and may well be somewhat less.[2]

The Distribution is only for the very top ranks of *klass*.

Unsurprisingly, ministries and institutes compete fiercely for access to it. An émigré with many contacts in the Soviet underworld told me on excellent authority that the KGB tried hard for months to convince one key Kremlin worker to divert food to the KGB from an ultraexclusive string of restaurants used only by the handful of men in the ruling Politburo itself. The man refused, thinking it better to be protected by the Politburo apparatus than the KGB. He miscalculated. The KGB tailed him until it caught him selling some food he had purloined from the restaurant kitchens (a common practice by employees with access to anything out of the ordinary), and had the man sentenced to jail.

Then the KGB officers gave him one more chance. This time they wanted a written statement implicating others in the kitchens in black-market sales. The man refused, hoping the Politburo apparatus would step in and save him. He heard nothing, and spent many years in Soviet prisons, convinced that the only reason the KGB wanted the statement was to use it to persuade Politburo members that black-marketeering was rife and that the only way to stop it was to let the KGB take over the Distribution. That would have given the KGB upper echelons access to the same food its bosses ate: a *klass* coup.

Privilege attached to membership in the Party Politburo is so great that, on occasion, it can continue into retirement. Anastas Mikoyan lived at Politburo level for decades as Stalin's minister of trade and later of foreign affairs, and was allowed to retire after being ousted by Nikita Khrushchev. A friend of his family (and a man himself linked to privilege at a high level) told me that as Old Bolsheviks (Party members from the early, revolutionary days), Mikoyan and his family simply filled out special *talony* (coupons) for whatever they wanted from the Kremlin clothes store as well as from food and other stores.

"He and his wife are embarrassed," the friend said. "The coupons are processed in a special department in the Party

Central Committee, so everyone knows when the Mikoyans order shoes and so on for their grandchildren."

Not to pay the price, however, would be unthinkable. A Mikoyan, even forced out of office, does not stand in line.

At lower levels, *klass* in food depends on standing and position at work.

At the headquarters of the Communist Party in Leningrad, for example, officials ate in three different *stolovayas*, depending on their rank. Not only was the privileged fare excellent, but prices were remarkably low. A friend, Tamara, who had been to a Party restaurant in the Tavrichesky Dvorets (Tavrichesky Palace), gawked at the fresh meat, at the boxes of imported candies, at rare plum and mint liqueurs about whose very existence she had forgotten. As she stood there she saw bowls of salmon soup and slabs of steak being ferried back and forth by well-dressed waiters.

"It was real communism," Tamara marveled. "The salmon soup cost twenty-five kopeks and the steak thirty-two kopeks per serving. Outside you have to pay two to three rubles—ten times as much—for the soup and at least two rubles for the steak."

Food itself is not *klass*, but a regular supply of good meat, caviar, and other luxury items certainly is. Few people starve in the Soviet Union. There is usually enough bread, potatoes, cabbage, and sugar, but in the last two decades the Soviet state has failed to produce enough meat and fresh fruit. Fewer than 20 percent of almost 800 Soviet émigrés surveyed in 1981 said that beef, chicken, pork, or sausage were regularly available to them. More than half reported that they could find butter, fruit, flour, milk, and even cabbage only irregularly. The exceptions are the Central Asian republics, whose citizens generally eat better than those in the colder north and west.

As we have seen, the government provides special food stores to citizens of *klass*, but is careful to hide them on side streets, whether in Moscow's ancient inner city, or in

Akademgorodok, the center for scientific research halfway across the country in Siberia. Elite food shops are kept in the shadows. They are not advertised, and their doors are either blank or posted with a misleading sign, such as the legend BURO PROPUSKOV ("Bureau of Passes") on the store for Kremlin officials behind a stone wall on Granovsky Street in Moscow.

Not only is the existence of such privilege kept from the public as much as possible, it is sometimes not even heralded among the privileged. When an individual is made eligible, generally through job promotion, he is sometimes handed a list of addresses of special stores; or he might have to ask colleagues of similar rank where he can go. A friend was amused that I should think everything was reduced to formal lists of names. "Where do you think this is?" he asked. "Germany? We are not as organized as that. This is Russia. All is chaos, confusion. Sometimes people are told about their privileges; sometimes they are not. Yet somehow, we all know."

Not all *payok* stores operate the way the Leninsky food shop for Academicians does. Those lower on the scale might be merely small rooms crammed with goods, such as the "Albatross" chain, which serves officers and men in the Soviet merchant marine. They display the superior export brand of vodka, sausage without the usual substitute ingredients, canned crab, and more. The seamen do not pay in cash but in coupons called "certificate rubles." Since it is against the law for the average citizen to possess foreign money, seamen are given a small allowance of certificate rubles for each trip abroad.

The privilege of superior food certainly extends to Soviet writers and their guests, who dine excellently in a comfortable restaurant in the Tsentralnyi Dom Literatorov, the Central Writers Union building, which serves some of the nation's best French cuisine in its main dining room. Under vaulted ceilings, lit by table lamps shaded with lace, Soviet writers, their families, and friends, leisurely enjoy fresh perch, *oeufs en cocotte* with mushroom puree, sturgeon served with lobster tails, quails *alla Genovese, potage printanière,* snipe, and grouse.[3]

For those who have enough status to drop the right word in the right ear, take-home food is also available directly from the kitchens of elite restaurants. One day a friend was invited to the exclusive restaurant at the Writers Union. After lunch he walked back into the kitchen with a prominent member of the union. He watched as the cook took two plump chickens, seemingly a different species from the anemic fowl sold in state stores, out of the refrigerator. The cook had them wrapped to take out and smiled as my friend pressed a ten-ruble bill into his hand.

Some clubs for Rising Class professionals regularly provide take-out food from their restaurants. At the Dom Zhurnalista, the Journalists Union, where my wife and I sometimes ate on foreigners' night, Thursday evening, the restaurant kitchen did a thriving trade in providing union members with fresh meat and even entire meals ready to take out.

Ivan, a quiet, intense writer, was surprised at the luxurious food available at one prominent magazine. He was invited to a meal by a man he described as "an ordinary editor" of the weekly publication of the Writers Union, the *Literary Gazette (Literaturnaya Gazeta).* After their discussion, the men left the editorial section and turned into a smallish room—a minirestaurant and minishop—reserved for medium-ranked editors.

It is common in such places to eat and buy take-out food at the same time. Ivan and his host sat down and a waitress served them coffee as they planned their purchases. Ivan tried not to look surprised at the array of fine food offered for sale, items almost never available in state food stores: red caviar, fresh sturgeon, fresh salmon, smoked fish, canned fish, canned orange juice from Greece, fruit compotes in glass jars from Bulgaria and Hungary, drawn and half-drawn Hungarian chickens wrapped in cellophane, and pork liver.

A week later, Ivan returned to the same offices to talk to a deputy editor, a man of higher rank than his first host. At the end of their session, the man suggested a quick meal. This time the writer was taken to a different room, one reserved for senior editors. The differences were subtle but definite. The coffee was better. The waitresses wore stylish white aprons and white headbands. The caviar was black, not red, and of higher quality. The tarts and cakes were superior. The liver was beef. These comparative minutiae are important in the variegated world of Soviet *klass*, for they are the acknowledged badges of rank.

Higher echelons of achievement merit access to even finer food shops. One prominent artistic figure described the canned crab and the other choice items he was able to buy in his special food shop. He casually mentioned that he had just picked up an order of liver—calves' liver. As I heard the story, I realized that a new tool of Soviet sociology had just been developed. One could measure Soviet *klass* by the simple phenomenon of liver. No liver at all for people without *klass*; pork liver for the lower levels; beef for middling privilege; and at the summit, calves' liver.

At the top of the Soviet food pyramid is the Kremlin, where the topmost Party elite have access to a Kremlin *payok* containing excellent quality food for eighty rubles a month. To buy similar food on the street would cost eight to ten times that amount; it would take days of shopping and would require contacts unavailable to most. Kremlin workers shop at the special shop on Granovsky Street, half way up the hill from Karl Marx Prospect. A glance at the line of black official cars lining both curbs quickly identifies its upper-class clientele. Well-dressed, smartly coiffeured women leave the Buro with oversized bags and slide them into the back seats of Volga and Chaika limousines. It is not possible to stand and watch this display of ostentation for long, for uniformed policemen move you on if you linger.

Whether at the Kremlin or at the lowest rungs of the Rising Class, status in food in the Soviet Union means meat. Russians love to eat beef, chicken, pork, and sausage and the Party knows it has to provide at least a minimum quantity in the major cities to avoid serious protest. The Party claims that the average Soviet citizen eats fifty-six kilograms (123.2 lbs) of meat per year, but the figure seems to be inflated for publicity purposes. Even that exaggerated figure is less than half the per capita consumption for the United States and well below that of West Germany. Many people turn to frozen or dried fish for protein.

Shopping for even small amounts of meat for the average Soviet citizen grows harder each year, even though the elite shops are seldom short of choice cuts. Shortages are particularly common in rural areas. By Western standards, much of what the Soviet Union sells as meat to ordinary citizens is almost inedible. It is full of bones and fat, cannot really be broiled, and sometimes needs to be boiled for hours to become digestible.

Street jokes in Moscow sum up how many people feel about unavailable food. In one, a man approaches a meat counter and asks one of the two assistants behind it for a fillet.

"No," says the assistant, "just out."

"Do you have any ground meat?" the shopper asks.

"No."

"Lamb?"

"No, maybe next week."

"Chicken?"

"No, last week."

"Beefsteak?"

"No."

"Sausage?"

"No."

The man turns and leaves the shop. The second assistant shakes his head: "Fancy asking for all that," he said. "What a fool!"

"Yes," says the first assistant, "but what a memory!"[4]

Even Party officials return from trips to the West impressed that meat is available all year round. One Party member said how surprised he was to see meat in the supermarket of a small American town in December. "All the Americans I met tried to be sympathetic and tell me the United States had problems, too—inflation, unemployment, racial tensions," he said. "I told them we have plenty of problems, as well. The difference is: we have problems; you have problems—and meat."[5]

Despite perennial meat shortages, the Party ensures that its senior members in the outlying Republics eat meat by sending frozen sides of beef and mutton in refrigerated railcars to cities where shortages are worst. The meat is unloaded at night and transported to cold storage. The only nonstatus Russians who can share in it are those who service the special food allotted to Party members. Boris, who worked in a cold storage vault where Party meat was kept in one Siberian city, realized that these shipments were so covert that no one made more than a cursory inventory. Before going home at night, he would hack choice cuts off a beef carcass and take them to his apartment wrapped in old newspapers. He later sold them to friends and neighbors at a small premium above state shop prices. The meat was so choice that he made a small fortune on his illegal enterprise.

The Party is discreet, but insists on taking care of its own. A special dairy farm outside Moscow produces top-quality milk, cream, butter, and cheese for the Kremlin's use alone. A separate state farm supplies cucumbers and other vegetables to Kremlin tables and simultaneously, of course, *na levo* ("on the left," or on the side) to the men and women who grow them.

How one eats in the USSR also depends on geography. In rural areas food is less plentiful, and its availability and quality rise as one approaches Moscow, Leningrad, and other cities of one million people or more. These are designated as

"A" cities. Below that population, the city receives a "B" designation and a poorer allotment of food.

The city of Kharkov in the Ukraine rejoiced in the late 1960s at being raised from "B" to "A" because its population had passed one million. The joy turned to disappointment when officials found they had been mistaken and the city was still 10,000 people short. The city finally did reach the million mark and with it the coveted "A" status.

Much hinges on location and climate. Kishinyov, the capital of Moldavia on the Romanian border, is forced to export so much fruit and wine that its people do not eat particularly well, despite its "A" status. Uzhgorod in the Ukraine has a lower ranking but eats better because it is allowed to keep more of the good food it grows.

So anxious is the Party to impress outsiders that the appearance of foreigners achieves miracles for the local population. When French and Italian mechanics arrived in the city of Izhevsk in the Urals to build a truck plant, the city rose from "B" to "A" status overnight. Local shoppers were delighted to see rare sausage and meat appear in the stores, and mourned a year later when the mechanics departed. Without them, the shelves began to empty.

Food can also appear in shop windows if Party leaders from Moscow pay a visit. Chickens went on sale in Tula, south of Moscow, when Leonid Brezhnev went there in the mid-1970s, and disappeared when he left.[6]

The food situation in the Soviet is strained, but it would be considerably worse without the help of the only legal capitalists in the land. They are the farm workers on Soviet collectives who are allowed to cultivate a private half-acre plot of land. The result is that 32 million private entrepreneurs raise livestock, potatoes, sugar beets, tomatoes, chickens, pigs, and rabbits.

Traditionally, the farm has had little status since 1917, or before. Between 1928 and 1930 Stalin killed and imprisoned most of the successful farmers, the so-called kulaks, seizing their lands to form state collectives. Today only farm chairmen and white-collar staff correspond to the Western idea of a "farmer," in that they make decisions about planting and harvesting. The rest of the rural population puts in an eight-hour day in the field, much like a worker in a factory.

Most rural workers do not have the same desire for privilege as sophisticated urbanites, but their expectations are growing. They achieve their measure of *klass* not from their state job, which is the lowest on the Soviet status ladder, but from the work they do for themselves early in the morning, at night, and during stolen hours put in cultivating their small parcels of private land.

The tiny patchwork of farmers' half-acre plots covers a mere 1.5 percent of the Soviet soil, but they are apparently a miracle of fertility. Men and women who laze through the day on state land are transformed into dynamos when they toil on these small pieces of their own land. In 1978, private plots produced 60 percent of all the potatoes in the country, as well as one-third of all the meat, milk, vegetables, and eggs.

Party hard-liners occasionally try to reduce the number of plots, seeing them as what they are, vestiges of capitalism. In fact their number has fallen off automatically in recent years as rural people have moved to the cities. But the Politburo knows it cannot do without the private farms while harvests remain uncertain. In fact, Soviet newspaper readers were recently informed that Hungary had become the largest food exporter in Eastern Europe, mainly because Hungarian officials lavished state aid on private plots.

Rural Class women like Irina Lukyanovna Lobinskaya, whom I met on the flatlands of the Ukraine, treasure these plots as their only hope of a middle-class existence. She greeted me in red cardigan and shawl, a sturdy, middle-aged, farm worker's wife. Three Soviet officials sat with me in her tiny house as we drank her tea and talked about farming. The home was clean, the walls spotless.

Irina's husband was tending hogs in low wooden buildings like aircraft hangars on a nearby hill; her eighteen-year-old daughter was in high school. Irina looked after the house, and at harvest time she helped dig up beets. Between chores she concentrated on the family's private plot, on which she raised livestock. Would she show it to me? I asked. The three officials frowned, but Irina nodded shyly and together we went out to see the prize of millions of Soviet rural families.

Fifty yards behind the farmhouse, we ducked our heads and entered a low, dark barn, teeming with life. A black and white cow, appearing huge in the confined space, stood protectively over her calf. Irina sold one calf each year and received 700 rubles for it—almost equal to half her husband's yearly salary. The Lobinskayas were saving for a car. Other income came from fifteen rabbits, sold for meat, some nutrias, hens, and chickens. If a calf died, it was a family catastrophe, and it was one of Irina's jobs to see that did not happen. Her calves were as well cared for as any Western bank account, and carried as much promise.

Food produced on private plots is fresh and available, but expensive when finally sold in state-authorized free markets in the cities. This successful capitalism coexists with a socialist food system that is inexpensive but poorly run and poorly stocked. Prices for meat, milk, fish, and bread at state food shops have remained almost unchanged for thirty years, held down by massive state subsidies that totaled some 40 billion rubles a year by early 1981.

But state food shops have a poor reputation with Soviet citizens. They are notorious for their ramshackle appearance, poor lighting, and brusque service, and, most important, for their lack of desirable food. Families complain about low butterfat levels in state-sold milk, fewer cuts of good sausage and salami, alarming absences of fresh fish. The Party can provide mouthwatering restaurants for the elite but many average citizens must leave their apartments each morning with plastic bag in hand, ready to hunt for food during lunch hours and after work.

The quality of the food he eats and how he is housed are two basic items that define a person's *klass* in the Soviet Union. As expectations rise, more energy of the new Rising Class is being devoted to that search for better food, to emerge from the survival stage that so long characterized tsarist Russia and still defines much of the USSR.

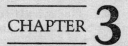
THE SYMBOLS OF PRESTIGE: COGNAC AND COMMODES

As I sat in a window seat of an Aeroflot Tupolev jet about to taxi away from the Domodedovo domestic terminal outside Moscow for a flight to Tbilisi, in Soviet Georgia, my eye fell upon a thickset Georgian struggling with a blue porcelain toilet bowl on the tarmac below. He disappeared under the wing, and a few minutes later collapsed breathlessly into a rear seat without his prize. He had persuaded, or paid off, a member of the ground staff to stow it carefully in the cargo compartment.

When we landed three hours later, the Georgian was the first off the plane. By the time I had reached the ground, he was a distant figure on the tarmac, walking briskly toward the terminal, his precious blue porcelain status symbol clutched in his arms.

Every society boasts a range of symbols by which its members measure status and rank. In America, a person might have an in-ground swimming pool or a mobile telephone or ride the supersonic Concorde jet to Europe. In the Soviet Union, symbols tend to be somewhat more basic. A Western-style toilet bowl, far from being regarded as a trifle, combines three essential elements of *klass* for the emerging Soviet bourgeoisie: it is rare, it is non-Soviet, and it is incomparably superior to local models.

Russian toilets are notable for a tendency to tilt to left or right, and a lack of lid. In the Soviet Union, any toilet seat is welcome, and anything better than a thin plastic model is a sign of status. Except in hotels patronized by foreigners, the water in most toilets I encountered did not shut off completely after refilling, and the clunk and drip of running water is an inevitable part of Soviet life. Finnish toilet seats will satisfy most members of the Soviet Rising Class, but American toilets are sought by Soviet sophisticates. Bolshoi ballet solo dancer Vyacheslav Gordeev and his wife Nadezhda Pavlova once returned from a New York tour with a turquoise toilet in their luggage. Installed in their home, it proclaimed their status as world travelers, as did their more conventional Scandinavian couches and chairs.

When I asked blond, effervescent Leningrad intellectual Irina what her status symbols were, she thought for a minute, and then replied, "Everything in our apartment talks about us and our status. Everything." Families in her building were competing to find door bells that chimed instead of buzzed, a contest that involved endless trips to special shops and warehouses. Her friends were caught up in a craze for indoor plants, the rarer the better. Telephones had become an obsession. Everyone wanted to replace their drab Soviet phones with better-looking red plastic models from Poland, or, even better, an Astra phone from Yugoslavia that was known as a *kolibri* (hummingbird) because its ring sounded more like a chirp than a bell.

The Soviet Rising Class can be gleefully ostentatious about many of its status symbols. At one end of a long bedroom in the apartment of an intellectual family stood its pride and joy: not the double bed with a large headboard; not the antique bookshelves stacked with rare, leather-bound books ordinary Russians cannot buy; no, it was a bar and two barstools. Glasses were neatly arranged on the polished countertop and bottles were stacked beneath. A carpenter had constructed bar and stools to order and the family regarded them as out-and-out status symbols. "We put them here because this is the largest room in the apartment," the husband explained. Ordinary Russians drink standing up in apartment stairwells, or in neighborhood canteens, or in dirty, crowded *pivo* (beer) bars with high counters. Their object is to get drunk as fast as possible. To drink perched on a stool, sipping slowly, is a rare Western refinement.

One physician kept American Nescafé jars from a special food shop as a status symbol and filled them with Soviet coffee. A chauffeur in the diplomatic service I knew proudly displayed a Finnish cigarette lighter and a red and white pack of Marlboro cigarettes. A writer's son begged me and other Western friends to bring him back a pair of Italian aviator-style sunglasses or a folding umbrella that fitted into a shopping bag. He would even accept an empty plastic shopping bag as long as it was splashed with bright color and printed in a foreign language.

An architect dropped casual hints of his recent vacations in Sochi, on the Black Sea, or to the status resort at Yermala, the long beachfront not far from Riga on the Latvian shore.

The relative of a writer spoke incessantly about her dacha in Peredelkino outside Moscow, about its mirrors and doorknobs, its floorboards and hearth rugs, its garden and exterior carvings. A government official used a state Volga limousine to take him to a superior *atelye*, a custom tailoring shop, so that the staff there would clearly recognize his status.[1]

Essential to a nouveau-riche, Rising Class way of life in Moscow, Leningrad, Kiev, Minsk, and other cities is anything that indicates contact with the outside world, particularly the West. Sometimes the boast is tasteful; at others it strikes Western eyes as almost sad. One family who had been abroad jammed its glass cabinets and tables with souvenirs that a Westerner, able to travel at will, would give away to small children: cheap metal models of the Eiffel Tower; plastic cocktail swizzle sticks and paper napkins from hotel bars and restaurants; ashtrays and postcards depicting Western capitals; stationery and ballpoint pens rifled from hotel drawers.

All were exhibited behind glass as tangible proof that the family had indeed touched foreign soil.

British tea towels made for drying dishes hang on non-kitchen walls as decorations. One Soviet acquaintance would ostentatiously leave his children's secondhand Fisher-Price toys on the floor of the living long after his children had gone to bed. One coveted item was a Western wall calendar. Russian friends constantly pressed Margaret and me for a Pan American or Barclay's Bank calendar, and displayed them prominently: the only Soviet calendars I saw were desk models. A roll of 35-millimeter American or Japanese camera film is also valued, not so much for the film itself, though that is also admired, but for its plastic cassette. In the Soviet superpower, film is still sold by lengths, in cardboard boxes. Gray plastic cassettes must be bought separately and the film loaded into them in darkness. One afternoon in Ashkhabad, the hot, sleepy capital of the Central Asian Republic of Turkmenia, I began to tear open a box of Soviet film after finishing my last Kodak roll. A young man beside me was horrified. "No, no," he said, and showed me the drill. He whipped off his jacket, laid it over film and Soviet cassette, and, using the coat as a minidarkroom, worked his hands back through the sleeves from the outside. "Didn't you know that?" asked a Moscow university student when I told him about it later. "All our film comes that way. In the summer we are always looking for shade so we can wind film onto cassettes." He paused. "Do you mean that film actually comes in its own cassettes in your country?"

Another sign of status, in a land of considerable sexual license in private but official Puritanism in public, is Western pornography. Officials and creative artists alike bring blue movies back from the West to show to friends. "It's curious," one Moscow intellectual told me. "Many Russians believe that blue movies represent the way the average Westerner behaves. If Russians think Westerners do something, it is status to do it themselves." The typical tourist cannot bring in pornography, but a businessman with high-level contacts can get it through customs.

Above all, it is the American touch that is valued. Teenagers in the big cities, with their thirst for foreign radio broadcasts, rock music, and jeans, prefer a "Made in U.S." label. Dmitri, a husky blue-collar worker, asked me on a street corner if I would bring him back some American jeans (*dzhinsi*) from Helsinki. "Not European but American Levis or Wranglers with the really strong denim—*chortova kozha* [literally, 'devil's skin']—with the sharp creases," he specified. He wanted a pair of sunglasses, but they had to have lenses as large and as sweeping as possible.

My wife and I once gave a pair of good American jeans to the daughter of a Russian friend. The girl was so thrilled that she could hardly speak. She kept covering her eyes with her hands and peeking through her fingers to see if the jeans were still on the table. She wore them every day for months.

Ultimate *klass* is a trip to New York for the opportunity to shop, to return with an American stove, a refrigerator, or other appliances. As a result Soviet officials visiting New York are not modest in their shopping splurges. Muscovites are convinced that some of these goods find their way into *kommissionyi* (secondhand) stores, where they bring enormous prices.

One senior official even brought back an American air-conditioner, though Moscow weather rendered it superfluous except for a few weeks a year. Japanese video recorders, many of which are purchased in New York, were popular in the artistic and diplomatic worlds. At the home of Victor Louis, in 1980, adult guests watched a cassette of *The Last Tycoon* on a Japanese video system while a group of children viewed an old Laurel and Hardy film on another at the end of the long living room. Japanese digital watches were also popular, especially the types with the most functions, such as chimes that beeped on the hour.

In the modern Soviet Union, the smallest item or habit can

become fashionable if it is Western. It was a status symbol in Moscow in 1980 to remark that you were reading detective stories by Western writers. The weekly intellectual and artistic magazine *Ogonyok* turned a Ross MacDonald novel, *The Far Side of the Dollar*, into a serial. Other treasured Western status symbols were cigarette lighters, fishing rods, miniature pocket calculators, even motorcycles. Since I left Moscow, an American personal computer has become the mark of immense *klass*.

The new bourgeois of the USSR are often envious of their friends and neighbors, perhaps more so than the middle classes that emerged before them in the West. Rising Class Russians study each other strenuously for status symbols that might have to be equaled. One army officer became annoyed when a relative acquired a small chandelier, since he and his wife considered it an affront to their own status. Several weeks later he tracked down a larger chandelier and had it hung where it could be seen from the front door. But his sense of achievement was short-lived: his relative's wife visited them one night wearing an imported sheepskin coat, and the officer was forced to spend more time scouring the black market until he had acquired a similar prize.

Another family we knew was incensed when neighbors covered their balcony floor with tiles imported from Finland. "What right do they have to show off like that?" demanded the wife. "Fancy displaying those vulgar tiles for everyone to see, and just where *we* have to look at them every day." Substitute the word "stunning" for "vulgar" and you see her point. "You wouldn't believe the pretty jealousies, the verbal battles, the cutting each other dead, that goes on when families compete over status symbols," one Moscow friend reported. "All our energies go into it, all our Slavic moodiness, our brooding uncertainties about life and self."

Status-conscious competition reaches into the Soviet Urban Class as well. One white-collar worker seemed to want little other than his end-of-the-day vodka, his Russian steam bath each Thursday after work, and an occasional day in the woods with his wife and daughter, but as he earned more he felt he needed to keep up with a friend with whom he went fishing. The friend had purchased some gaudy West German lures and the worker would not rest until he had a matching set. He kept on asking Western contacts until one bought him a set in Helsinki. The worker was delighted.

Not all Soviet Top and Rising Classes behave in a nouveau-riche manner. A number of Moscow, Leningrad, Minsk, and Baltic intellectuals, including scientists, mathematicians, writers, and artists, positively shun display. They want *klass* as much as anyone else, and spend as much time chasing it, but they consider restraint in public to be a sign of grace. Perhaps the worst epithet one can apply to a Soviet person is *nyekulturny*, "uncultured." It impugns his pride in having left backward, often rural, ways for a more modern world. The refined intelligentsia regard ostentation as *nyekulturny* and do not hesitate to say so. "Certainly not," replied one highly privileged man when I asked if he had thrown a large party to celebrate his Moscow wedding. "That is for others. We simply went to a restaurant with a few friends." He felt himself to be in the minority, however, and he was convinced that Russians en masse adored display.

At the top political levels, status symbols are often hidden from public view, except for the black limousines used by top Party men. This is not the inverted snobbery of the rich to be found in the United States and Britain, but rather a sense of self-importance, a feeling that superior ways of living are no one else's business. The higher the *klass* in the Soviet Union, the more Western and the more hidden it tends to be. The lower the status, the more Soviet it is and the more open it becomes.

The Politburo's own status symbols create the standards to which all aspire: the ZIL limousines, and luxurious government dachas such as the one at Pitsunda, south of Sochi, with its plate glass and marble and large swimming pool. The late

Leonid Brezhnev's own retreat near Moscow was a series of Victorian-style wooden cabins, simply but comfortably furnished with old-fashioned chairs and tables. Brezhnev had a penchant for hunting boar and deer, and for driving one of his dozen or more cars, including Cadillacs, Mercedes, Rolls-Royces, and others presented to him by foreign leaders who knew of his love of large non-Soviet automobiles.

Not all Soviet status symbols come from the West. Some are home-grown, particularly if they are antique. Experienced families assign students or other friends to browse through *kommissionyi* stores that sell prerevolutionary furniture and china, a new fad among the Rising Class. On the lower rungs of Soviet society lies the peasant suspicion that what is old is bad, but Western-oriented Russians delight to discover what Victor Louis did: two antique doorposts and a lintel for 100 rubles, or an entire walnut fireplace with carved figures holding up the mantel. Louis sent a photo of the fireplace to a friend in England asking him to find a heater to fit inside in lieu of a hearth.

The Soviet Urban Rising Class shop eagerly for fine Bukhara and other carpets from Soviet Central Asia, for gold jewelry and coins, for books with ornamental bindings. So great is the demand that the Kremlin keeps raising the prices for such antique goods, knowing that the new bourgeoisie will pay.[3] Some families collect wood and metal icons, and antique jewelry is also valued as a way to use excess rubles that would otherwise lie in the state bank accumulating only 2 percent simple interest.

Eastern European items also have their place in *klass*: Polish shirts and cosmetics; leatherware, ceramics, and canned vegetables from the Yadran shop in Moscow operated by the Yugoslavian government; crystal from the Czech Vlasta store. French cognac is prized, but so is Armenian cognac, usually accompanied by explanations that it was drunk by Winston Churchill himself. Scotch whisky and American rye or bourbon were uncommon in my time, except among diplomats, or officials of the Ministry of Foreign Trade or others who dealt regularly with foreigners. Vodka was a necessity; families of higher status served the best export grades. After dinner, they could offer guests genuine American cigarettes, made under license in Soviet Moldavia, or brought back from the West by returning travelers.

Some of the clothes and household cleaning compounds from the East German store on Lenin Prospect were also thought to be worth having. One special touch of *klass* in Russia is a radio antenna in the center of a car roof, a sign that the occupant has enough rank to be hooked into the radio-telephone communications link, "Baikal," that covers Politburo members, KGB chiefs, senior generals and admirals, and the upper levels of the Council of Ministers.

At least one Soviet intellectual coveted that antenna for the instant respect it would evoke from friends and police. He already possessed an imported car, itself a sign of privilege, but he felt that the central roof antenna would be the ultimate touch. It would provide access to the center lane on larger roads, enable him to drive at top speed and park wherever he wanted. When I last heard, he was still trying to figure out how to get such a restricted item. Another man reported as having close ties to the KGB was proud of the amber headlights he had installed on his car, similar to those on official cars that flash a warning to police to stop other traffic. When he flicked on his special lights, traffic police held other cars back.

As in the West, private cars are a major symbol of status. For those who have enough *klass* to warrant an official car, traffic jams are no problem. Police wave them through and onto reserved center lanes on major roads.

The ride to Moscow's VIP airport at Vnukovo usually took me the best part of an hour through heavy traffic on Lenin Prospect and beyond, but I soon discovered that Soviet officials routinely made the trip in half the time in their special lanes. After watching former secretary of state Cyrus Vance depart after one visit, I found my tiny Zhiguli (Lada) four-cylinder subcompact behind the dark blue Chevrolet sedan of *The New York Times*, its driver, David Shipler, was in his turn behind two American embassy Plymouth station wagons pulling out for the ride back to the embassy. Driven by experienced Russian chauffeurs selected by the KGB, the black Plymouths hurtled back down Lenin Prospect in the center lane at the busiest time of the afternoon, David keeping pace easily with me hanging on desperately behind. I knew that if I lagged too far police would consider my small car "nonofficial," in spite of its foreigner's plates. The magic path opened by police for the longer cars would vanish.

Rocketing faster than I thought the Zhiguli could go, I caught glimpses of crowds of pedestrians held back, and long lines of cars and trucks backed up on side streets. I realized how different Moscow was to the elite: faces vanishing in a blur, no delays, traffic cleared away. We reached the embassy in twenty-five minutes. It took me another twenty-five to recover.

Government cars are available to the elite even after working hours. It is a sign of prestige to be able to pick up a telephone and be collected from dinner by a black government car, even if only a four-cylinder Volga. I watched *Pravda*'s chief writer on the United States, the shrewd and shaggy Sergei Vishnevsky, telephone for a *Pravda* Volga from an American correspondent's apartment on Kutuzovsky Prospect in a discreet example of *klass*.

Inside the office, it is prestigious, as it once was in the United States, to have several telephones on the desk. I never encountered a switchboard in Russia, only single lines. A senior official who wants one line for his family and friends, another for ordinary office use, and a third for his chiefs has three separate telephones.

By Western standards, Soviet offices are small, except for

someone like Djerman Gvishiani, who was deputy chief of the State Committee on Science and Technology. He derived his privilege in two ways. He dealt continually with American, European, Japanese, and other foreign businessmen and was granted spacious quarters to show that Soviet officials, too, had large offices. He was also married to the daughter of the then premier, the late Alexei Kosygin. Lower-ranking officials, such as Vselevod Sofinsky when he was head of the Press Section of the Foreign Ministry, occupied offices Westerners would find cramped.

The higher a person's *klass* in the USSR, the more exalted the status symbols. When Grigorii Romanov, formerly the Party chief of Leningrad, still a full voting member of the Politburo, and one of the youngest leaders in the country, threw a wedding reception for his daughter in 1979, rumors raced around Leningrad and Moscow that he had given orders for priceless imperial china to be taken from a state museum. It was used, the rumor said, at his daughter's wedding to serve the Leningrad elite. Some of the china had been broken, the story went, and Romanov had been forced to take a telephone call from the Kremlin rebuking him for his ostentation and carelessness. Some said the call came from Leonid Brezhnev; others insisted it came from the late Mikhail Suslov.

A former American diplomat who had served in the U.S. Consulate in Leningrad had no doubt that Romanov had used the china. Too many people had confirmed the story to him. When I questioned Leningrad friends they raised their eyebrows. "Of course he used the china," said one. "That's what our leaders do. They live like tsars while we look for meat every day." I still can't swear that the story was true, but I found it interesting that my friends took it for granted, without question.

Leisure, especially expensive leisure, can be a sure sign of *klass* in the Soviet state. Late one lovely summer afternoon, I fell into conversation with a man festooned with privilege as he stood on the deck of the long white sightseeing ferry named the *Maxim Gorky*. Ivan, as I shall call him, had traveled abroad, owned a car, and earned considerable royalties from books that criticized the United States. As we floated along the Moscow River, a small sailing boat drifted toward us, its trim picked out in faded red paint, its lines boxy, its jib and mainsail patched and torn.

"How much would a boat like that cost?" I asked. It probably belonged to a trade-union sports club.

"Well, that's not a very good one," said Ivan as he squinted into the sun. "Let's say about 3,000 rubles, but much more for a proper type."

A dinghy approached, propelled by a tiny outboard motor. "Would many people have such boats?" I asked, having just read in the government newspaper *Izvestia* that a total of 813,000 motorboats jostled for mooring space on the Volga River alone; officials were trying to decide how fast they ought to be allowed to go, and whether more depots should be set up to sell fuel.

"Yes, yes," said Ivan, "many on the Volga. You see that outboard motor? The best ones are made in your country, in America. The best, I think, is the Mercury. But I don't have a wooden dinghy like that one." Ivan was in an expansive mood now, showing off his *klass* to a correspondent who undoubtedly thought there was nothing more to Russia than golden onion domes and snow.

"My boat is French, inflatable," he went on. "It can carry half a ton. My friends and I, we take extra fuel in cans, and bottles of vodka and whiskey, and we go down to where I keep the boat on the Moscow River not far from here, and we load it up. We cruise along until we find a calm stretch of water, and we switch off, and drift, and drink, and drink some more, and drift . . . beautiful."

One of his children was a member of a boat club, earning the right to sail in the summer by spending the winter cleaning and painting. He compared the merits of inflatable and fiberglass hulls. The sun set over the river. Birds called, and the *Maxim Gorky* slid smoothly through tranquil water between banks on which factories had given way to fields and trees. It could almost have been the Potomac, or the Hudson, or the upper reaches of the Thames, instead of Moscow, USSR.

In many ways Russians in the Rising Class are reminiscent of the early consumerist days in the United States and Western Europe. Their status symbols often reflect the enormous status attached to traveling outside their own country. They show the constant effort of men and women to use whatever influence they have to acquire possessions that make them different from the sea of uniformity around them.

Their joy in bringing back from a trip a tin of Twinings tea or a box of After Eight mints or a pair of American Levis is the joy of those who have set themselves apart from their fellows by exerting *klass* to achieve the foreign travel denied to all but a very few.

Their restless desire to acquire a new telephone or a private car or a period mantelpiece is partly the pent-up need for comfort and style after decades of war, purges, and economic hardships. It is also in part an assertion of their own belief that they have "arrived," that they know someone influential or have access to a trade union or professional club, or have landed a job with access to special food shops, elite custom tailors, or a privileged dacha in a cool pine forest.

The rush for status symbols is the Western rather than the Asian side of the Russian character. It represents modernity to a Rising Class that prides itself on having left behind the peasant manners of a rural, prerevolutionary society. It seemed to me that my Rising Class friends, while intensely proud of their own country, and patriotic to the core, nonetheless wanted to be accepted by the West as enlightened, civilized, respectable Europeans. They didn't want to be seen, and they tried not to see themselves, as backward, uneducated, Asian, or old-fashioned.

The Rising Class is largely an urban class. It wants a bigger

share of the *klass* that the Top Class possesses. It listens to
foreign broadcasts. It reads foreign books in translation
(though not many are permitted to leak through the censors).
It sees foreign tourists in the streets in the bigger cities. It is
convinced—rightly—that it lives a more comfortable life
than its parents and grandparents did.

Only a minority of the Rising Class are dissidents, though
many of them pay far less attention to Party ideology than the
Party itself would prefer. Given the chance to go abroad to
live, the majority would go to see the world for themselves,
and then would return to home and family and the country
they know best. The Party errs in believing that a desire to
know about and to imitate the rest of the world means automatic disloyalty to the USSR. Many of the Rising Class are
disillusioned with Marxist ideology, but not to the point of
taking the momentous step to leave their country, families,
and friends forever.

Back in 1839, a remarkable French nobleman named the
Marquis de Custine traveled through Russia by coach for six
months and wrote a book as perceptive in its way about the
Russia of the tsars as Alexis de Tocqueville was about the
United States of America at about the same time. Noting a
desire of the tsar's court and the nobles and other upper levels
of society to imitate the West, the Marquis wrote, "I do not
blame the Russians for being what they are. I blame them for
pretending to be what we are."[4]

His point was about more than just status symbols. Yet
millions of urban, Rising Class Russians are still aiming to be
"what we are" in the way they live and exert *klass* influence.
In a society that in theory is supposed to be narrowing the
cleavages of social distinctions, they search constantly for a
comfortable, carpeted, relatively affluent middle-class identity. They do it in part by reaching for status symbols from
cognac to commodes. They yearn for sophistication, with all
the hunger of a people whose country is still a relative new-
comer, in historical terms, to urban, Western social ways.

CHAPTER 4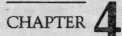

HOUSING *KLASS*

V anya wanted to write poetry, and to dream, and to read books. He did not want to follow the career the state had marked out for him as an engineer. He was tall and pale, with an air of distraction, oddly out of place in the down-to-earth, materialistic Soviet society of today. He had upset his bosses with his lack of application, and he no longer worked at his institute. Since his file, or "work book" *(trudovaya knizhka)* now carried a critical comment in it, and since Soviet citizens cannot get a second job unless they present their books to prospective employers, his chances of another good job were minimal. He eked out a living by translating documents for university friends (he spoke several languages).

His wife, Galya, felt much the same about the workaday world of Soviet society as he did. All she wanted to do was paint pictures. She and Vanya had no children when Margaret and I met them, and although their parents both held what seemed to be solid jobs in their fields, they seemed to have few prospects either.

But they did have an apartment. In Soviet *klass* terms it was a good one, though they thought it more of a trial than a triumph. "Come and see how Russians live," said Vanya in a gently self-mocking way characteristic of him. "We think you ought to see."

One night in winter we met him on the sidewalk close to his apartment building. He held a finger to his lips to indicate that we should not say a word: the moment we tried to speak

Russian our accents would give us away, and he was in enough trouble without neighbors knowing he was entertaining Westerners—worse, an American, and worse still, an American correspondent from whom Soviet citizens were constantly exhorted by the official press to stay away.

I'm not sure what Margaret and I expected to find. By Moscow standards the area was good—about a mile and a half from Red Square itself. The building was solid but anonymous from the outside, as so many Russian buildings are. It looked pre-Revolution. Vanya led us silently into a dark and odorous lobby. The floor was thick with dirt. The light was dim. The air smelled of stale, boiled cabbage, and old potatoes, and imperfect plumbing, and neglect.

The gray paint on the elevator shaft was peeling. The elevator itself creaked and groaned to an upper floor. We emerged, turned left, and made our way down a dim hallway to a door at the far end covered with black sound-proofing material. Vanya fumbled for a key. The door swung back to show another hallway lit by one dangling bulb. Seven doors were set into the wall to our right, and three to the left-hand wall. Another key, and Vanya opened the first door to the right and we slid inside.

We were in a large room. Americans would call it a studio apartment. Vanya and Galya had divided it into a painting area for her at the far end by the tall windows, a sleeping area, and a living area. The floor was parquet but caked with mud and slush from winter boots that had dried where it fell. A refrigerator against one wall did not work (to save electricity) but it hardly mattered: fruit and vegetables and odds and ends of meat hung in bags between the standard double panes of the windows, frozen solid by the winter weather.

The room was shabby-genteel. The furniture was solid, clearly expensive in its time, which I estimated to be fifty years ago.

Gradually Vanya and Galya told the story of the apartment. Before 1917, a wealthy merchant had lived in all of it; the three doors in the opposite hallway wall opened into a bathroom, a small lavatory, and a kitchen. But now a separate family lived in each of the seven rooms, which meant that twenty-three individuals shared the facilities across the hall. Things had been worse: several people had recently moved out for one reason or another.

Vanya and Galya dreamed, not of a penthouse or a car, but of a kitchen and a bath of their own. Whenever they visited their parents who lived in a newer building, they refused to eat as a point of principle ("we can afford our own food") but always accepted the offer of a long, hot bath without other people hammering on the door every few minutes. "Tell me," Galya asked, "how many apartments in your country would have their own bathrooms and kitchens?"

Vanya pulled open the door of the bathroom across the hall. Lit by one twenty-five-watt bulb without a shade, the room contained an ancient tub with a broken leg tilting it to one side; a low, cracked toilet without cover or seat; an overhead cistern tank coming away from the wall; and graying tiles dropping to the floor.

In the communal kitchen, four small gas stoves stood side by side. Seven small tables were piled high with pots and pans. Cockroaches rustled underfoot. A list pinned to the door set out the days each family was responsible for cleaning. "I try never to come into the kitchen at all," Galya said. "I'd rather buy food and eat it in our room." I indicated seven pegs on a bathroom wall, from which hung seven zinc tubs. "Where else are we to wash our clothes?" Galya asked. She shuddered at the thought of raising a child in such an atmosphere. She and Vanya had inherited their communal room from an aunt who had lived there for fifty years. She had raised children in it, and she had died in it.

Grim as it seemed to our outsiders' eyes, the apartment was actually a superior one of its kind. It was centrally located, and occupied far more floor space than the young couple would have been entitled to had they applied for new state-built premises. If they had not inherited it, they would probably have been living in worse circumstances, with less room to write and paint, although, as they pointed out, they might have had their own kitchen and bathroom.

Margaret and I returned to our own foreigner's apartment, to find it palatial by comparison. It has been estimated that 20 to 30 percent of the residents of downtown Moscow and Leningrad still live in communal apartments. The Party builds many new apartment blocks every year. New ones are superior to most of the older ones (even though friends complained all the time that walls were thinner and the neighbors much more audible, especially when the husbands were drunk). Yet the rate of construction cannot keep pace with demand, and millions of Vanyas and Galyas keep making do, and sharing bathrooms and kitchens.

"What do you do if you feel ill or you need the bathroom in a hurry in the mornings?" I asked. Vanya smiled in his self-mocking way. "I do what all of Russia does," he replied. "I wait."

Lives, literature, marriages, and dreams in the Soviet Union are all permeated with the hope of finding an extra room. The writer Vladimir Voinovich wanted one, but had to struggle with a man with Party connections for so many months that he felt compelled to write a book about it, the satirical *Ivankiad*. At one point he says, "Now I will be able to have my own room, where in blessed silence I will be able to create my own works . . . as long as I've lived I've never known such luxury. If some kind magician were to appear and ask my one desire, I would say, 'I want a room to myself.'"[1]

When the Party asked for approval of the new Soviet constitution, one citizen suggested that Section 44 be amended to include the words: "The aim of the Socialist state is to provide each member of a Soviet family with his own room." It was merely an aim, not a call to action, but it was not adopted by the Party.

While millions of Russians scheme for their own space, those with sufficient *klass* live in relative splendor in the "workers' state." Artist Ilya Glazunov lives in a handsome, high-ceilinged apartment in central Moscow with three large bedrooms, a living room, and a kitchen with dining alcove, all for three adults and two children. On the floor above is his penthouse studio. Maya Plisetskaya, prima ballerina of the Bolshoi, had five large rooms on Gorky Street comparable to a Park Avenue triplex, complete with imported stove, refrigerator and dishwasher, coffee-table art books, and a collection of drawings, paintings, and lithographs by Picasso, Léger, Braque, and Chagall.

Victor Louis lives in a converted summer dacha at Bakovka, outside Moscow. The area is filled with luxurious tsarist-era estates, one of which was used by Leonid Brezhnev, another of which is reserved for the staff of *Pravda*. The Louises—his wife is British—have a two-storied dacha that could be in any fashionable area outside of London or New York. Built in the style of a hunting lodge, its walls are paneled in dark wood, its dining room floor is tiled with squares of Italian marble, and the study is reached by a spiral staircase leading down from a lounge.

"Is Louis KGB?" I once asked a veteran Soviet analyst. "No," he replied. "He is a lot higher. He speaks with the voice of the Politburo itself."

Moscow, the most privileged of all Soviet cities, still suffers from inferior construction and cramped quarters, but it has islands of supreme *klass*. The better apartment buildings are found in the most fashionable areas: a quiet street called Alexei Tolstoy that runs from the Sadovoye Koltso south toward the Kremlin or on Ryleev Street, which links inner and Sadovoye ring roads not far away. Attractive new apartment buildings are also located in a number of unobtrusive streets in the southwest arc of the circle by the Sadovoye ring with the Kremlin at its center. A trained eye can spot them: solid, well-built apartment houses set back from the sidewalks.

Neighboring apartment blocks are pre-fabricated concrete,

with walls straying from the perpendicular, badly painted, old before their time. Others have ancient stone façades behind which several families live in communal style. Luxury apartments for the elite are conspicuous by contrast. Each is at least nine stories tall, built not of concrete but of honey-colored bricks. Unlike most Soviet brickwork, these are laid to regulation Western standards, straight and true. Their windowpanes are larger than usual, fitted with clearer, more expensive glass.

One of these apartment houses, on Alexei Tolstoy, has its own spacious parking lot instead of the usual surrounding patch of untended ground. Black official cars wait with engines idling as drivers read newspapers or smoke in silence. A police car is parked around a nearby corner, its own engine running. In the lot are the usual official Volga cars, four-cylinders, badly finished; one or two old-style Chaikas, chrome and black and finned like a 1955 Chevrolet; a new-model Chaika; and a bright red Mercedes sports car so immaculately clean that it has clearly emerged from another status symbol: a garage. On the day that I spotted this building, I noticed a massive, black, custom-built ZIL limousine nose out of the driveway at 8:30 A.M. following a silvery BMW sedan converted for police use with its roof light flashing. It was followed by the Volga parked around the corner, which sprang forward at a sign from a policeman who had stopped all traffic.

On Ryleev Street, another new brown-brick apartment house has chandeliers in its large lobby, a strong contrast to the naked twenty-five-watt bulbs that distinguish the standard apartment-house entrance. No gray-uniformed *militsioner* (policeman) was to be seen, but attendants inside the glass entrance doors checked each face as it came and went. Natasha, a Moscow friend, laughed when I told her what I had seen.

"You cannot imagine," she said, "the maneuvering that goes on to get an apartment in one of those places. You need really high rank in the Party or the KGB, or in a ministry with more than usual influence—heavy industry, or metallurgy. Or you have to be a really outstanding and politically 'safe' ballet dancer or composer or something like that." Another friend of some status agreed: "It can take years to get in. You have to start the battle as soon as you know a brown-brick building is going up. Wait until construction begins and you don't have a chance."

Both women were struck by the mixture of individuals who share the buildings. In the Soviet Union, intellectuals and artists can live in separate co-op buildings built by unions: composers here, dancers there. But within some of the new brown-brick walls there is at least a measure of upper-class diversity. A general in the KGB can share an elevator with a noted professor whose political views are closer to dissent than to the Party; a member of the Party Central Committee walks to the parking lot a few paces behind a famous actor.

The apartments are expensive, but money alone does not gain access at these exalted levels. Only high station will provide an apartment in a brick building and ensure another privilege: quiet in a city of seven million people and thundering government trucks. When the first brown-brick apartment was completed on Alexei Tolstoy, a new sign went up in the corner where traffic turns into the street from the main ring road. "No entry," it proclaimed, "between 11 P.M. and 7 A.M."

Many of the superior apartment houses in the Soviet Union, as in the West, are cooperative buildings, generally purchased and owned by members of the Rising Class. Middle-rank professionals—scientists, writers, actors, doctors, musicians—join together and give the state 40 percent of the construction cost. The state lends them the other 60 percent, and builds the apartment. The 60 percent loan is paid back to the state at one half of one percent interest, monthly. One friend of ours was paying twenty-five rubles a month for the two rooms he and his wife kept in immaculate condition; another couple paid fifty-five rubles a month, about a third of an average monthly salary, but only about an eighth or a tenth of the income of typical Rising Class couples.

Two decades ago, electronics engineer Viktor Elistratov deposited 1,500 rubles as his share on a building not far from the Leningradsky train station in Moscow. A decade later, other friends had to lay out 6,000 rubles for the same privilege. In co-op apartments, children are also registered as occupants, and they can inherit the apartment. They can also sell it, but only for the original cost. To make a profit by selling an apartment would be speculation, and therefore illegal. But in reality, speculation in apartments is rife, with payments made in secret.

The advantages of owning a good co-op apartment are many. The workmanship can be better than in state housing; the fixtures can include such details as parquet floors and foreign kitchens; the rooms may be larger; it is one of the few major private investments possible in the socialist state; the apartment can be inherited by one's children; and the buildings are built more rapidly than others. Even with the red tape involved, a family can move into a new co-op faster than if they wait on a government list for a regular state apartment.

However, at the very top levels of klass—academicians, senior Party figures, marshals and generals—even better apartments are provided by the state at purely nominal rents. It is an irony of klass that only two types of people have "public" or state-provided housing: the poor in the Urban and Rural Classes (and most of the Rising Class as well) together with the ultraprivileged, who get the best the state can offer both as a reward for loyalty and an inducement to remain loyal. A prominent scientist I knew lived in a fine co-op on Lenin Prospect, with several large bedrooms; an academician just a few doors away was so senior in klass that he had an even larger apartment in a building belonging to the Council of Ministers, at a diminutive rent.

Most apartments in the Soviet Union are small, particularly

by American standards. Lenin himself established the tradition by decreeing that Soviet citizens were to be allowed only nine square meters of living space per head. No one seems to know why Lenin chose nine, but he did; and much of Soviet life revolves around that awesome statistic. Nine square meters is 96.86 square feet—or a room slightly smaller than ten feet wide by ten feet long. The quota excludes kitchen, bath, and hallways, but even so it is hardly Utopian. By 1979, *Pravda* was reporting total usable space of 12.1 square meters per person, but that included kitchen and bathroom, and even then it was only one-third of the corresponding figure in the United States.

One measure of *klass* in the Soviet Union is the ability to increase living space without crowding in more bodies. A member of the Writers Union is entitled to an extra twenty square meters by virtue of his union card. A scientist with a doctorate can also claim an extra twenty square meters, another incentive for academic achievement. The higher a man rises in the Academy of Sciences, or the KGB, or the Party Central Committee, or a district soviet (council), or a trade union, the more space he is allotted. I knew of one academician's apartment of 200 square meters for a family of three.

For an urban family already living in a comfortable apartment, the next step up in status is a dacha outside the city. It can be a one-room wooden shack without water or electricity, a two-story chalet with carved window frames and winter insulation, or the plate glass and chandeliers of Party dachas on the Black Sea.

Olga and Anatoly used their privileged positions in the artistic world to build their own dacha outside Moscow. As lumber, nails, glass, and cement poured into the city for the 1980 Olympic Games, their contacts diverted enough building materials to them to build their summer place. Another couple, now retired, created a jewel with an open fireplace, a sauna bath imported from Finland, and gleaming parquet flooring. Irina, a translator, lived with her mother and son in a

smaller dacha outside Moscow in July and August, carrying
cutlery and sheets back and forth by train. She was happy to
make the long train ride to work each day if it meant she
could escape Moscow pollution and breathe fresh air at night
and on weekends.

Marina, a musician, talked animatedly about her own
plans. A good dacha, she explained, costs about 9,000 rubles.
But despite *Pravda*'s articles about falling crime rates, thieves
often broke in while owners were in the city.

"No, no," she said, "it's better to buy into a country club."

I had visions of a low clubhouse, tennis courts, ice-skating
rinks, a restaurant, but Marina had something more prosaic in
mind. "You know, like an apartment building, but in the
country," she explained. "You buy into it, like a *kooperativ*
really, and there are men to guard the lobby and you have
friends in the building. We Russians like to be together.
That's far the best way, really it is." She had already bought
her own "country club" apartment and was calling upon a
formidable array of contacts to furnish it in a way that, she
hoped, would stun her neighbors.

Marina was following a pattern set by the Party itself. It
unobtrusively constructs some of the best housing in the
country, doing what it can to hide it from the general public.
Nikita, an artist with the shoulders of a weightlifter, was
asked by a friend if he wanted to help sculpt abstract designs
on a stone wall going up at a new apartment complex. The
pay would be good, so he agreed. He found himself outside
Moscow the following day staring at the most luxurious
apartment block he had ever seen. He had not known buildings of such quality existed in his country.

The wall he was to embellish ran for fifty feet from an access road to a main building set in a grove of trees. Each apartment had a wide balcony, with a view of rural tranquillity.
Kitchens were equipped with stoves and refrigerators from
West Germany; rooms were carpeted and furnished in Scandinavian design from Helsinki. Living rooms had brick fire-

places. Nikita suspected the complex was for weekends and vacations for Central Committee members of the Party, but not even construction crews on the site could confirm that. Nikita marveled at the building, but he was disturbed that such privilege could exist in a country mired in a perpetual housing shortage.

How do most Russians, even those with only a modicum of *klass*, manage to get more living space? The answers include connections, ingenuity, and swapping. People gather to swap apartments either in tiny offices provided for the purpose, or on snowy street corners, or at Metro (subway) entrances. Private deals are legal, but must be registered with the local authorities immediately.

Tanya, a professional woman of some distinction, lived with her young son, another grown son and his wife, her own mother, and a large dog in two rooms in an old building. In an adjoining room were a man, his wife, and three small children. Both families—ten people—shared the same bathroom and kitchen. Tanya's sons were not on speaking terms with each other; neither family liked the other. Life was a grind of tension without privacy.

At last Tanya was able to pull some trade-union strings and make an elaborate swap, which was highly admired. She traded her two rooms for one room in a cooperative apartment for herself, her mother and her dog, and for two more rooms further out of town for her two sons and her daughter-in-law.

Tanya laughed when I asked why the swap had taken so long. "You can't just go to a local *raion* and ask," she said, indulgent at my ignorance. "They have long lists and they give preference to families with less than nine square meters per person. Oh, you can try to slip an official a thousand rubles if you want, maybe two thousand." She paused. "You would do it in private of course, without witnesses, so that if he tries to inform on you later, it's only his word against yours . . . Well, I don't do that sort of thing."

Another housing saga illustrated the use of government swapping offices, and some of the problems of life in the Soviet for those without *klass* privilege.

When her father died, Olga was left with her sister Natasha and her mother in a two-room apartment suddenly larger than the twenty-seven square meters to which the three of them were officially entitled. The choices were bleak: either they waited for local officials to put another family in with them to alleviate the housing shortage, or they would face higher rent, double the standard rate for every square meter over twenty-seven. Rumor had it that the excess rental rate was soon to rise to five times the normal one, which would break the family budget.

The only other choice was to move. Olga's mother pestered the local housing office every day for weeks, and contacted a relative who worked for a construction enterprise. Olga, Natasha, and the mother succeeded in swapping their old place for a single room of barely twenty-seven square meters with its own kitchen and bath, and they congratulated themselves. But new problems arose when Natasha married and needed a place of her own. A separate apartment meant a long wait, so the family agreed to put up a thin wall across its one room. Olga and her mother lived on one side; Natasha and her new husband lived on the other. All shared kitchen and bath. Although they had less than the minimum nine square meters per person, they lacked sufficient *klass* to break out of the dilemma.

Four years later Natasha gave birth to a baby girl, and her husband's excellent work and ideological record finally produced a separate apartment: two rooms of their own. One room was twelve square meters, the other eight. The move left Olga and her mother alone in the twenty-seven-square-meter room, and the same old fear surfaced: the two of them were entitled to only eighteen meters. What would happen to them now? Would another family be foisted upon them?

Suddenly, Natasha and her husband were divorced. Natasha

visited a local housing office and leafed through one of the many swap registers kept there. She found an offer: "two rooms for two single rooms." She landed one room for herself and her child (sixteen square meters) and a single communal apartment room for her ex-husband. All this required taking time off from work, paying a small fortune to hire a truck to transport belongings, and more rubles for vodka and bribes to induce the men to finish the job.

Meanwhile, Olga and her mother had decided to give up the room of twenty-seven square meters before another family moved in. They finessed a swap for a room of eighteen square meters close to Natasha's new room. Olga had taken the bus over to Natasha's area many times to stick small handwritten notices to walls and doors asking if anyone wanted to swap, only to see janitors take the papers off each morning.

The finale to this marathon was yet to come: Olga and her mother wanted to live with Natasha again after her divorce. Months of extra effort, use of contacts, pleading, traveling, hunting, and poring over registration books enabled them to swap Natasha's sixteen-square-meter room and Olga's eighteen-square-meter room for one three-room place. The family was pleased . . . and exhausted.

Sometimes nothing avails in the perpetual fight against bureaucracy, and a small Soviet apartment can become a veritable prison. Igor, forty years old, lived in a two-room shoebox with Anna, the woman who was once his wife. They had divorced years ago but neither could find another place. When they broke up, Igor found a girlfriend who was now back in her East European home with the baby she bore him. Anna remarried and left the apartment. Igor applied for an exit visa to live with his girlfriend, only to see it rejected. Anna divorced her new husband and she and Igor drifted together again in their former apartment, which Igor had never left. They sleep in separate rooms, each with its own lock, two lives made more complex by the lack of living space endemic to Soviet cities.

* * *

When Soviet citizens emigrate, they cannot imagine a housing system different from their own. "Those houses," said one émigré as he drove from the airport in London, "how many families live in each?"

"Just one," replied his friend. "Just one."

The émigré's disbelief slowly turned to wonder as he drove the fifteen miles to his friend's own home. He had lived in Leningrad, where rumors circulated that the Party was about to reduce allowable living space from nine to seven square meters. The concept of one family, one house, took time to accept.

Within the constraints of its emphasis on military hardware and heavy industry, the Party has tried to fill the urgent demand for housing, but it is hobbled by Soviet inefficiency and the lasting effects of World War II. In the Crimea, in the western border areas, and in Leningrad, the Nazi invasion wreaked terrible damage. One in every five buildings in Leningrad was flattened during the 900-day siege there. Construction of new apartment buildings goes on regularly, and the older city centers of Moscow, Leningrad, Kiev, Odessa, Yalta, Smolensk, and Sverdlovsk are ringed by the pale, rectangular shapes of new apartment buildings, lined up like soldiers on parade.

These buildings are thin-walled, generally poorly built, noisy, and crowded, but a step forward from pre-1917 wooden *izbas* (cottages) which had no plumbing and no running water. Each year the Party says it completes 110 million square meters of housing and that 11 million people move into new apartments. Thirteen million square meters are built in cooperative buildings in the cities, and 14 million more in the countryside. The Party keeps rents low; for ordinary apartments they have not risen since 1928, and constitute as little as 4 percent of the joint income of a working couple. "Rent isn't something we think about," said Volodya, "or heat or the phone or electricity or water. That's the one good thing about Soviet housing: it's cheap."

If you are a worker, it helps to have a job with a powerful, favored ministry such as those for the chemical industry, machine tools, or the fishing industry, which invest twice as much money in apartments for their workers as do the non-status ministries for railroads, light industry, food, and trade. *Pravda* comments from time to time on workers who deliberately seek jobs at computer factories, qualify for housing, move in, and then switch back to less prestigious but more congenial work. Those who work in industries of low priority are discriminated against.

Millions still live in Nikita Khrushchev's contribution to better housing: oblongs of five-story walk-up buildings. Residents think he did a good job in recognizing the housing crisis and building new dwellings, but they complain that he lowered ceilings and, in particular, made kitchens smaller to cut costs. The slang word for these oblongs is *krushchoby*—a pun on the former leader's name and on the Russian word *trushchoba*, or slum.

The tendency to build poor-quality housing was not restricted to Khrushchev's era. In too many new Soviet apartment buildings, floors consist of poured concrete with thin linoleum stuck directly onto it. Holes are bashed in new bathroom floors and walls for water, sewage, and drainage pipes, and left that way. The wife of a French contractor working on Moscow's new Kosmos Hotel lived in a new Soviet apartment that, she says, aged a decade in a single year. Fittings pulled away from walls, tiles fell and smashed, mailboxes were vandalized.

Even buildings for the privileged, unless they are made of brick, quickly show signs of age, sometimes before they are occupied. A concrete edging was slapped into place on the outside wall of a renovated building opposite our apartment, but fell off soon afterward, breaking the windshield of a car belonging to the *Daily Telegraph* of London. When sandbags were placed on an inner-courtyard balcony in the just-constructed French embassy, the whole balcony slid spectacularly to the ground, though the bags were only half the weight that the balcony was designed to bear.

Soviet families take for granted paying for necessary repairs before they move into a newly built apartment house. Windows don't fit, walls sag, floors are rough and unfinished. Inspectors at factories where housing components are made constitute a mere one percent of total staff, and no one checks quality on the site.

Fortunately for the government, the expectations of the Urban and Rural Classes are still relatively low. For many, one new apartment in a lifetime fulfills a dream. But for the Rising Class, quality and size are more important than cost, and it is these factors that are generally lacking. The elite at all levels would like to get one of the new, larger apartments in solidly built brick buildings. Lacking that, they bribe, swap, fix, build cooperatively, and devise other strategems to find an extra room, a balcony, space for a mother-in-law or a new baby. There is little chance that their drive for more space, more Finnish kitchens, more dignity in living, will abate soon.

The most desirable Rising Class housing is to be found in the major cities, where food, jobs, and opportunities are best: Moscow, Leningrad, Kiev, the three Baltic capitals, and so on. It is not easy to move to those cities if you happen to live somewhere else; you need a police stamp (*propiska*) in your internal passport showing that you have permission to live in the city of your choice. One sign of *klass* can be whether an outsider has managed to gain such permission, and one way is to work in an essential trade or profession, such as building construction. Bricklayers, carpenters, crane operators, and others simply turn up at construction sites. If qualified, they are quickly hired. Foremen wink at the absence of a *propiska*. If a man or woman holds down a job in a city for five years, he or she can simply apply for a *propiska* and receive it. Some men and women resort to the *fiktivnyi brak*, or fictitious marriage, to become the spouse of someone with a coveted residence stamp and thus acquire a similar stamp for themselves. The cost to the person seeking residence can be high: it cost one out-of-town construction manager 5,000 rubles for a cooperative apartment for his "wife" and carrying charges of fifty rubles a month. He wanted so badly to live in Leningrad that he paid the money for two years, after which the "marriage" was dissolved by agreement.

Big-city chauvinism, and the status it bestows, is common among the Soviet Rising Class. "The provinces, anywhere more than 200 miles from Moscow, are just a blur," says the son of one renowned Soviet scientist. "No one I ever knew went there. Somehow, they didn't exist." In the same snobbish manner, the lower classes are derided by those above them. In the world's first workers' and peasants' state, to be a worker or a peasant, or the descendant of these classes, carries little status. Only older Party leaders and officials boast of their humble origins, while the urban elite who make up most of the Rising Class try to hide theirs.

"The worst thing you could be," says Alexander Levich, a child of privilege in Moscow until he emigrated a few years ago, "was to be known as someone descended from a worker or a peasant."[3] Levich, tall and fair-haired, lived in a home wrapped in *klass* because of his father's elevated status as a member of the Academy of Sciences. Dr. Benjamin Levich, now living in New York, was also a full professor in Moscow before he emigrated.

"If you had a grandmother or a grandfather who came from a village," Sasha explains, "you didn't talk about it. You hid them, so to speak. You didn't let your city friends know about them. As in all things in the Soviet Union, there is a public show in which the worker and the peasant are all important, and a private, more real one, in which they are not."

CHAPTER 5

KLASS AND *KULTURA*

I n the name of communist equality, the doors of Soviet theater, ballet, concerts, and exhibitions should swing wide to all comers, and especially to the ranks of workers and peasants in whose name the Party rules. In theory the people ought to be exposed to the finest cultural traditions the country has to offer.

In fact, Soviet society is an interlocking cliff face of *klass* distinctions. To get a ticket to a show or concert that is worth attending, a Muscovite or a Leningrader or a Kievan or a Siberian in Novosibirsk or Yakutsk needs status, influence, or privilege—in a word, *klass*. The result is that only a few see the best. Most have to make do with the worst.

It is in the nature of ambitious, restless, growing middle classes the world over to express themselves, not only through jobs and possessions, but by demanding a share of the culture that the classes above them have long enjoyed. The new Soviet Rising Class emerging in the cities is no exception, but it finds the struggle far from easy.

Take, for instance, Sunday, April 25, 1982. Across Moscow that day, thirty-one theaters were playing matinee and evening performances, and some were open in the morning for special children's programs. Moscow families could, it seemed, choose between the Bolshoi Opera and Ballet companies; the giant stage of the 6,000-seat Kremlin Palace of Congresses (white marble and imported glass, roughly equivalent to Washington's Kennedy Center); two state circuses; a world-famous puppet theater; three children's theaters; and even a new animal theater where four-legged actors (and birds) staged tableaux and stumbled through elemental story lines.

Twelve halls were open for concerts, from the impressive conservatory to smaller, simpler auditoriums. Art museums and galleries included the interior of the Kremlin itself and the legendary Tretyakov Gallery.

On the face of it, a Muscovite had a wide choice of both post-Revolution and pre-Revolution offerings, in one of the best-known cultural capitals on earth. It appeared to compare well with a typical night in London at the same time, which saw four operas, one ballet, two big concerts, fifty-seven theaters, two talked-about exhibitions ("Painting in Naples" and paintings and manuscripts by Richard Adams, the author of *Watership Down*), and eighteen art galleries.

All over the world there is competition to see the best on offer: Moscow is hardly alone in that. It always helps to know someone in the cast or in the theater, or to have access to block-booked tickets, wherever you are. A number of shows in London, especially musicals, were sold out for months.

In Western capitals, though, ordinary people can get to see hit shows if they wait long enough. In Moscow, mere waiting won't do it. *Klass* might. Even the higher ranks of the Soviet Rising Class have difficulty getting into the Bolshoi; lesser Muscovites have little hope at all.

The only people in Moscow who could count on seeing the opera *Boris Godunov* at the Bolshoi that afternoon, or the ballet *These Charming Sounds* that night, were foreign tourists whose seats had been booked in advance as part of their itineraries, or members of extremely senior Party, government, KGB, and intellectual elites. A Bolshoi ticket is an immense status symbol. Those in the Top Class of Soviet society guard such privileges closely. Numbers of tickets are held for each performance until the last minute in case someone of high rank might suddenly decide to show up.

"I don't say I couldn't get in," remarked one Muscovite with good family connections as we discussed *klass* and culture one day. "I know some people, and there's always the opportunity to slip someone in the box office a ballpoint or felt-tip pen from America or some chocolates, or even some rubles. But you need *klass* enough to find the opportunity in the first place. It's not easy."

Another friend was in the office of the box-office manager of the Bolshoi one day, ostensibly to congratulate the man on the opening of a new Bolshoi season but in fact to hand over a plastic bag containing cognac and chocolate as a bribe for tickets. The manager was called out of the room for a moment, and my friend noticed an official document lying sideways on the desk. It listed some of those in the Rising Class entitled to tickets for any and all performances. At the top were holders of the highest civilian and military medals, the Hero of Socialist Labor and Hero of the Soviet Union. The medals are always worn on the left lapel: a red ribbon and a small gold star. The list also contained the information that any of the 1,500 people "elected" (actually, appointed) to the rubber-stamp legislature called the Supreme Soviet (which meets in the Kremlin twice a year) were entitled to tickets, as well as ranking officials in the KGB and the police, in the Council of Ministers, and in the Supreme Court.

The topmost levels of all—the Politburo and Party Central Committee apparatus—were not mentioned. They didn't have to be. A telephone call ahead of time suffices to obtain a VIP box and a champagne reception for them.

At the Moscow Art Theater's contemporary brick headquarters on Tverskoi Boulevard, on the inner ring road in Moscow, were two plays, Maeterlinck's *The Bluebird* in the afternoon and Chekhov's *Ivanov* at night. They were in Russian, so not many Westerners would attend, but Eastern Europeans go, and the Soviet *klass* elite retains first choice. "Getting in is easier than at the Bolshoi," my Russian friend observed.

Further east on the Sadovoye Koltso, close to the foreigners-only apartment house in which my family and I lived, the Obraztsov Central Puppet Theater was busy with a splendid children's production in the morning *(Funny Little Bears)* and a highly sophisticated and somewhat satirical program for adults at night, *I-Go-Go* (roughly translated, *Yo-ho-ho*). The race to see the adult program was so great that only the best-connected officials or foreigners could get in for months ahead. A Rising Class parent might eventually get in after a long wait; anyone below the Rising Class could forget about it altogether. The puppet theater is widely known in Europe for the caliber of its work, and it is appreciated by many intellectuals in Moscow for the sly ways in which it manages to comment on contemporary Russian life and its difficulties.

The two state circuses are popular with Muscovites and foreigners alike. There's no language barrier, and in the USSR the circus has long been an art form of its own, with its own training schools around the country. Many times our family went to see Popov the clown at the sharply raked original State Circus. A newer State Circus has opened beyond the Lenin Hills in a much bigger, domed, arena, and we liked that, too. On the night of April 25, 1982, the new circus was showing a "grand fairytale performance"—a circus ballet on ice, while the old circus was offering a peculiarly Soviet brand of entertainment entitled *Love, the Young Communist League, and Spring.* Both were packed with senior Rising Class elite people and foreign tourists, and would remain so.

Any child who wanted a quick ticket for the Sunday-morning performance of the Russian musical-ballet *Dr. Aibolit* at the Stanislavsky Musical Theater needed parents of considerable *klass* standing. (Similar to Hugh Lofting's stories about Dr. Dolittle, *Dr. Aibolit* is a Russian classic, with pirates, adventures, and animal capers: the words *ai, bolit* are an exclamation meaning "Ouch, it hurts!") It was also a struggle to get tickets for a translation of *Mary Poppins* at the Yermolov Theater and *The Adventures of Pinocchio* at the Operetta Theater House.

Adults found it hard to get into the Soviet play at the Vakhtangov Theater; almost impossible to see a translation of a West German play at the theater of the Moscow City Council; and difficult to land a ticket for an evening of Pushkin poems at the Taganka Theater, famed for the political daring of its controversial (and now exiled) director, Yuri Lyubimov.

Even below these levels, much of the Rising Class found it hard to get into a nineteenth-century play by Ostrovsky *(Guilty without Guilt)*, or to a good play in the main hall of the Central Army Theater, or to an opera at the Stanislavsky-Nemirovich-Danchenko Musical Theater on Pushkin Street.

As for music, only influence, *klass*, or the black market could get you in to the Tchaikovsky Concert Hall where the Moscow Symphony played Sibelius, Dvořák, and Janáček in the afternoon, and organist Leonid Reisman performed Bach and Handel in the evening. At the Moscow Conservatory on Herzen Street, violinist Boris Gutnikov gave a subscription concert of Beethoven and Brahms in the Big Hall and cellist Mikhail Khonitzer played Vivaldi, Gabrieli, Boccherini, Rossini, Paganini, and Donizetti with the Moscow Philharmonic in the Small Hall. Both concerts were booked solid by tourists and intellectuals.

Also beyond the dreams of most Muscovites was a production by legendary satirist, comedian, and actor Arkady Raikin that happened to be taking place beyond the Lenin Hills in the main hall of what was originally built as the Olympic Village for the Summer Games in Moscow in 1980. Most Russians can only hope to hear Raikin on records or see him on television.

"Of course," said my influential Russian friend, "there are some shows that anyone can go to see. But who would want to? I mean, look at this." He shook out a page from his copy of *Pravda.*

"The Khorvatsky touring group from Yugoslavia at the Satire Theater. Yes, it's foreign, but not foreign enough, if you take my meaning." He meant Western enough.

"And look at this: the provincial drama company of

Sevastopol (a naval base in the Crimea) in the Small Hall in the Red Army Theater . . . that's the kind of thing platoons of army draftees are taken to see on their night off . . . well, anything is better than the usual army routine, after all."

A charmed circle of the Soviet intellectual elite is always able to obtain tickets through status and contacts. Members of this group meet each other time and again in theater buffets and foyers, in aisles and cloakroom lines. In a classic setting of *klass*, Margaret and I would frequently see them drifting, arm in arm, in a promenade of privilege on the first floor of the Bolshoi, or around the cavernous marbled lobby of the Kremlin Palace of Congresses, or under the chandeliers of the Tchaikovsky Hall. The circle would move slowly, counterclockwise, seeing and being seen, nodding to friends and acquaintances, savoring the moments all the more because of the effort it took to fight through *klass* barriers to achieve them. Many were professional people who turn not only to contacts in the cultural world but to their own trade-union clubs. Even here tickets are by no means automatic: architects, doctors, musicians, composers, physicists, engineers, painters, writers, geologists, and others have to cultivate and lean on their trade-union contacts, and give them "gifts" as well. The more hard-to-get pens and cosmetics and items of clothing that they can casually push across the table "for your birthday" or "to celebrate our friendship" the better chance that tickets will appear.

Some trade-unions *dom*s, or clubs, can win better tickets than others. The Dom Kino, or film-industry club, trades movie tickets for theater tickets, or provides prints of movies themselves. The Central Writers Club offers hard-to-find books. The Dom Kompositorov (composers' and musicians' club) offers concert tickets and records. Behind the Detsky Mir (Children's World) department store near the KGB headquarters in the Lyubyanka, members of the Performing Arts Club swap tickets among themselves.

Some professions do better than others. A surgeon discovered that a woman he knew had access to tickets and was willing to let him have a steady supply if he would recommend a surgeon to operate on her mother without the customary long wait and inconvenience of the state health system. A dentist regularly accepted payments in tickets for work he did after normal working hours. A department-store director set aside portions of the best warehouse deliveries to the store—clothes and household goods—to dole out to contacts whom he knew were in a position to provide tickets in return. The permutations are endless.

Ingenuity and persistence are usually among the *klass* keys to obtaining tickets. "Well, you find a woman in the central *kassa* (ticket office) for Moscow theaters," explained one young man to me, "and you go to her, and she says she has nothing for the performances you want.

"You look at her, and she sees you are not a blue-collar worker or anything like that. You say, 'Well, I really want to see such performances, and I think you and I can do business.' If she likes you, she will find you a ticket for something, and you buy it, even if you don't plan to go. The important thing is to build a relationship with her, personal recognition. That's vital. If people like you, they'll help you. We have the old saying, 'Better a hundred friends than a hundred rubles.'

"Anyway, after a few times, the woman at the *kassa* knows me. I begin to give her a little gift here, a little present there, especially anything from the West—lipsticks, stockings, tights. You bring her something every now and then, and soon she has tickets for anything you want to see whenever you want it."

Access to an occasional ticket is minor *klass*, but possession of a steady flow of tickets to cultural events is major privilege. There is a flourishing illegal market in tickets for the Bolshoi. Margaret recalls one freezing winter night as crowds poured across a stone bridge built in 1516, through the Kremlin Wall, and up a cobble-stoned slope to a Bolshoi Ballet performance in the Kremlin Palace of Congresses. She had an extra ticket that evening because I was back in the office covering a late Kremlin speech. Around her were the same pleading eyes and outstretched hands to be found outside any Bolshoi or other popular performance. "*Lishnii bilyet?*" the desperate voices asked. "Do you have a spare ticket?" Margaret could hardly bear to walk past those for whom a seat would be such a longed-for treat. She decided to sell her extra ticket for its face-value only.

One tiny, elderly woman pleaded so touchingly that Margaret stopped, nodded, and held out her spare ticket, asking for the two rubles and forty kopeks written on it (at the time, about $3.60). The woman was grateful and offered to pay more, but Margaret would not hear of it. She volunteered to walk with the woman to the Palace, but was told that she was "waiting for a friend." Margaret went on alone and found her seat. When a stout West German tourist sat down beside her, Margaret was puzzled. The seat she had sold was next to her own. Where was her tiny friend?

"I was lucky," confided the German. "I had no ticket for tonight, but I met this old woman down on the street and she let me have her ticket for only ten rubles [at the time, $15]." The old woman's gratitude had actually been for the scalper's profit.

Even theater programs are bartered items of *klass*. Only a few are printed, and usherettes hold back supplies for friends and for contacts who might return the favor later. These same usherettes whisk friends and paid contacts swiftly past colleagues taking tickets, and sit them on folding chairs so they can watch the performance from aisles and sides at the back.

Muscovites who lack genuine *klass* connections often find themselves having to buy tickets *s nagruzhkoy*, an expression that literally means "with a load." It means that a ticket for the coveted Taganka Theater is available only if you buy another for the Khorvatsky players or the Sevastopol drama company. It is the same principle that food stores and factory canteens use: to get good cuts of meat you have to accept bones and fat at the same time.

Soviet cultural *klass* is not just about getting tickets. It includes a Top and a Rising Class layer of performers, and a similar layer of Party censors and watchdogs who try to regulate culture in general and control the flow of potentially dangerous ideas.

One of the cultural superstars who lives a life of privilege is portrait painter and historical artist Ilya Sergeevich Glazunov. Thin, chain-smoking, and intense, he shuttles from room to room, from guest to guest, from telephone to telephone, in an apartment in one of Moscow's best areas, the southern end of Kalashny Pereulok (Lane), below the embassies of Japan and the Netherlands.

The apartment is super-*klass:* a splendidly disheveled salon furnished with French Empire pieces fashioned from mottled Karelian birch and decorated with brass. Ornate mirrors line the walls. Massive oil paintings of the Romanov rulers stare down: Catherine the Great, Paul I, Alexander I, each in a wide gilt frame topped by a replica of the imperial crown. Doors have crystal knobs. One of several Japanese stereo sets around the room provides soft music while Glazunov writes and works. His wife Nina, slim and well dressed, relies a good deal on her mother to cook and care for her two small children, and on friends to help shop and entertain. One flight up, past a Glazunov horse outlined in red on wood paneling, is a tall black door. "*Kto tam!*" (Who's there?) Glazunov asked if I knocked unexpectedly. Recognizing my voice, he would throw open the door and welcome me to a penthouse studio.

At the far end of the larger room was a stunning dining room, its lofty walls crowded with wood and metal icons, a carved stairway leading up to an ornamental balcony on which are arranged a score of antique samovars. A long wooden dining table is set into the wall beneath the balcony. At late evening meals, candles shimmered. The table was crowded with friends and hangers-on, a Westerner or two, perhaps a bearded Orthodox priest in black robes with a glass-and-metal cross swinging from his neck.

Ilya Glazunov illustrates the achievement, the controversy, and the tension of a Soviet creative artist. On the one hand, he has painted the portraits of Gina Lollobrigida, Indira Gandhi, Kurt Waldheim, the king of Sweden, and more. Before I left Moscow he won one of the Party's highest awards, "People's Artist of the USSR." He drove a white Mercedes 230 sedan. The antiques in his apartment and studio come partly from his wife's family, the Benoits (distant relations of the Russian-born actor and playwright Peter Ustinov), and partly from connections in the Russian Orthodox Church.

On the other hand, tension was always close to the surface. A number of Westerners and Russians alike believed he had sold out to the KGB. How else, they asked, could he travel so freely and live so well?

To me he was genuine in a devotion not to the communist world of the present but to the Russia that existed before 1917, and to the Russian Orthodox Church as the repository of Russian—Slavic—roots and ideals. He had to make choices that Western artists can avoid. He was required to measure, almost daily, how much to placate the Party and the KGB and how much to stand up to them; when to refuse an exhibition because one or two paintings in it had been banned and when to submit. Like all Russians who are permitted to travel abroad, he was subject to the pressures of the KGB, and he had to decide how much to yield. Sometimes he miscalculated; once he was dispatched for several weeks to Siberia to sketch scenes from construction sites along the second Siberian railroad.

An artist like Glazunov cannot get away with undiluted defiance; and every time he made a concession, critics said he had sold out once again. There are aspects of his philosophy, particularly about Jews, that I cannot share or condone. Yet he seemed consistent in defending his own view of Russian nationhood, and he was apparently able to appeal to Slavs in high position who privately shared his glorification of the Russian, Slavic world of pre–1917. He was always interested in publicity abroad, and was not above courting it.

One of his paintings showed a woman seated by an apartment-house elevator. She was not happy, as the Party wants to see her, but grim and sad-mouthed, a survivor of war and famine, typical of old women everywhere in the country. Another large canvas showed a kindly working-class man with an array of Party propaganda posters behind him, wearing an army medal on a threadbare lapel and raising a glass containing clear liquid. The title was *To Your Health (Na Zdorovye)*. A tribute to the working man, his life enriched by the Party's care? Or a sharp, bitter comment on a state that builds its world image on the backs of the ordinary man and leaves him stripped of everything except his poverty, his medals, and his vodka?

Like Glazunov, soloists with the Bolshoi Ballet in Moscow and the Kirov in Leningrad are also household names. Nadezhda Pavlova is no rebel. She is a graduate of a school set up by Bolshoi graduates in the Urals city of Perm. Married to dancer Vyacheslav Gordeev, she lives in one of the apartment blocks reserved for the Bolshoi, surrounded by furniture imported from Scandinavia. She and her husband drive an imported car, shop at special food and clothing stores superior to ordinary state shops, travel abroad on Bolshoi tours, and are careful to stay in the good graces of Bolshoi chief choreographer Yuri Grigorovich.

Pavlova has her own own semiofficial fan club made up of ballet enthusiasts who collect photographs of her performances. It is a minisample of *klass:* the object is not gossip but the tickets she can arrange for particular performances. The fans enthusiastically lead the applause at the end of each act and the final curtain.[1]

If the creators of Soviet *kultura* stay in the good graces of the state, they can live lives of relative luxury. Not necessarily as grand as Ilya Glazunov, but comfortable. The core of their privilege is membership in cultural unions and clubs, socialist palaces of privilege for composers, actors, writers, critics, and others. The Central Club for Writers in Moscow is famed for its restaurant and unofficial take-out food from the kitchens. The Dom Kino, or club for the movie elite, has an attractive lobby, broad central staircase, and large auditorium with tip-up seats and the latest projection equipment. The club shows up-to-date Western films that the average moviegoer will never see. It is open only to those holding union cards or who have received special invitations.

On Gorky Street, on the southern side of Pushkin Square not far from the Kremlin, is the headquarters of VTO, the All-Union Theater Organization, a kind of National Arts Council. It keeps track of theaters across the country, sending out speakers and compiling information. Its restaurant is another haven: clean tablecloths, fresh meat and fruit, and a secluded, clubby atmosphere with good service.

The Dom Kompositorov (Composers' Club) is on Herzen Street, not far from the country's main concert hall, the Tchaikovsky Zal. Near it I met Dmitri Kabalevsky, a veteran composer whose work is known in the West. He lived in a large apartment block reserved for composers on the other side of Herzen Street, where the units are large and soundproofed. The late Dmitri Shostakovich had lived on the same floor, he said; the late Aram Khachaturian had been upstairs. Behind Detsky Mir (the Children's World department store), in another prerevolutionary mansion, is the club for workers in the Performing Arts, where stage actors have a good dining room, a theater, and other *klass* benefits.

It is almost impossible for a creative person to have a privileged life without belonging to the right union. Its KGB section controls such essentials as the right to publish, or to travel outside the USSR.

A free-lance theater critic such as Zinovy Zinik (now living in London) who did not belong to the union, could manage to exist by combining a tour of the theaters of Daghestan on the Caspian Sea with lectures to local theater companies at twenty rubles an appearance. But his opportunities were limited as long as he refused to join a magazine or newspaper staff and comply with union regulations.

For a cultural artist with the right *klass* credentials, accolades rain down. One ballerina, Natalya Bessmertnova, found herself sitting in the Supreme Soviet as one of its 1,500 deputies, gathering fresh privileges to add to the many she already enjoyed. A Bolshoi soloist, she was also the wife of chief choreographer Yuri Grigorovich. In 1978, the Bolshoi Party caucus put forward her name as candidate for deputy from the Sverdlov district, in which our apartment on Sadovoye-Samotechnaya was located. As the only Party candidate she was duly elected, serving only for a few days a year and attending the full sessions held twice a year in the Kremlin itself. I asked a Soviet acquaintance, a supporter of the Party, why the ballerina was qualified to sit in the Supreme Soviet. She was surprised at my ignorance.

"Do you think," she asked, "that a famous *kollektiv* like the Bolshoi doesn't know what it is doing?"

But why a ballerina, an artist busy with her own career?

"I've told you. The Bolshoi nominated her. She is well known."

The creators of *kultura* earn large salaries as part of their *klass* privileges. Cinema studios, ballet companies, theaters, and publications pay monthly salaries and extra payments per performance, article, or book. Moscow actors, for instance, might earn 100 rubles a month when starting out with a cinema group, and five rubles more every day spent on a set shooting a film. A veteran actor can earn 300 rubles a month plus another seventy-five rubles a day on the set.

As with performers' salaries, royalties to authors are determined by the state rather than by reader demand, by popularity with the cultural watchdog rather than among the people. One night, an editor of a national publication explained to me how at least some book authors are paid. A writer, he said, received 1,500 rubles (at the time, $2,250) per 100 pages for the first printing of 100,000 copies of a book. Relatively few books achieved such printings, and the state made sure that royalty percentages decreased with volume. The same 1,500-ruble figure was paid for the next 100,000 printed, but only 60 percent of that sum applied to the third 100,000.

Popular and ideologically sound authors can become wealthy. The late Mikhail Sholokhov, author of *And Quiet Flows the Don*, piled up more royalties than he could ever hope to use. A full member of the Party's Central Committee, he lived in a baroque three-story villa in the Cossack village of Stanytsa Veshinskaya, and hosted gala evenings for workers on the local collective farm. Sergei Mikhalkov could expect huge printings for his children's stories, as could Julian Semyonov, the USSR's most popular mystery writer.

Theater reviewers are not wealthy, but they too can make a reasonable income. They receive between sixty and a hundred rubles for ten written pages. The ten-ruble-per-page rate is also true for magazine journalism and the Novosti press agency. The longer the article, the more money.[2] One well-connected journalist I knew earned a base salary of 200 rubles a month and doubled it by writing five four-page articles every month.

To ensure that its rewards to the creators of *kultura* are not wasted on provocative ideas, the Party has set up an elaborate system of watchdogs. One night in the late 1970s, the lights in the Malaya Bronnaya Theater on Moscow's inner ring road darkened and a play began. It was no light comedy or Shakespearean tragedy, but a work with a theme that Party censors generally approve, life on the factory floor—an "industrial play," as Russians nickname the genre. The theater was empty except for ten men sitting shoulder-to-shoulder in the orchestra seats. It was an early dress rehearsal under the guidance of director Anatoly Efros, and the Glavrepertkom was seated. It was a commission of Party ideologues from the ministry of culture and from the Central Committee cultural department, which was headed by an old friend of the late Leonid Brezhnev, Vasily Shauro.

Without interrupting the performance, the commission watched the story of a factory whose workers revered their director, and were shocked when he was replaced by a more dictatorial, ruthless man. The play had long speeches about organizing the production of steel, and continual references to factory life—not a trace of politics or criticism of the state. True, one of the veteran workers committed suicide rather than submit to the new director, but it fitted the plot.

If the Glavrepertkom finds fault—if the actor playing the new director has a Stalin-type mustache, or there is any criticism of the political system—the commission raises its points at a long meeting with the cast and director immediately after the rehearsal. The director will fight for his interpretation, gauging carefully which points he must yield and which he can defend. The meeting will adjourn and the commission will file a report. What it wants changed will be changed, though some subtleties might creep through unnoticed. "The commission might contain men of artistic merit and judgment," one theater critic told me, "but only by accident. Its job is ideological. Sometimes it does miss a subtle point and the cast sighs with relief." Other points could be deflected if the director has good contacts in the Central Committee.

Watching the Efros play, the commission found it in order. Performances began. Audiences left the theater smiling: they had effortlessly discerned the point of the play. The plot was really about the relationship between a tyrant and the people, and the lengths to which some will go to escape dictatorship.

The parallel with Stalin was there for those who looked for it, though the play contained not a single political word.

Party censorship is ever present, though its intensity varies depending on the power of the director, the theater, the author, and the play.

One of the most daring plays I saw was an adaptation of the novel *The Master and Margarita*, by Mikhail Bulgakov, at the Taganka Theater, staged by Yuri Lyubimov. Bulgakov was a brilliant, dissenting playwright and novelist who had a running battle with Stalin for years before he died in 1940. Stalin banned the book outright for its thinly veiled satire on the one-party state, though the book has since been published in the Soviet Union, albeit censored and in a small edition. Lyubimov managed to win permission for a stage version that retained some of the more famous scenes. One has the devil mocking Muscovites' greed for rubles and consumer goods. Another commits the Master (a writer) to a psychiatric ward for telling the truth. Another shows Margarita trying to win the Master's salvation by presiding without clothes at a ball for the dead organized by the devil. The actress sat with her back to the audience, which was nonetheless stunned by the shock of such a sight on a Soviet stage.

The quickest way I could get tickets was by interviewing Lyubimov ahead of time and getting them directly from him. He was in the midst of a political balancing act between his theater and the Party which eventually caused him to stay abroad in 1983 instead of returning home, and which has now led to the Party's refusing to let him return at all.

Lyubimov thought he could use his reputation abroad to win more and more concessions from a nervous and uncertain Central Committee and Ministry of Culture. For years he succeeded. His Taganka Theater was a mecca of political outspokenness and good drama. When Leonid Brezhnev died and Yuri Andropov took over, he felt he could continue, counting on Andropov as a protector and friend. When Andropov died and the Chernenko team came to power with the old cultural orthodoxy of the Brezhnev years, it was the beginning of the end.

Now Lyubimov is an exile, directing plays and operas in Western Europe, his Taganka Theater emasculated. It can happen to any Soviet superstar, at almost any time.

Dissident writers such as Voinovich and Zinoviev send their works to the West, and finally emigrate themselves. Poets Yevtushenko and Voznesensky reap huge state rewards but run into trouble when their verse becomes individualistic. In the late 1970s, even a man like Yevtushenko was taken off the television screen because a senior Party man objected to four lines in a reading that was to have lasted four hours. Sergei Lapin, chairman of the State Committee on Radio and Television, took exception to a stanza that called television viewers "bewitched male and female fools" impaled "upon the beloved tower of Ostankino . . . like onto a skewer." Ostankino is the central transmitting tower for Moscow, visible for miles in all directions. Mr. Lapin judged the four lines to be insulting to Soviet television, its employees, and its viewers.

Star poet Andrei Voznesensky also went through some anxious moments after contributing to an unofficial collection of 480 pages of essays, drawings, and poems called *Metropol* in 1978. Party watchdogs were angered that a copy was sent to Ardis Publishers in Michigan and published there. The Politburo itself was said to have considered the problem at two separate meetings. Two of the twenty-four contributors, Viktor Yerofeev and Yevgeni Popov, were expelled from the Writers Union, and the first secretary of the union, Feliks Kuznetsov, attacked *Metropol* in the *Literary Gazette* as the work of "renegades."

But for those in the professional world of *kultura* who stay within the system, the rewards can be considerable. From the left-hand lapel of the tall, graying figure of Sergei Mikhalkov droops the coveted gold star of a Hero of Socialist Labor. It entitles him to Bolshoi tickets, good hotel rooms wherever he travels, a larger than usual apartment, free vacations, and a host of other *klass* benefits. A writer of children's stories, he is also well known for having written the words of the Soviet national anthem, twice. He did it for the first time in 1944, when Stalin wanted a new anthem to replace the "Internationale" and to rally Russian resistance against Nazi Germany. Thirty-three years later, in 1977, Mikhalkov was again on hand when the words had to be changed to eliminate the word "Stalin."

Creative people like Mikhalkov move with the times, nourishing their *klass* prerogatives. One of his sons, Andrei Mikhalkov-Konchalovsky, has had a spectacular career. In the late 1970s he directed a six-hour epic, *Sibiriada*, which depicted the development of Siberia since 1917. Andrei's half-brother, Nikita Mikhalkov, is an actor as well as a director. "Nikita has an American car," breathed one Soviet acquaintance. "His brother has a French wife, and they go to Cannes for the film festival. They can see any Western movie they want, and they buy their clothes in the West, and their royalties are very large." His voice trailed away with the enormity of it all.

The cultural watchdogs who hounded Lyubimov belonged to a network of Party officials headed by the Politburo itself, on which sat Minister of Culture Pyotr Demichev, a nonvoting member, and the head of the KGB. Beneath them was the powerful department of the Central Committee, which supervises all cultural, educational, propaganda, and scientific affairs. It was headed by Mikhail Zimyanin, a former editor of *Pravda* and ideological chief of Belorussia after World War II.

Reporting to Zimyanin on cultural affairs was Vasily Shauro, a veteran specialist in ideological supervision whose career rose in parallel with Zimyanin's after they worked together in Belorussia. Georgii Markov, first secretary of the Soviet Union of Writers, was a full member of the Central

Committee. Aleksandr Chakovsky, chief editor of the *Literary Gazette*, was a nonvoting Central Committee member. They were some of the men who decided what would be read, seen, and heard. Possessing the *klass* of high Party rank themselves, they rationed official approval and rewards and dispensed punishment to those in their cultural domain.

Censorship varies in intensity from period to period. It relaxed somewhat when Stalin died, but appeared to become more rigorous in the later Brezhnev years, although some writers, including Valentin Rasputin, the late Yuri Trifonov, and the chronicler of the decline of the Russian village, Fyodor Abramov, were allowed to portray varying degrees of Soviet reality.

Censorship is no mere red pencil slashed across a page. The Party controls the basic tools of cultural life, as well as the finished products, including all printing equipment. Every office typewriter in the Soviet Union is registered with the police, and a sample of its typing is supposed to be on file. Despite this, ingenious dissidents have circulated typed manuscripts called *samizdat* (literally, "self-published") for years. Every copying machine is controlled by the KGB and the average citizen is forbidden to copy anything, except in the large libraries, and only with special permission.

Control is also maintained through the granting, or withholding, of supplies. Painters require oil or water paints, preferably from abroad; actors need makeup and musicians instruments; sculptors require marble, bronze, and other materials. Without a supply-and-demand economy to provide them, creative artists must depend on the state, on friends from abroad, or on the black market, which charges a fortune for those few items it can find.

Of all the arts, music is the least heavily censored because it is the hardest to interpret. When asked about the meaning of his famed Seventh Symphony, Dmitri Shostakovich would give a noncommittal reply. But in the most believable of two recent biographies, one published in the West by Solomon

Volkov who said he spent many hours with the composer, the symphony was described as a requiem for those who died in Stalin's purges.[3]

At the other end of the scale, the most closely regulated art form is the cinema. Even when censors do permit edited versions of such Hollywood epics as *Cleopatra* to be shown, the average fan has to line up for hours. The Party has built no fewer than 154,000 cinemas, or 58 percent of all the movie houses in the world. The movie-mad United States has only 16,000. The state uses them mainly to show propaganda films on industry and Soviet patriotism.[4] Although the local movie house is still one of the few places of relaxation in many a Soviet town, more and more Soviet citizens are turning to television. The nightly news on television's First Channel (*Vremya*, or *Time*) is now said to reach 160 million viewers in the USSR.

Party censors show up on movie sets and at script conferences. Clever directors such as Eldar Ryazanov of Leningrad can include revealing slices of daily life in comedies and dramas, but no director is permitted to criticize or to be satirical beyond a certain ideological point. Some everyday shortcomings of Soviet life can be mentioned, such as the abuse of official cars, or alcoholism, or low productivity, but the basic legitimacy of Party power cannot be questioned. These rules also apply to the weekly satirical magazine *Krokodil*.

For the controllers of *kultura*, one priceless privilege is that of avoiding their own controls. They can read any books they care to, obtaining them through Soviet embassies or trade officials abroad. They can see Western movies in their original, uncut state at special screenings arranged in Party and Kremlin offices. The films are often copies of prints brought in by Westerners for exhibitions or festivals.

American movie people told me that they disliked bringing in their precious prints. "The Soviet customs people take the films away for a day or two when we fly in," said one Los Angeles producer, "and we know they have made illegal and unauthorized copies. They show them at private screenings and they pay us nothing. We have too many reports about Soviet officials seeing black-and-white copies to disbelieve them." A Soviet scientist once told me he had seen *Rosemary's Baby* at the club for professors of science on Kropotkin Street. The film had been black-and-white, and he shrugged when told it was originally in color. "A copy," was all he said.

It was common for senior diplomats and trade officials to buy color video cassettes of Hollywood movies in New York and to view them in Moscow using imported video sets unavailable in the shops. Some Western businessmen brought in film cassettes, which they handed over to Soviet officials to curry favor.

The system can destroy what could be great artistic creation in a society long noted for the richness of its culture. It is difficult to judge the precise depth of artistic unhappiness, but it was profound among the creative elite I knew in Moscow and Leningrad, who believed that the system rewarded many who could not maintain a high standard of art in an open society. Satirist Vladimir Voinovich said that many members of the Writers Union were Party hacks who have never published a genuine literary word; in his book *The Ivankiad*, he dreams that a large white saucepan has been elected to union membership on the grounds that, although it has never written a good word, it has never written anything politically unsafe either.

"Socialist realism" in Soviet painting often produces paintings that look like Western picture postcards. Propaganda movies and television are repetitious: the Party always right, the country always heroic. To read short stories in national magazines like *Ogonyok* is to read high-school realism with few subtleties of plot or language—in the country that produced Tolstoy and Dostoevsky. Literary monthlies and quarterlies sometimes reach higher standards, but not since the days of the "Thaw" under Khrushchev have they maintained uniformly good levels.

So *klass* in the world of Soviet *kultura* cuts several ways. It is alluring for Party watchdogs and censors. It enables Top and Rising Class elites to obtain tickets. It rewards performing artists, and by being withheld, punishes them if they stray from the Party's chosen paths. Ultimately controlled and rationed by the state, it does not create an atmosphere in which creative genius flowers: cultural achievements since 1917, with some exceptions, are shallower and more ordinary than those under the tsars.

Social class per se is no barrier to creativity, of course; but the Party allows no Soviet Charles Dickens to pour out his moral outrage at poverty and inequality. The Party is instead a patron—not like the royalty and the wealth that commissioned great art in Europe in the Middle Ages, but a patron of conformity, reinforced by the use of *klass*. The wonder is not that there is so little genuinely creative expression in the post–1917 land of the Soviets, but that there is so much.

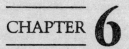

CHAPTER 6

MONEY: IT DOESN'T TALK
AS LOUD

At the end of a gray winter afternoon in Moscow, Nina Petrovna and I were chatting over a cup of tea. The subject drifted around to money. I knew that Russians carry larger amounts of cash with them when shopping than Westerners do, and I was about to ask Nina how she managed her own money each day when she held up an authoritative hand. An ample woman with a husband, a mother, two children, a dog, and a heart of gold under a stern exterior, Nina counted herself a person of considerable social *klass*. She was a graduate of a prestigious Soviet institute; she possessed a modicum of access to privilege; and she was not about to let an American harbor what she believed to be a mistaken impression of her motherland.

"Well," she said, "yes, we carry plenty of rubles, but we do have something new. I don't suppose you have heard about it, since you are a foreigner, but I can tell you anyway." She paused.

"We don't have to pay rubles for some of the things we buy anymore." She looked to see how I would react to this momentous announcement.

"That's right," she said. "I can go into a shop, and buy something, and I don't give the shop any money. I just hand the assistant a piece of paper from the bank with my name on it, and the cost of the item, and so on!" She sat back, pleased to have been able to place the USSR in the front rank of financial sophistication.

"That's interesting," I replied. "You know, we have something similar in the West. It's called a check."

"Yes, we sometimes call it that, too," she said. "*Chyek*. It's one of the words on the piece of paper. Usually we call it a money *dokument*, though. It's a good idea, isn't it? Do you use the *chyek*s a lot?"

I began to explain that millions of people used checks all over the Western world, but she interrupted again. She wanted to tell me how it worked in practice. In typical Russian style, she had given the theory first and now it was time for the reality.

"Of course," she said, "it's not very common here. I don't use the documents. I mean, why should I? You can only use them if you buy something worth 200 rubles or more, and when do I buy something that costs 200 rubles? You can't pay bills with the checks. You can only pay to shops. Even then, most shops don't accept them. Sales assistants have never seen one and wouldn't know what to do with one. No, I wouldn't say they are convenient to use every day." But then she brightened.

"But we do have them, and so we have what you have in the West." On that, she was firm.

Rising middle classes the world over know the value of money. Throughout the West money opens doors, buys luxury, affirms status, and acquires at least the outward trappings of class. It cannot buy the blue blood of a Boston Brahmin or perhaps quite atone for a wrong accent or the wrong clothes in England, but on the whole, money in the West not only talks, it shouts.

In the Soviet Union, money is also important, but to the Rising Class, less so than access to privilege, job status, and *klass*. On the whole, money doesn't lead the way upward: *klass* connections and job promotion do. Except in some of the freewheeling Central Asian Republics, money alone cannot always acquire a private car or a larger apartment, but an extra portion of *klass* can. Only *klass* gains access to a special food or clothing store, and only considerable *klass* can win the ultimate status symbol of a trip abroad. Money still talks, but with another accent. Privilege, status, access: these are the really valuable commodities, the hidden currency of the Top Class, and the Rising Class of Soviet society.

"In the West money has more power," remarks Marina Voikhanskaya, a psychiatrist from Leningrad who now lives in England. "It can buy so much, including social position. In the Soviet Union, money buys only things. You need it, but it has its limitations."[1]

I asked Volodya, another Russian friend, whether he would rather have more money or more *klass* privileges. He laughed out loud. "The privileges, of course," he replied. "You Westerners would probably take the money, but we Russians know better."

First, Volodya said, he would choose a friend who was the director of a large food store. Next, the director of a department store (*univermag*) selling clothes and household goods. Then, someone in authority in a hotel. Even a doorman would be enough to guarantee him a bed if he wanted one. "You have no idea how hard it is to find a hotel room if you are a Soviet citizen," he explained. "Foreigners book in advance and get the best, and Party officials have their own special establishments all over the country. We Russians usually have to sleep in hotel lobbies when we travel." The Soviet press regularly prints stories about hotel administrators who receive bribes of chocolate and champagne, vodka and wine to book rooms for nonstatus citizens.

Volodya wanted a friend who was a hairdresser for his wife, and a barber for himself. That he felt, would save hours of standing in line. A friend who was a doctor was essential. As well as providing private medical care or rapid free care at the clinic or hospital, doctors are needed to satisfy the bureaucratic demand for a medical certificate for the slightest absence from work. Next, and in quick succession: "a chief at my office who likes me" (handy for arranging vacations, being promoted, avoiding dismissal, acquiring more canteen privileges, and more), and a friend at the local district housing council, for aid in swapping his tiny apartment for a better one.

Of course he would accept and enjoy more salary. "But as the comedian Arkady Raikin says, the people we Russians really love are the meat-counter assistants and all the others who can supply us with *defitsitnyi* goods. If everything was plentiful we might not love them. But nothing is plentiful, and oh, how we love them."

Money is still needed to pay for good food and to buy such things as cars or cooperative apartments—but only after the privilege to do so has been granted. Money can bribe and soften. In the southern republics of Georgia and Azerbaijan it is used to buy lucrative government and Party posts. Without rank, however, and without access and connections, its uses can be limited. In the West, money can help to make up for the absence of social class, while in the Soviet Union the elite classes succeed twice: first in their access to privilege, then in receiving sufficient money to exercise that privilege.

Nina Petrovna is one of the new Soviet bourgeoisie, the Rising Class, who agree that rank talks louder than rubles, but who never have enough of either. It is a common state among her friends. The basics cost her little, but everything else is expensive when measured against her salary of 150 rubles a month.

At the top levels of society, rubles shrink into insignificance. During Konstantin Chernenko's presidency, his salary was said to be only 900 rubles a month, but it seemed irrelevant when set against his array of state cars, state dachas, state apartments, and state-supported travel, food, and clothes.

As both rank and status begin to dwindle, money begins to reassert its importance. Most factory and office workers, women, pensioners, draftees slogging through their two years' national service, and teenagers know the value of a ruble to grease a palm, to ensure a cut of meat from the man behind the counter, to jump places in a tedious line, to buy food at the few officially approved farmers' markets in the big cities, to store in pocket or purse to snap up an imported umbrella, or rolls of toilet paper, or net curtains, or a tube of lipstick, the very moment that such *defitsitnyi* items appear on sale.

When Russians speak of money they don't mean checkbooks or credit cards. These concepts still don't exist for most people. They mean cash—ruble notes in thick rolls or wads in pockets or purse. A bank has little glamour; the local branch is merely a temporary resting place, or money box, where rubles sit briefly before being used.

Nina took me to her dingy branch, one room of the state *sberegatel'naya kassa* (savings bank), distinguished only by its utilitarian branch number above the door. There was no plate glass, no carpeting, no customer-service desks behind velvet ropes. Neither were there security guards in sight. Nina sat at an old rickety table, picked up a nib pen, dipped it into a dirty blue plastic cup filled with sludgy ink, and filled in a series of deposit slips, blotting them carefully with the same kind of half-moon roller blotter that lay on my grandfather's desk a half-century ago.

We joined the line at one of the two openings in the glass above the counter, and waited. At last, Nina slid her deposit slips to the teller to have them checked, then crossed over to the second window to have the deposits recorded. The sums were small, and to her uninteresting: seventeen rubles (at the time, $26) for one month's rent for three rooms, one hour from Red Square; two rubles for a month's telephone bill; three rubles for a month's electricity and heat; forty-eight kopecks (at the time, 72 cents) for gas. She could have arranged for the bank to pay the bills automatically for her each month, but in the traditional Russian way, she preferred taking her salary with her to the bank in cash and dividing it up herself. "That way," she said, "I can feel what I have earned. I hold it in my hands, and I know it is mine."

She already had 1,000 rubles in her account—five months' salary, earning a standard 2 percent per year simple interest. One thousand rubles was, in fact, the average savings account for the 27,800,000 individual accounts in the state bank. Nina Petrovna was saving for a winter coat.

Nina's use of money demonstrated another difference from the Western middle class. Her spending patterns were reversed. She hardly gave a thought to rent, telephone, heat, light, or basic health care. Only owners of cooperative apartments had to pay back housing loans. The Party boasted that this gave Nina a fine standard of living, but that is exactly what it does not do. It gives her subsistence; but for anything better, she has to be ingenious. She needs privilege. She needs *klass*.

Because food is so expensive, Soviet families spend more of their income on it than Westerners. Official figures say that one third of a family income goes for food, but no one I knew believed it. Five rubles a day for three people seemed a minimum. That was 150 rubles a month, only ten rubles a month less than the average wage. If both husband and wife work, as is most often the case, almost all the wife's income would be spent on food. Food costs can in fact run as high as 50 percent of a family's income, or even more. In winter, in cold northern and western cities, the figure can reach 80 percent, if enough good food can be found. Clothes and shoes can bite heavily, especially if they need to be bought when food costs are high.

Nina Petrovna did not deposit any of her salary on the day I went with her. She preferred to keep it loose in her purse for shopping. She was preoccupied with finding some meat, and with trying to arrange a chain of favors that would culminate in having her child's teeth examined by a dentist outside the overbusy local polyclinic.

*   *   *

There is one kind of money that virtually shouts in the Soviet Union, a currency with as much, or more, power than the dollar has in the West—a currency that is available only to those with considerable *klass*.

It is the "certificate ruble," a hard-currency coupon issued by the Soviet government in exchange for foreign money, which is itself illegal to own. When I was in Moscow Soviet citizens could receive foreign currency as gifts from abroad which they then exchanged for certificate rubles at the state bank. But most of these valued certificates were earned abroad by Soviet scientists, artists, diplomats, engineers, and other officials who received part of their salaries and all their travel allowances in foreign currency.

When they returned to the Soviet Union, they converted them into certificate rubles for use in a chain of special, semi-hidden shops that sell food, clothes, and other hard-to-find items, generally of Western or East European origin.

The most valuable form of "certificate" was known as the D-coupon. It could be acquired only in exchange for the hardest of all hard currency: dollars, sterling, and other West European currencies.

When we were in Moscow, we would receive dollars from the *Christian Science Monitor*, which would come into my account at the Bank for Foreign Trade by telex from a bank in New York. I would convert some of the dollars into rubles to pay the salaries of our translator, our maid, and our driver, and to use in Soviet stores. I converted more dollars into the famous D-coupons, which looked and felt rather like Monopoly money, to use in the diplomatic food store, to pay staff salary bonuses twice a year, and to make purchases in a number of "Beriozka" stores, which sold Western goods and superior Russian items, including souvenirs, to residents and tourists for coupons only.

The whole system was a part of the fabric of *klass*. It was partially designed to reward those Russians who worked for Westerners, and to make sure that the special Beriozka shops could not be patronized by any hapless Russian possessing rubles alone. The certificate rubles permitted to Russians who had worked abroad were one step lower on the fiscal *klass* scale but highly coveted nonetheless.

In 1982, the government suddenly withdrew the D-coupon privilege from Western journalists and businessmen in Moscow. It gave no reason nor formal advance announcement: those appearing at the Bank for Foreign Trade were simply told that the coupons were not being issued any more. The reason appeared to be that the D-coupons were a black marketeer's dream, and were fetching up to twenty times their face value in rubles on the street. Foreign diplomats were the only non-Russians still allowed to use the coupons, which meant that the special supermarket they used, which accepted only D-coupons, remained open to them but was suddenly off-limits to all other foreigners. This presented immediate problems to those with small children and large families, and led to higher expenses (and customs bills) on imported food and other items from Helsinki. It also meant the end of Beriozka shopping in all of the special stores that took coupons instead of dollars or other Western cash.

A good Beriozka shop in Moscow, such as the one opposite the Novodevichy Monastery, and another in the Rossiya Hotel, sold the best vodka and caviar, packaged ham and other delicacies, Japanese stereos, foreign whiskeys, and clothes from Western and East European countries. It was, by Soviet standards, a fairyland. No amount of ordinary rubles would buy even a Czech ball-point pen in a Beriozka.

Before the ban, one privileged Moscow woman went shopping with my wife, Margaret, to the hard-currency store in the Rossiya Hotel, where the staff knew her. She bought a fur coat for a friend, using certificate rubles obtained after a recent visit to West Germany. Another woman went with us to another store to buy a Russian *pododeyalnik*, a double sheet casing into which blankets are inserted on a bed. She also purchased some ordinary Western sheets patterned with light blue flowers, a pair of Western sunglasses, six balls of baby-blue mohair wool, and a pot of Revlon face cream. None of the items were available in Soviet state shops. Another woman bought a box of European chocolates to take to a male friend (not her husband).

Since certificate rubles are regularly granted to Soviet diplomats traveling abroad, they spend as little of their hard-currency earnings as possible in foreign countries. This desire to save them for use in a Beriozka shop at home makes the Russians the stingiest of travelers.

The Soviet bank exchanges one American dollar for one certificate ruble, but Marina Voikhanskaya, about to emigrate, found its true value on the street. "Someone in America sent me $200," she said, "and I soon found out how wonderful it was. I exchanged it at the bank for 140 certificate rubles—the bank took sixty dollars in tax. A friend and I went to a special food store, but we were so overwhelmed at the sight of all that caviar and smoked tongue that we bought only a bottle of Black and White Scotch whisky and a German liqueur because we liked the colors on the label. Later we bought a couple of other things, and I had a hundred certificate rubles left.

"I had no other money and I was going to emigrate," she continued. "I needed money for tickets and the taxes you pay when you leave and so on. So I found someone who exchanged my 100 certificate rubles for two thousand ordinary rubles. That paid for my tickets, a fur hat for a friend, and left 700 rubles for another friend who was emigrating." The Soviet government had taken her $200 and given her certificates at a ratio of one to one. But on the street, where supply and demand rules, each certificate ruble was not worth one ruble but twenty.

Central Asians and citizens of the southern republics with thousands of ordinary rubles from black-market deals are anxious to find foreign currency, especially dollars, which are valued and hidden away like gold pieces. One Uzbek woman in a shawl and long dress stopped her taxi directly in front of Margaret and me outside a hard-currency store in Moscow, waved a huge roll of Soviet bills, and shouted, "Dollars! Dollars!" at us. When we shook our heads, the taxi roared away.

The certificate ruble is a powerful lever for the Soviet government, for as soon as it is bestowed on someone, he has true purchasing power in the Western sense. But it is also a potentially dangerous instrument for the government. Unlike other special shops for Party and Academy members, the Beriozkas are patronized by foreigners and are highly visible. Should the Soviet government's largesse become too widespread, more and more people would come to know about it and the envy that now exists, but is contained, would expand rapidly. The Party prefers its privilege to be hidden, not openly displayed.

The possession of mere rubles is often frustrating when one cannot use them to get what one wants. This is particularly true in areas away from Moscow and from republic and district capitals. A farm worker in Siberia who has made a considerable amount of money selling the produce of his private plot wants a telephone and a car, but he knows that the local Party branch has allocated only seven telephones and three cars to the entire farm for that year, and that they have all been assigned. Nothing short of close kinship with the district Party chief could change that. A bribe might help, but it would probably only move him a few notches higher on the list. One reason to choose work in Siberia is that it places a man at the top of such lists in his home city when his tour ends.

The situation changes again in some of the southern, non-Russian republics, where money assumes true power, particularly through the purchase of favors. In Azerbaijan, Georgia, Armenia, in the Central Asian republics of Kazakhstan, Uzbekistan, Turkmenia, Tadjikstan, and Kirghizia, bribery, the black market, and the buying of school degrees are a way of life. Money changes hands in enormous quantities and with extraordinary rapidity despite a chorus of complaint in Party newspapers and even an occasional prosecution.

In these regions the climate is better, the people are spirited, proud, and independent-minded, and they have more links to the outside world through Armenia and nearby Muslim cities. At the upper levels of society, privilege and rank are still more important, but unlike the situation in European Russia, money can buy comfort, and even a degree of *klass*.

Throughout the Soviet Union a kind of capitalism flourishes at the lower end of the class scale. Taxi drivers, for instance, can be rapacious, deriving their power from the shortage of transport, especially late at night and on weekends. As we drove back to our apartment in the evenings, it was routine to see knots of Russians, mainly men, standing in the road, holding up hands with one, two, three or more fingers upraised, showing how many rubles over the meter they were prepared to pay. Taxi drivers have been known to hire out their taxis to prostitutes for use as brothels. Drivers make deals to deliver packages and to carry furniture, especially if their Volga taxis are station-wagon models. This *na levo* work is illegal, but it is done on such a huge scale that the state looks away.

If a member of the new Soviet bourgeoisie wants to hire a moving crew, he must deal with these gougers. A limited number of "taxi trucks" stand at some Moscow railroad stations, but their drivers are even greedier than their comrades in taxis. The amounts of vodka and rubles they require is beyond the purse of most Russians. In such cases, the answer is once again personal contact, the granting of favors in return for favors to come. It is a constant calculation of benefit given and taken, a part of the fabric of Soviet life captured in the phrase *ty mnye, ya tebye*, "you scratch my back and I'll scratch yours."

Chauffeurs of government cars and drivers of heavy trucks also find ways to convert their jobs to extra cash. My first ride from the Ukraina Hotel to the *Christian Science Monitor* apartment was in a black government-owned Volga whose driver caught my eye as I looked vainly for a cab. He bounced me across town for one ruble. The officials he had just delivered to the Hotel would be in meetings for several hours. Any money he made by hiring out the state car, filled with state gasoline, was his.

While there seem to be few interior decorators in Soviet society, many a Rising Class family bribes a state crew of *remont* (repair) painters on a nearby job to work in their own apartments at night or on a Sunday. Trained auto mechanics can earn as much as their stamina allows after hours in their state repair garages, using tools borrowed from the garage. Hairdressers visit clients in their apartments after hours, bringing state-owned rollers and lotions with them.

This is not capitalism in the Western sense. Soviet "capitalists" do not buy the materials they resell or improve: they take them from the state. Villages in the Caucasus send their menfolk flying to the cold cities of the north with knitted winter garments to sell at high prices, but the wool is not their own. It is stolen from the backs of state sheep. Only the small private plots that feed the expensive free market in food are legal.

The Party wants to reduce this erosion of its resources, but finds it difficult. The bourgeois need for services and ownership is an unstoppable wave as long as the state denies the Rising Class the goods the West takes for granted.

Laws against money-making and investment are strong. Most individuals in the Soviet Union cannot sell their apartments at will. One family can own only one dacha and one single apartment. Unofficially, the black market sees many variations, all of them illegal. The elite cannot bequeath their cooperative apartments to their children unless those children are registered as occupants of the apartment when the parent dies. Anyone inheriting an apartment must give up other dwellings he may be using, except for a dacha. Renting out rooms in houses at the seashore is legal but is subject to taxes of up to 80 percent. Owning an aircraft is prohibited by law: someone might defect in it.

Only earned income is supposed to be deposited in the state

bank, and any unusual amounts are likely to be reported to the local KGB, which promptly sends a man around to ask questions. Individuals who have amassed money illegally cope with these regulations in various ways. One told me he kept money in his mattress. The families of some senior Party officials collect stamps, gold, icons, jewelry; the daughter of one prominent Party figure was widely rumored to collect diamonds and cars.

"Always have an excuse, a reason, if you are buying something people will notice," Boris, an office worker, told me. He had bought a stereo set and he had already been asked about it by several people. "Older women living on pensions sit around the apartment house all day and gossip endlessly," he complained. "They see you come and go. One or two will report you to the district KGB."

Another friend preferred to buy gold rings with black-market money. "You can always say your mother gave it to you," he shrugged. One well-dressed Russian woman tried to enter an elite shop in Kiev but was turned back at the door. "But I have certificate rubles, look!" she said. A Western friend had given her some foreign currency, but she could not mention his name for fear of compromising both herself and him. Unlike other Eastern European countries, possession of foreign currency is illegal in the Soviet Union.

"Where did you get that money?" another guard asked.

Necks craned. An incident was developing. The woman was tall, and her face was expertly made up. She made her decision, swayed her hips, and looked straight at the guard.

"I am a prostitute," she said. "My clients are Western."

The guard let her in without another word. A well-dressed woman plies that trade in a Soviet city only if she is informing for the KGB.

Cash is not all in the Soviet Union, but when it is needed, it is important. Credit exists, but only in a limited way. One morning in the Orbit radio and television store close to the Foreign Ministry building in Moscow, I went to the desk marked KREDIT to ask about buying a color television set. "*Da*," said a plump girl with dyed blond hair. She explained the terms: 25 percent down on any item costing 150 rubles ($225) or less, and the balance over six months at an interest rate of one percent. For more expensive items, it was 20 percent down, and six months to repay at an interest rate of 2 percent.

Before anyone could start filling in the forms, he had to produce his internal passport with the stamp showing he had permission to live in Moscow, and a letter from his office or factory showing he had a blameless record. The state can control credit by withholding letters of permission. As I left the store, I found that it had all been academic anyhow. A small sign on a wall announced that the store had sold all its color television sets, and the date of the next shipment was not known. Most people would rather pay cash and eliminate the hazard of such red tape and a possible investigation.

Money may be secondary to *klass* at higher levels, but the state acts as though most Urban and Rural Class workers consider money their ultimate goal by offering a range of cash incentives. The standard bonus for a factory or office worker is one extra month's salary a year (the "thirteenth month"), with more bonuses for exceeding output targets. Many managers falsify production reports at the end of the month to ensure that quotas are met and bonuses paid. The largest bonuses go to workers in steel mills, coal mines, oil and gas rigs, and to geologists, cotton combine drivers in Uzbekistan, scientists applying ideas to factories, and workers in Siberia. Some workers can double their salaries, aggravating the very class distinctions communism is supposed to be diminishing.

I met a blue-collar worker who adjusted color television sets in a showplace factory in Lvov in the Ukraine. He pushed a basic salary of 160 rubles a month up to 300 with bonuses based on quality as well as quantity, even though the usual criterion is quantity alone. A proud woman, Alexandra Alexeyevna Abrosimova, used an eight-ton press to stamp out leather uppers for children's shoes at such a rate that, when I saw her, she was two years ahead of herself. When I asked what would happen if someone decided to change the designs of the uppers, all I received was a blank look. Design, I gathered, rarely changed.

In four and half years as an American correspondent traveling inside the Soviet Union, I was officially allowed to meet only "good" workers, earning up to 320 rubles a month. "Bad" ones with lower salaries were not placed in my path. Three cotton combine drivers in Uzbekistan said they made 220 rubles a month most of the year, but at harvest time, they worked almost around the clock and each earned 500 rubles a month. They were about to spend 1,000 rubles (then, $1,500) on an imported motorcycle.

Directors of state and collective farms told me they earned salaries that ranged from 350 rubles a month in Krasnodar in the west, to 490 rubles near Novosibirsk, far above the standard 160-ruble figure. White-collar farm staff—agronomists, administrators—earned 80 to 100 percent more than milkmaids. An agronomist near Novosibirsk received three times the standard wage, 490 rubles a month, while a woman tending farm machinery earned only 220. The director of that farm admitted to making 490 a month, but earned far more in privileges such as a private car, special food, and cheap vacations.

Klass differences in the Soviet Union are symbolized by wide wage differentials, though not caused by them.[2] An academician earns 1,000 rubles a month or more, six times as much as the average working wage, which is estimated by the government at 150 rubles a month. To get an idea of how big that gap is, think of an American earning a salary of $15,000 a year; six times that would be $90,000. A marshal in the Soviet armed forces earns about 2,000 rubles a month—twice the academician's salary.

In cities, scientists, engineers, and researchers earn two to three times the national average. One member of the Academy of Sciences, Dr. Sergei Polykhanov, explained to me that he received an extra 500 rubles a month simply because he was an academician. Another academician who emigrated to America was also a full professor at Moscow State University, and his combined salary exceeded 1,100 rubles a month, 200 rubles more than the official salary of the late Konstantin Chernenko.

One of my colleagues, Peter Hann, interviewed three chemical engineers and learned that one of them, a forty-one-year-old woman, earned 450 rubles a month as chief of a plastics laboratory employing 25 people. Her husband, a doctor of science, made 500 rubles a month. The couple were models of Soviet *klass.* They had studied in Toronto, lived in four rooms, and planned to buy a motorboat and water skis as soon as possible. Another man lacked a higher degree but had risen to the post of deputy chief engineer at a chemical planning enterprise. He earned only about 400 rubles a month, but could use an official car and spend twenty rubles' worth of taxi vouchers a month. He rented a dacha each summer for about 200 rubles, jogged, played volleyball and badminton, and swam.[3]

As in the West, entertainers are often very well paid. One popular Latvian composer of songs and film scores, Raymond Paulls, has earned 2,000 rubles a month in royalties and fees. Successful film director Alexei Mikhalkov-Konchalovsky received 5,000 rubles for completing one film, his six-hour-long *Sibiriada.* A Bolshoi prima ballerina earned eight times more than a qualified engineer in addition to bonuses for every performance over four a month. Her privileges outweighed her salary: a large apartment, imported cars, and travel abroad.[4]

In Siberia, well-orchestrated bonuses push salaries high, though the privileges that accompany the salaries are even more attractive. I met dozens of workers in Siberia who lived a frigid frontier life, but were allowed to retain apartments in their home towns in the Soviet west. They could buy cars without the usual long delays. They were entitled to either take forty-two days of vacation a year, or work thirty-two straight months followed by six months off with an all-expenses-paid trip to and from their home towns. These Russians can run up large savings accounts without arousing the suspicion of the KGB.

In temperatures of minus thirty degrees centigrade, an hour by bus from the far eastern frontier town of Chegdomin—itself an hour's jet ride northwest from Khabarovsk, which is nine hours nonstop in a jet from Moscow—muscular Vladimir Zudilov led a team throwing a bridge across a ravine and earned 500 rubles a month. His wife drove a crane on the same job, for 300 rubles a month. It was so cold that metal sometimes snapped like twigs. At Oil Rig Cluster 64 on an endless white plain of snow near Surgut, north of Tyumen in Western Siberia, foreman Alexandr Kisilyov earned between 500 and 600 rubles a month for leading a rig team seven days a week. He had become a wealthy Soviet citizen. After ten years' work he had 15,000 rubles in the bank, a car, and hopes of moving his family back to the warmer skies of his native Bashkiria before long.

As darkness began to fall at three P.M.; as I saw Kisilyov talking to his crew in an orange hard hat over a fur cap; as I watched flares of gas burn at the top of oil towers and turn the horizon into a congregation of ghosts; as I sensed the bleakness, the unremitting toil and Party pressure at the center of Soviet oil production, it seemed to me that men like Alexandr Kisilyov earned every kopek of their salaries and their privileges. The Party gets its money's worth.

Wide gaps between salary levels in the "classless" Soviet society are not a recent development. Lenin argued in his pamphlet "State and Revolution" that differences in wealth would remain in the first phase of Communism. Only in the second could men be rewarded "according to their needs" instead of their ability. But Lenin was a realist. Seeing the need to keep skilled managers and technicians working in the chaos of 1918, he ordered that the specialists were to receive 1,200 rubles a month, 400 more than People's Commissars, and 850 more than clerks. The same decree of June 17, 1918, curtailed cost of living supplements, long-service awards, subsidized food and lodging, business expense accounts, and other tsarist perquisites.[5] All of these privileges—and more—have long since reappeared in the modern socialist state.

Perhaps Isaac Naiman put it as well as anyone. While amassing one of the Soviet's largest underground fortunes from an illegal fabric empire, Naiman played cards at night with other underground chiefs. The stakes were always gold or American dollars. "Rubles," Naiman used to say, "are not very interesting."

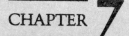

CHAPTER 7

THE CULT OF THE CAR

On the other side of Leninsky Prospect I could see a knot of people, but I couldn't make out what they were studying. I had to cross over anyway, so I decided to take a look for myself. First, though, I had to wait for a stream of Moscow traffic to pass.

It was the kind of traffic to be expected from an isolated country whose government devotes much of its productive energies to the military-industrial complex and permits a mere 3 percent of its people to own private cars. Snub-nosed trucks bolted together in World War II–style in Ulyanovsk and Gorky carried loads in what looked like tin drums cut in half and laid between cab and rear wheels. Shabby, light-green Volga taxis were driven by men and women whose calculated and calculating search for profit constituted a subclass of capitalism. Tiny models called Zaporozhets buzzed along like oversized lawnmowers looking for work. Prim Moskvich sedans, designed decades earlier, looked as stern and unyielding as Victorian maiden aunts. Subcompact boxes known as Zhigulis and made on a Fiat 124 assembly line bought by the Kremlin in the mid-1960s were bright with newer paint and colors. Larger but still four-cylinder Volgas in government black or military khaki, their dashboard wiring snaking over the front floor, handled with all the grace of tanks on a sand dune.

The occasional heavier government limousine, all black paint and lumpy chrome and copied from an American

Chevrolet of the early 1950s, swayed like a ship at sea as it sped down the center lane cleared by vigilant militia police. When Soviet officials asked Henry Ford II at a Brussels motor show what he thought of the then-new Chaika ("Seagull"), Ford is said to have glanced at the cumbersome car and remarked, "Well, I guess I could make two cars out of that." The Soviet officials were pleased rather than insulted. Size and weight have status in the Soviet Union.

When a break in the traffic came, I finally saw what the group was admiring. It was a status symbol that would turn heads in Paris and Peoria as well as in Moscow: a long, low, two-door 1936 Bentley convertible, carefully refinished in a dark and gleaming green.

The black convertible top was fixed in place over leather upholstery and a splendid dashboard and steering wheel. Russian men in thin overcoats and well-worn caps studied the details. Two chrome-plated horns stretched out like silver trumpets. The grille was vertical and chromed in classic Bentley–Rolls-Royce style. Circular headlamps loomed as large as searchlights. A black-and-green enamel badge on the grille bore the legend "Bentley Owner-Drivers' Club." I was puzzled; I could think of no Westerner in Moscow's small foreign community who had brought in a Bentley. Then I glanced down at the license plates, and I understood. The plate was Soviet, and the Bentley belonged to a Russian of supreme *klass*.

Any private car is an automatic status symbol in the Soviet Union, where the Party, and not supply-and-demand, decides how many cars will be produced, how many will be imported and exported, who can qualify to buy one, what they will cost, whether and how they may be sold secondhand. To own a car of his own, a man must either be in a high social position, or know someone who is, or pay an exorbitant amount on the black market. Using official channels, he might wait ten years.

But the Bentley belonged to the legendary, shadowy Victor Louis.

I learned later that Louis had arranged for the car to be imported and refurbished, but he was not content with only one status symbol on wheels. One night some weeks earlier, after we had both attended a dinner given by the Finnish ambassador, Louis fished for the keys of a silvery Volvo sedan which I had not seen before. It shone in the streetlights of Kropotkinsky Lane. He explained: "It's a new one, Italian styling. See the windows? Electric. Air-conditioning, of course, and see here, this is a thermometer built into the sideview mirror so that the driver can tell the temperature outside." The Soviet Embassy in Stockholm had arranged the details of purchase and importing. He said that he had looked at a Cadillac Coupe de Ville in New York shortly before, but had been unimpressed. He seemed to think that the Volvo would do.

Later, after lunch in his luxurious private home in Bakovka, near the elite colony of dachas used by the staff of *Pravda* in Peredelkino, west of Moscow, Louis showed me and some other guests his garage. It was as large as a small house, beautifully decorated and painted in traditional Russian style outside. That day it held no fewer than six cars: the Bentley; the Volvo sedan; an Oldsmobile station wagon with a diesel engine and blue and yellow New Jersey license plates; a Zhiguli; a van fitted with official yellow lights to ensure priority treatment by the police; and another eye-catching sports car, this one a white 1936 two-seater BMW made in Austria and bought by Louis from an auto club in Riga, the capital of Latvia. The few classic cars that remain in the Baltic states are from the days between the two world wars when those countries were independent. Louis also owned a Mercedes 450 sedan, very like the one owned at the time by Leonid Brezhnev.

Louis's love affair with cars might pass unnoticed in London or New York, in Munich or Marseilles. But in the Soviet Union, it could hardly be improved on as a way of proclaiming *klass*. Russia has always been a largely rural country situated well away from the main European trade routes, and when Lenin seized power in 1917, people still traveled by train, horse, cart, or coach. The number of motor vehicles ap-

propriated by the Bolshevik government in May 1918 totaled
a mere 2,582,[1] at a time when car production in the United
States was rising toward the 2 million mark.[2] Stalin then sub-
ordinated private transportation to public, and Khrushchev
did the same. The needs of the military and of heavy industry
have always come first.

By 1950 the country was still turning out only 64,500 cars a
year, as compared with almost 300,000 trucks. In the 1960s
Soviet cars were almost a laughingstock abroad. With the
Party itself seeking status in the post-Stalin era, and the Top
Class and an emerging Rising Class wanting more rewards,
the need for a better passenger car became apparent. Moscow
turned to the West to provide the skills it lacked itself. The
West German Volkswagen Beetle would have been the logical
choice: rear-engined, easily maintained, and slow-revving. It
was also air-cooled, which made it ideal for cold Russian cli-
mates where radiators can quickly freeze. But a deal with
West Germany was politically impossible in the years immediately after the Berlin wall appeared, and the Kremlin turned
instead to Italy. It bought the assembly line for the Fiat 124,
even though that car was made for warmer weather, had a
water-cooled, high-revving engine, and required a greater degree of tuning.

The plant was built on the banks of the Volga River, an
hour and a half southeast of Moscow by plane. Soviet workers
were trained by Fiat experts. Soon the 1200 cc. Zhigulis began
to turn Russian heads and draw crowds as they appeared in
bright reds, greens, and yellows on roads from Minsk in the
west to Vladivostok in the east. Instantly the Zhiguli became
a leading status symbol for worker and intellectual alike. It
was far more desirable than home-grown Soviet models,
mainly because it came from "There," meaning the West.
Eventually, a sportier 1600 cc. model came out, followed by a
four-wheel-drive version called the Niva. By 1972, the country was finally producing more cars than trucks. Today it
builds about 1.3 million private cars a year, of which some

600,000 are Zhigulis. A few years ago the Renault company in France helped modernize the Moskvich plant in Moscow.

However, none of this means that a genuine auto age has dawned in the Soviet Union. Motoring in the USSR is still not a part of everyday life. A car is not a necessity in order to get to work or leave on vacation. Carburetors and shock absorbers are certainly not part of the fabric of Soviet adolescence. Streets are not lined with used-car lots, or the plate glass of new-car showrooms, or the clutter of gasoline stations. Soviet motoring is a world of *klass*. In a country of chronic consumer shortages, it requires ingenuity, improvisation, and *klass* influence to keep a car on the bumpy roads and, of course, to buy one in the first place. "A private car, and especially a Zhiguli, is the difference between someone with some status and someone with a lot," one Moscow friend remarked.

Around the world, middle (and other) classes count automobiles as one of their prime symbols of prestige. The process has been slower in the Soviet than in the West and in Japan, but since the mid-1960s it has picked up speed. Official policy has helped. By keeping passenger-car production down, the Party has ensured that competition for each new car is fierce—that the car, once obtained, is an even stronger symbol of socialist rank and *klass*.

The number of private cars on the road in 1980 was about the same as those on American roads in 1920: by 1990, the number will have risen only to the U.S. figure in 1925. When I left Moscow in 1981, about one in every thirty-one Soviet citizens owned a car, compared to one in every two Americans, one in every four Britons, and one in every six Japanese. Even Bulgarians owned more cars per head than Russians.

Soviet pedestrians step off curbs oblivious to traffic lights. They spend their lives waiting in lines for buses and electric trolleybuses, and riding escalators to and from the Metro. Ask a city-dweller for directions, and he will almost always give you the name of the Metro or bus stop nearest your destination. Party policy emphasizes public transport over private cars partly because Soviet production is geared to military use and partly because buses carry more people for the budgets available. "We have a good public system," Moscow city officials told a visiting Australian diplomat, "and we expect people to use it. We don't want the pollution and traffic problems you have. We think public transport is best."[3]

Domestic demand for cars must also take second place behind the Party's need for foreign currency. Fully one third of the 1.3 million passenger cars made each year by 1981 was exported, mainly to Eastern Europe and Soviet-bloc allies. Some were sent to Western Europe as well. Most of them were Zhigulis, renamed the Lada for export. They sell well enough in Eastern Europe, but run into difficulty in Britain, even though they are relatively cheap. Export models have demonstrated uneven manufacture and a lack of attention to detail.

One London dealer told me that he was selling a Lada a day because they were cheap—less than £3,000 pounds—but he did have problems. The Soviet export agency insisted that he accept some Moskviches as well, which were difficult to sell, and he had to modify every Zhiguli he received. He installed new rear windows fitted with electric-heating wires, new shock absorbers, new spark plugs, and he adjusted the carburetor and throttle linkages to improve fuel mileage. The dealer was less than impressed with Soviet fine-tuning, but still believed the car was good value for its price.

Another garage in Surrey, England, stopped selling new Ladas in 1982 because it said the workmanship had fallen off badly. The paintwork was poor, spark plugs wore out every 1,000 miles, trim and upholstery were stuck down so carelessly that glue lay in unsightly blobs. "It's basic transportation," said the service manager, who still carried out warranty repairs. "I have one for my wife, but I service it every 1,000 miles."

It is one measure of Soviet status that a car considered so

simple and cheap in the West should be a life's dream to ambitious Soviet social classes.

The highest *klass* is found in an imported car. Bolshoi prima ballerina Maya Plisetskaya imported a Citroën from France, and used a British Land Rover to negotiate the rutted track to her dacha thirty miles northeast of Moscow. Poet Yevgeny Yevtushenko drove a foreign car. Another prominent member of the Moscow cultural world settled for a Soviet-made Volga, but to compensate, he equipped it with a two-way telephone and a television set and antenna.

In the sunny strip of land between the Black Sea and the Caspian Sea, Georgians, Armenians and Azerbaijanis revel in the cult of the car, turning the Caucasus into the California of the Soviet Union. Outside my hotel in Yerevan, the Armenian capital, I was greeted one afternoon by a swarthy man about as wide as he was tall, who wanted to practice his English.

He was Norig Musheghian, and he immediately stamped himself as a man of *klass* by announcing that he was a former world-champion Graeco-Roman wrestler, just returned from teaching the sport in Nepal. To check his status, I had only to look at his car. True, it was a white Volga station wagon, made in the USSR rather than imported, but anyone who knew the Soviet car market would acknowledge a man who owned the largest passenger car his country has to offer, priced at a sum that equals almost ten years of an average salary, 18,150 rubles. The seats were covered in red plush and tufted with squares of black fur. Background music was not the static-filled crackle of a normal Soviet car radio, but had a pure and even tone. "Quadrophonic?" I asked as I spotted several speakers. "Yes," he nodded. "American music, Japanese set."

Norig treated the car as his due. After all, he was a local hero, an Olympic Games medal winner, and a frequent traveler. He lived in a large apartment with his striking, black-haired wife and several children. It was scattered with other *klass* symbols: imported tape recorders, movie cameras, and stylish clothes.

In Tbilisi, capital of Georgia, I saw cars adorned the way they sometimes are in the West. Each adornment was a sign of *klass*. Inside Zhigulis and Volgas, custom gearshift knobs were filled with red and yellow plastic roses, or colored pictures of Jesus and the Virgin Mary. (The Georgian Church is one of the oldest Christian churches in the world, established in A.D. 337.) Bright carpeting reached halfway up floor-mounted gearshifts. Racing stripes flowed along hoods and doors. Long whip antennas were bent back and attached to rear fenders.

Rear windows were decorated, and shaded, by strips of material in thin vertical lines. Dolls, bears, skeletons, and medals hung from rearview mirrors. Most common of all were decorated hubcaps, many made to imitate the star emblem of the Mercedes. They looked real from a distance, but when I knelt for a closer look, the star turned out to be two pieces of metal. The surrounding paint matched the car.

It takes at least Rising Class status to own a car. At the very top, Leonid Brezhnev collected at least ten foreign cars from a Cadillac to a Rolls-Royce. A former Soviet international tennis star drove a Ford Mustang in Tbilisi. Senior officials of the MVD police roar through Moscow in imported Mercedes, BMWs, Volvos, and even Jaguars, all painted in pale blue and gold and fitted with flashing red roof lights and sirens. Volgas and Zhigulis would be cheaper, and do indeed form the bulk of the police fleet, but there is little point in having sufficient *klass* to acquire foreign cars without displaying it.

High in the Rising Class, directors of offices and factories used their black official Volgas to ferry them to and from work each day. Party and government officials rode in heavy Chaika limousines, and there was even greater status in having access to one of the newer model Chaikas, squared off like a 1970s Chevrolet Caprice.

The higher the personage, the more government cars travel with him, usually with rear and side windows curtained. Margaret observed this at extremely close quarters when the engine of our Zhiguli died as she was driving in the outside lane on the far side of the Sheremetyevo airport. Regular traffic had been stopped in both directions on the road, but she had been allowed to continue, apparently because of her white foreigner's license plate. She was trying to start again when a silvery BMW police car bore down from the other direction at eighty miles an hour. A few minutes later a veritable cavalcade of *klass* hurtled toward her: a black Volga, followed by the ultimate of official cars, the lordly ZIL, used by members of the ruling Politburo and said to cost about $75,000. The noise of sirens and the eight-cylinder ZIL engine was deafening. Behind the first ZIL was another, and behind it still another, with its windows curtained, and another police car. Eventually Margaret's engine fired and she drove on as other traffic gradually reappeared.

What Margaret had seen was Leonid Brezhnev returning from his Victorian-style dacha at Zavidovo. He often used two ZILs for security reasons, each traveling at high speed so that no one could tell which one was carrying him. The closed-in ZIL was an ambulance that followed him everywhere in his declining years.

The ZIL is to the Politburo what gilded coaches were to the tsars. I inspected one at close range in the courtyard of the American embassy as it waited for Secretary of State Cyrus Vance. Its seats were thick gray plush and the dashboard was wood. Steering and brakes were power-assisted. Suspension was heavy duty to cradle VIPs over poor Soviet roads. A two-way radio, part of the Baikal network that links the ruling elite, was on a console between the front seats. The ZIL is made on a single assembly line in one corner of the Lenin military plant in Moscow and its three-letter name is formed by the initials of the plant's Russian title, *"Zavod Imeni Lenina."* Most of the work is done by hand, and it is said to be the most expensive car in the world to produce. By Western standards, it is a gas-guzzler, and incorporates no more extras or refinements than an upper-middle-class American or European would expect in a top-of-the-line limousine.

To buy an automobile in the West, you walk into a showroom or scan the paper's used-car advertisements. To buy one in the USSR you use *klass*. Even so, the purchase is an ordeal of red tape that can take ten years of a man's life and salary. The process is so intricate that not even the men and women who make the Zhiguli at the Fiat plant by the Volga River find it easy. When a visiting delegation of British auto unionists remarked on the almost empty staff parking lot at the plant, Soviet escort officials were upset. The visit, intended to promote goodwill between union members, ended unhappily.

With only 1.3 million passenger cars produced a year, a citizen needs connections, or at the very least a blameless work and ideological record in a factory belonging to a prestigious ministry. Sergei was a young scientist at an Institute of the Academy of Sciences. He was only in his late thirties but he had been abroad for a one-year study program. He had saved most of the foreign currency he had received there and by 1980 had converted it into enough "certificate rubles" to buy a car outright.

If Sergei had not been abroad, he would have had to pay a deposit of 25 percent, or about eight months of his salary, and wait from two to ten years, depending on his *klass*. Prices of cars rose 18 percent in June 1979, and since he had applied after that, he had to pay the higher price. Sergei's certificate rubles gave him two advantages: he did not have to wait more than a few weeks for the car, and he was able to buy at a discount. He did not have to keep raising the issue with his trade-union representative, through whom such requests are usually channeled. He did not have to offer a bribe disguised as a gift to anyone in the auto distribution system.

Another Soviet couple we knew made a down-payment and began to save the rest as they waited for what they imagined would be several years for permission to buy. The husband was rather taken aback to be told a relatively short time later that he could pick up his car within three days. He assumed that the waiting period had been shortened because he worked in a prestigious institute. It was a privilege, but a problem as well, because he hadn't saved enough. He dared not let the three days go by because he had no way of knowing when his turn to buy would come around again; so he and his wife spent all of one night on the telephone borrowing money from friends. "Some wanted the money back in six months," the husband said later, "and some in a year. Some said to pay it when we could. We gave everyone written promises saying when we would repay. Our friends were wonderful: we raised thousands of rubles in just that one night."

On the morning that Sergei was told he could pick up his authorization to buy, he was also advised that he must choose his car within three days. Delighted, he gathered his certificate rubles together, rushed to the trade-union office, picked up his precious permission slip, took time off, hopped on a Metro train to the Lenin Stadium on the bank of the Moscow River, and began the Soviet ritual of Buying A Car, a tortuous, difficult, and very Russian exercise.

In front of the stadium was an expanse of tarmac, half of it covered by Zhigulis and Volgas. No sign; he had to find his own way to the end of the tarmac where a small crowd of bystanders peered through a black iron gate into the Promised Land beyond.

Once through the gate he saw a small wooden trailer without wheels, the kind used on construction sites. He stood in line before the first of three women behind the counter. As he waited, he read a list of new car prices tacked to the wall, ranging from 5,390 rubles for a mini-Zaporozhets (at the time, $8,000) to 18,150 rubles (about $27,000) for a station-wagon Volga model GAZ 24-02. Even the Zaporozhets would take three years of an average salary to buy.[4]

"Not here," said the first woman when she saw his permission slip. "Outside."

A wizened old man in overalls took his paper, spat, and waved a dirty hand at the cars. "Choose one," he said. He brightened only when he heard the chink of bottles in a plastic bag Sergei was carrying. Vodka was a vital detail, as it is in many other areas of Soviet life.

The old man stopped at a line of Zhigulis. All of them were red, and covered in the protective wax that Western sales rooms polish off before customers appear. All were darkened by days of sitting out in the open. A rear passenger door of the first one refused to shut properly. The driver's door of the next was loose. Another had a large dent in the rear fender. Eventually Sergei found one that seemed in good condition except for a rear door that would not stay shut, and a notable absence of hubcaps, cigarette lighter, and windshield wipers.

Chink, chink went the bottles. The old man sprang into action, pulled out a Phillips screwdriver, undid the bolts attaching the rear door latch plate to the body, moved it slightly to the left, did up the screws and slammed the door shut. It stayed closed. The old man grunted. He was long accustomed to the oversights of the Volga River assembly line. The missing parts were in a plastic bag on the rear seat, perhaps to prevent theft en route to the sales lot.

Sergei offered his plastic bag. The old man took it, glanced inside, climbed into the driving seat, and drove to a distant corner where he used a hand pump to splash a small amount of *benzin* (gasoline) into the tank. He revved hard, shot the car forward to a point just short of the wooden trailer, and jumped out. Sergei never saw him again.

The line inside the trailer was long, and when Sergei reached the first woman again, she shut up her books with a slap.

"One o'clock," she said. "Lunch."

Sergei was distraught. "But I've been away from the Institute all morning already."

"Lunch," she said. "Don't I have the right to lunch as well as other workers? Am I not a citizen, like you? Don't I have the right to *otdykh* (rest)?"

Sergei did not dare leave the tarmac area in case he lost his place in the line. He sat on an upturned oil drum for an hour, clutching his certificates wrapped in brown paper. At 2 P.M., he went through the formalities, received a set of keys, and walked over to the car. Under the eyes of the crowd beyond the gates, he opened and closed all four doors, looked under the hood, discovered a good set of tools, put on the hubcaps, fitted the cigarette lighter, and attached the windshield wipers.

At long last, he grasped the steering wheel in his hands. Someone pushed open the iron gates. The crowd parted, and he drove slowly away, the shouted comments and advice of the onlookers in his ears, triumph in his heart, and a red light on the fuel gauge blinking to warn him that he would be fortunate to reach a gas station before exhausting that thimbleful of *benzin*.

To Sergei it was all well worth it. It was privilege and convenience combined. He had not bought the car to commute, but to use at night and at weekends in spring, summer, and fall, to free himself and his family from waiting in line for buses, trams, and the Metro. It clearly marked him as someone special.

I went through the procedure myself twice, buying Zhigulis for my newspaper office in 1977 and 1979. Because I paid in dollars, the state cut the price of a Zhiguli station wagon by two thirds, granting a bargain that made a mockery of its own official exchange rate. The red Zhiguli I bought cost not the 6,636 rubles list price to the Soviet buyer, but 2,200 rubles in special D-Coupon certificates obtainable at the time at the Bank for Foreign Trade.

The same bank was forcing Americans to pay $1.50 for every ruble, but I was actually paying only thirty-three cents per ruble for the car. That was much closer to the unofficial rate of twenty-five cents offered for rubles at Geneva and Vienna airports, which were the only two places in the West quoting any ruble rates at all. The same car that took a Soviet citizen three years' salary to buy cost an American earning $30,000 a year only six weeks' income. My price was unfair to Soviet buyers, but they shrug: foreigners have always been favored; there is no point in worrying about it.[5]

A Soviet citizen impatient with government bureaucracy and low production can try to buy a car on the secondhand market. It is possible but costly. The further east one goes, the higher the price. I saw a used Volga parked outside the farmers' market in Yakutsk, in eastern Siberia, going for 20,000 rubles (at the time, $30,000), which was more than the price of a new one in Moscow. All used Volgas are to be doubted. They are the standard Soviet taxi, so there is always the danger that a car for sale is a resprayed taxi with the odometer wound back. Whatever the condition of the car, the state charged a commission of 7 percent on all secondhand deals in 1982.[6] Many a used vehicle changed hands on the black market.

The black market was also active in supplying the needs of frustrated motorists. Some drivers flagged down government trucks on highways or on urban backstreets and negotiated with the drivers to buy gas directly from them. They siphoned gasoline from the truck's tank, and the driver altered his log book and his odometer to account for the missing liters. He pocketed the extra income. When I left Moscow the official price of *benzin* was between 85 cents and $1.10 a gallon, depending on octane, but illegal gasoline was often cheaper.

Spare parts were in such flagrantly short supply that the black market did a substantial trade in windshield-wiper blades, spark plugs, side mirrors, steering wheels, shock absorbers, contact points, tires, snow tires, hoods, fenders, chrome stripping, hubcaps, wheels, and more. To obtain parts from the ministry of the automobile industry, bribes of no less than 1,000 rubles a time were paid to the deputy director of the ministry's supervisory board and his closest colleagues, who countersigned all requisitions. Clients even rented an apartment in Moscow for ministry officials to use for parties.[7]

Drivers' licenses could also be obtained through bribery. The fixed bribery rate in Moscow was 200 rubles for a normal license and 150 rubles for the lowest grade (no. 3) of a professional driver's license.[8] Militiamen who inspected road transport before issuing safety certificates took ten rubles per approval and traffic police were often bribed not to record or impose fines. Motorists would slip police one ruble for a small violation, and up to fifty if caught with alcohol on their breath, an offense severely punishable by law.

In non-Russian republics, even higher officials have used their status to deal in black-market cars. In January 1979, the then Party chief of Azerbaijan and former KGB official Geydar Aliev publicly castigated senior Party men below him for sidestepping long waiting lists of cars, then reselling them for considerable gain. One official had bought and sold three new cars in succession. "Incidentally, comrades," Aliev asked at a Party meeting in Baku, "we wonder where the secretary of the Komsomol Committee in the Radio Plant found the money to acquire a vehicle."

Driving a car in Moscow, Leningrad, Kiev, and other parts of the western and southern USSR might denote *klass*, but it is fraught with problems as well. Soviet drivers display both caution and braggadocio. Many proceed slowly, unaccustomed to traffic and fearful of the police at most large intersections. Other drivers, particularly taxi and government chauffeurs, speed like demons.

Foreigners stopped by police could pretend not to speak Russian and were usually allowed to drive on, since the police were just as happy to avoid the paperwork connected with giving a summons to someone with a foreign passport. Soviet motorists were treated roughly unless they flashed red Party cards or other *klass* credentials. One Russian who worked for foreigners used to avoid fines by offering a copy of *Playboy* magazine from his glove compartment. He claimed it always worked. Soviet drivers were flagged down all the time and lectured for minor infringements and even for driving dirty cars, even though it was almost impossible to keep a car clean during Russian winters. I never found a Western-style car wash.

Roads ranged from poor to appalling. Rarely were they laid with a camber, so snow and rain lay flat, freezing overnight in winter, cracking the macadam in the spring. Moscow is the pothole capital of the world. Drivers exchange information about avoiding new giant craters that suddenly appear. Traffic rules are so complex that the Moscow evening newspaper *Vechernyaya Moskva* often printed diagrams of the more difficult intersections with dotted lines, arrows, and text describing how to negotiate them.

One of the few properly marked and graded roads led to a diplomatic beach reserved for foreigners at Uspenskoe, and on to the dachas of the Politburo at Zhukovka. Swiss friends who took a wrong turn near the beach found ragged nature strips and unpainted buildings magically replaced by tended lawns and chalets that reminded them of home. Security was also tight. They had not followed the excellent road more than several minutes when a police car appeared and shepherded them back to the main road. By contrast, the main highway between Moscow and the Polish border at Brest is a strip of wavy concrete.

Despite Moscow's quarter of a million private cars, many more trucks, and a large fleet of government cars, only a handful of gas stations had been built to serve them by 1981. Unless you had *klass*, buying gas could require waiting in line for a half hour or more.

The *benzin* station near the diplomatic food store off Gorky Street was typical. While ordinary citizens waited in line one afternoon to serve themselves from two 97-octane pumps at the front, or from a 93-octane pump on the right, a black government car overshot the line and reversed toward a special pump on the left. The driver leaped out, took the hose and nozzle, and filled his tank, tossing hard-currency vouchers at the woman in charge. I confess that at times, I too would use the *klass* pump, relying on my white license plates, even though I would have twinges of guilt as I looked back at the endless line in the street.

Oil was another challenge. One morning I received a special favor without even knowing it. The standard procedure was to rush from the car with your own can and fill it from one of several filthy metal faucets dripping different grades of oil around the back of the gas station. The process covered hands, clothes, and shoes with thick oily stains. The first time I needed oil I asked the woman in charge, an Amazon in a black, belted raincoat and a headscarf. She demanded my *bak* (can). When I could not produce one, she shrugged and turned away. I drove back to the apartment, found a can that had once contained pineapples, and drove back. She filled it for me.

With the now-brimming can in hand, another dilemma presented itself. Would I hold up the line behind me while I hunted for the oil cap under the hood and tried to pour in the oil without a funnel, or should I put the oil can on the front floor and drive out of line, risking disaster if the can tipped over? I chose the latter course. The can stayed upright.

Payment for gasoline was always in advance, so motorists had always to estimate how many liters they wanted. On highways outside Moscow, I paid at a small window and ran back to the pump to try to reach it before the attendant, usually a woman, turned it on. If I was too late, I would arrive to find the nozzle spraying gas wildly as it bucked against the piece of string suspending it from a nail. I would shove the nozzle in the tank, and the flow shut off when it reached the number of liters I had paid for. If I had overestimated the amount, the tank overflowed onto the car and the ground and sometimes on me. If I underestimated, the tank stayed less than full. Rather than go through the entire process again, I would usually drive on, hoping I had enough gas for the next stage.

Klass was certainly needed to service a car. Government Chaikas easily qualified. They sped up Petrovka Street from the Kremlin and swung right a few yards past the intersection with Karetny Lane into an unmarked gate guarded by a soldier. Seen from the street, the gateway opened at the end of an anonymous, ocher-colored façade that could have been an office or a warehouse. As I walked down Karetny Lane and followed it around to the left, however, the size and purpose of the building became apparent. The sounds of a large garage and repair shop were unmistakable. Large windows were glazed over to allow light in but to keep prying eyes out. From the gate on Petrovka, meanwhile, Chaikas and even ZILs swept back into the traffic, still dripping from being washed as well as serviced at state expense.

Service for private cars was more difficult. Russians with foreign cars have the *klass* to go to Repair Garage Number Seven off Gorky Street. There I have seen senior military officers waiting patiently for mechanics to return from lunch, and discovered just how much power a skilled mechanic can wield in a society of chronic shortages.

Moscow listed only thirteen repair garages by 1980, yet many Soviet owners refused to go near them. Stories were legion about garages' stealing parts from cars brought in for routine servicing and replacing them with inferior types. The better auto parts often found their way to a thriving black market.

One driver came to pick up his car, drove it away and suddenly noticed his black steering wheel had been replaced with a light brown plastic one. When he stopped to make a more thorough check, he was horrified to discover that his dashboard had been robbed of all ornamentation. Another story, apocryphal but widely repeated, has a driver complaining to a mechanic that he would not accept his newly serviced car because it had a wheel missing. "It was like that when you brought it in," the mechanic replied.

I included a few anecdotes about car servicing in a *Christian Science Monitor* article that was broadcast back to Soviet audiences on the Voice of America. A foreign ministry official approached me at a reception a few days later. I braced for criticism: how dare I slander Soviet reality by implying shortages existed? But I was surprised. "Yes," the official said, "you were right. We do have problems with spare parts. But we are correcting them."

A professor of physics discovered that gasoline was pouring out through his carburetor and learned that even for someone of his *klass*, car repair in the Soviet Union could be a nightmare. He drove thirty kilometers to the nearest garage from his apartment in Moscow's Izmailovo district. At the garage, on Starokoptevsky Lane, the line of waiting cars was so long he could not find its end. Several days later he returned early in the morning, and secured a number in the waiting list for the following day. Back he came at 6 A.M., hoping to be at his institute before lunch, but it was not until early afternoon that a mechanic checked the carburetor and agreed to repair it, two weeks later.

On the appointed day, the professor made his fourth trip to the garage. He waited several more hours for the carburetor to be inspected again. Returning several days later, he learned that the actual repair had taken only ninety minutes. The weekly *Literary Gazette* in Moscow, which told the story, calculated that the professor had driven a total of 270 kilometers (162 miles) and used about ten gallons of fuel for a simple repair job.

The alternative to official garages was finding a mechanic or a pensioner who had the tools and the opportunity to repair cars *na levo*, on the side. Skilled mechanics could earn fortunes by moonlighting after hours at the thirteen Moscow repair garages. Others took government tools home and worked at night in alleyways or side streets. The level of skill could be high: one mechanic repaired an American's Volkswagen Beetle clutch cable in a single night, though he had never been under a VW before. The cable held through a two-day drive to Helsinki, and was pronounced a first-class job by VW mechanics there.

Russians with *klass* ask Western contacts to bring them back Champion or Bosch spark plugs from abroad. I found it quicker to telex Helsinki for a Zhiguli mirror, shock absorber, or set of snow tires than it was to drive out to Varshava Chaussee and be told by the central spare parts bureau that nothing would be available for months.

For a family that has never before owned a car, simple tasks such as adjusting spark plugs or changing over to snow tires could be overwhelming. They would pay large sums to have the work done. One official told the *Literary Gazette* that 14 percent of motorists used *na levo* mechanics, that 56 percent were covered by state garages, and that 30 percent did their own repairs. Friends of ours scoffed. They said that a far higher percentage used *na levo* services, and a far smaller number bothered with official garages.

By the year 2000, the USSR will have 40 million private cars, but Moscow may still have fewer than twenty garages and fewer than forty registered parking lots. It could still have its single "washing point," supposedly built by 1981 but which no one I knew had ever seen. Cars were either driven dirty, or taken in the summer to the banks of the Moscow River outside the city, where children fetched water in plastic buckets while parents swabbed off the dirt with handfuls of rags.

Summer is car time in the Soviet Union. Families pack themselves into small vehicles and set off to the dacha, or for picnics by the river or in the woods. Men wear knotted handkerchiefs on their heads while women cream their noses or stick small tree leaves to them to block out the sun. Cars are piled with blankets, bread, pickles, cheese, apples, books, boxes, balls, buckets, spare clothes, and the inevitable bottles of vodka.

Winter is more punishing for cars. Owners can keep their cars going in the Central Asian republics, the Caucasus, and the southern Ukraine, but in western, northern, and eastern areas, the bitter weather takes its toll. Most cars stand outside all night. Batteries freeze, engines will not start, and oil congeals. Truck drivers light fires under their vehicles to thaw the oil, a risky practice. I paled when I saw a British air attaché advancing toward his own Zhiguli with a Japanese hibachi grill filled with coal, determined to thaw out his radiator, but he later claimed success. Lacking antifreeze, Russians use vodka in radiators and windshield washer containers.

They lack the means to follow the example of one Japanese journalist, who connected a number of electric wires and strung them from a power plug through an upper-story window in our apartment building and down to his engine in the street below. Nor did many repeat what I did in the minus-thirty-degree cold one Christmas. I unbolted the battery in a freezing gale, thawed it out upstairs, and reconnected it the next morning. The car started.

Many Russians take their cars to parking lots, put them up on blocks, cover them with tarpaulins, and leave them for the winter, having first removed their windshield-wiper blades, side mirrors, and anything of value. Theft of these items is so common that many motorists remove windshield wipers each time they park. My office cars lost half a dozen side mirrors while parked on the street outside our apartment block.

In Siberia, winter driving is as hazardous as it is necessary. Motorists place an extra layer of glass over windshields to prevent fogging. In Canada, motorists can plug engines into outdoor electrical sockets, and Scandinavians use gasoline-driven heaters operated by time clocks to warm up engine and front seats before drivers appear in the mornings. One Soviet answer to the cold is simply to leave the ignition on all night. I drove past a suburban bus parking lot in Leningrad one winter evening to find dozens of buses nose to tail, all vibrating, engines filling the night air with exhaust smoke and sound. How people slept in the apartment blocks nearby I could not imagine.

Though the auto age has yet to dawn fully in the Soviet Union, the automobile provides a new way for the Party to exercise control through reward. It has also had another effect, less valuable for the Party. The private car has opened the eyes of the Soviet urban elite to the freedom of being in command of one's own coming and going. Independence is hardly a state of mind the Party wants to encourage.

Pressure is growing to expand light and consumer industries, particularly auto production, but this can only be done by taking investment funds away from the military-industrial complex. Yet the 1980s were hardly a time when the Kremlin felt able to relax. Relations with the United States were strained and the Soviet economy was growing more slowly than at any time since World War II. Oil and natural gas cost more to extract from deeper and deeper sources beneath the Siberian tundra.

This helped to explain some of the urgency with which Party publications advised against an unbridled love of automobiles. *Sovietskaya Kultura* warned what could happen if a Soviet man became obsessed with his car. A Leningrad owner, it claimed, parked his car outside his apartment and kept running to the window to see that it was safe. After finding a garage some distance away, he preferred to drive from there to work, even though it took longer than by public transport. In the summer, he really wanted to go to the woods, but felt he should drive his family hundreds of miles south to the Crimea. Such warnings continued, but they were ignored by the Rising Class who saw those with status rushing to buy new cars and did not want to be left out.

The Party worried about one more impact of the car, a high accident rate largely caused by the Russian addiction to vodka. Although the Soviet Union has only a fraction of the number of cars on American roads, it has a considerably higher auto accident rate.[9] In Soviet Georgia alone one survey showed that there were 300,000 accidents, many times more than the Western average.

The Soviet automobile is many things: a status symbol, a problem to operate and maintain, an export item exploited to earn foreign exchange, an instrument of Party control, a staple of the black market, and a symbol of individual independence. The Party will try to blunt that opportunity for independence. So far it has succeeded by keeping cars out of the hands of all but a small minority. Most Soviet people are still more rooted to one locality than Westerners. They are still less mobile.

At the same time, a generation of Soviet young people is growing up with cars for the first time. By the year 2000, about 40 million cars will compete for *benzin*, spare parts, and repairs. More and more families will come to know the freedom of the open road, away from prying eyes and ears. Pressures on the Kremlin will keep rising for more gas stations, more spare parts, and more cars.

The jaunty feeling of jumping into a private car is hardly compatible with the social discipline the Party prefers. In the long run the Party may find that Rising Class mobility will be harder to contain.

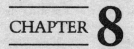
THE CHILDREN
OF THE PRIVILEGED

Tall, fair-haired and nineteen years old, Nikita Nikolaev
was at the age when most young men in large Soviet
cities worry about being drafted into the military forces,
about passing examinations at university or institute, about
how to lay hands on a decent pair of jeans and a record or
cassette of Western rock music. And yet, if you studied him
long enough, you realized there was something different
about him. Unlike many other young people around him, he
was not in a hurry.

He lived in a rarefied indolence of his own. He never
seemed to have anything particular to do, and he readily fell
in with suggestions from others in his circle of friends. He
would lunch in an exclusive hotel restaurant, or listen to records in someone's apartment, or make a sudden, late-night
decision to jump in his parents' Mercedes sedan and drive 400
miles north to Leningrad, singing, drinking, and ignoring the
speed laws all the way.

In a country of unpressed, utilitarian clothes, he stood out
in expensive, imported European or American sweaters with
high, round necks over imported shirts, always with a pair of
sharp Wrangler or Levi Strauss jeans from the United States,
immaculately clean, with creases like the edge of a knife.

Nikita was the son of a former major-general in the Soviet
artillery who had married a beautiful woman much younger

than himself. Both father and mother had connections with the highest political figures in the Kremlin. On a table in their large apartment stood a photograph of his father with Leonid Brezhnev, taken years before, and the word was that his mother had once had an affair with a man who had since risen to immense rank on his own.

Nikita grew up in a world of maids, of dachas in the countryside and on the shores of the Black Sea, of Western clothes, good food delivered to the door by the privileged network known simply as the "Distribution." He was one of Moscow and Leningrad's *zolotaya molodyozh*, "Golden Youth." With access to cars, travel, to almost unlimited amounts of cash, he took for granted privileges that most Soviet people can never know.

Never particularly bright, he did poorly in grade school and in his early high school years. His father impatiently transferred him to a military high school, where he boarded for several years. But he failed the examinations there as well, and returned to Moscow where his mother hired a battery of tutors to push him through evening classes to complete his high school education.

Exams over, he proceeded to have a good time. Nominally he was enrolled in an institute of foreign languages, where he studied English. In reality, he whiled away his days and nights in a way familiar to the affluent classes in Western societies.

He woke each morning in his private room in the family apartment, in a country where most people can only dream of a room of their own. Some friends had persuaded their parents to set up separate apartments for them, but Nikita found it more convenient to live where his parents' maids could see to his daily needs.[1] For lunch he often took his parents' Mercedes to the National Hotel on Karl Marx Prospect, or perhaps to the exclusive restaurant in the VTO (theatrical union) building, or to the excellent one in the Dom Zhurnalista, the Journalists Union, on the inner ring road near Kalinin Prospect. Joining a group of friends, he nodded to the doorman, who knew him by sight and by tip, and spent several hours eating and drinking in leisurely style.

He drank only cognac, a personal trademark which he used to demonstrate his wealth and *klass*. He preferred Georgian, Armenian, or, if he could get them, imported brands, especially French. From lunch until he retired in the early hours of the following morning, he was inebriated to a greater or lesser degree. Physically strong, his system had great resistance to alcohol, but the continued drinking began to take its toll. He smoked American cigarettes, mainly Marlboros. In a society that uses matches, he casually flicked the wheel of an American lighter while others stared.

His friends were the children of other senior figures in the Soviet hierarchy. One father was in the Party Central Committee; another was a government minister; a third had a relative at a dizzying height in the MVD, the ministry of the interior, in charge of the police. There were always girls: at lunch, in his car, at dinner, at parties, on his arm, around his neck, in his bed. Sometimes they were of the same social rank as he—daughters or granddaughters of famous writers, ranking ministers, or other generals. Often, however, they were Moscow University students out for a taste of privilege, or aspiring actresses looking for contacts, or simple social climbers.

Nikita was particularly friendly with the children and relatives of other generals. The fathers were themselves the sons of peasants or blue-collar workers and were straightforward men, relatively unschooled but shrewd survivors of post–1917 purge and war, now reaping the rewards of their survival. Their lack of formal education combined with their status often produced the most egregiously nouveau-riche ways of living; and Nikita was a classic result. "He is more *haute bourgeois* than the Rockefellers," was the acid comment of a Moscow acquaintance who liked Nikita personally but was repelled by his display of opulence.

Almost inevitably, the time Nikita spent in hotels and restaurants brought him into touch with the *fartsovshchiki*, the subclass of black-market dealers who frequent the places where foreign tourists stay. Nikita did a little buying and selling himself, as a lark, and at one point he was arrested. For most young Soviet men, an arrest ends their chances for the future. But for Nikita, custody lasted only moments. In his wallet he had a telephone number his mother had given him in case of emergencies. He dialed it and found himself talking to the staff assistant of a Politburo member. A few minutes later, police told him he was free to go and that his case was closed.

Last heard from, Nikita was still indolent, a dedicated member of the *zolotaya molodyozh*.

Nikita's kind of life disturbs many other Russians. "There's a Central Committee resort just outside Moscow," one friend told me, "and you should see those black cars driving up to its doors. Children get out, some of them only about ten or so, their noses in the air, with hardly a backward look at the drivers. I never expected to see such attitudes in our country."

However, not all Top Class, or Rising Class, Russians are like Nikita. In a separate category are those who use, rather than abuse, their *klass* privileges. They tend to be the children of scientists, of intellectuals, of better-educated Party and government officials, or of middle-level armed-services officers, and of factory and office managers. These parents want their sons and daughters to have independent careers, preferably in fields sheltered, as much as possible, from the unsettling winds of internal Party and government politics. If the parents should suddenly lose influence or patronage, the child with a university degree or a prestigious post has a chance of surviving.

The parents know how the promotion game is played in the

Top and Rising Classes and they work hard to ensure that their children gain admission to superior universities and institutes. After graduation, they keep using family *klass* to secure them good jobs.

A graduate from a university or an institute is assigned his or her first job by the state, and is supposed to stay in it for three years before seeking a change. Each time he moves, he must take with him his *kharakteristika*, or references, and his *trudovaya knizhka*, or work book, in which details of each job are recorded along with comments on performance. The children of the privileged, however, have their parents as their *kharakteristika*, and they often aim for jobs that take them abroad or bring them into contact with foreigners.

One man with the highest personal reference during my time in Moscow was Yuri Leonidovich Brezhnev, elder son of the late General Secretary. He graduated from an academy of foreign trade, worked in the department handling the import of light industrial equipment, then landed a much-desired job overseas in the Soviet trade mission to Sweden. In five years he was head of the mission. He rose swiftly in the prestigious ministry for foreign trade, itself headed by an old friend of his father's, Nikolai Patolichev, and became first deputy minister.

One prestigious job for children or relatives of the upper elite is academic research or analysis. Foreign Minister Andrei Gromyko has a son, Anatoly, who has directed the African Institute of the Academy of Sciences, and an urbane daughter who lived in Paris as the wife of the Soviet ambassador to UNESCO, Alexander Sergeevich Piradov. Lyudmila, the daughter of the late premier Alexei Kosygin, directed the All-Union State Library of Foreign Languages. She was married to a deputy chairman of the State Committee on Science and Technology, Djerman Gvishiani.

The grandson of Old Bolshevik Anastas Mikoyan is slender, graying Sergei Mikoyan, director of the Latin American Institute of the Academy of Sciences. Then there was the tall, dark, self-assured young man in a black leather overcoat who talked to Margaret during an American women's group tour of Lenin's home outside Moscow; he turned out to be the grandson of Anatoly Dobrynin, the Kremlin's ambassador to the U.S. for many years. His fluent English was punctuated with American colloquialisms as he recalled living in a large house with his grandfather on Lenin Hills overlooking Moscow.

The daughter of the late Yuri Andropov graduated with a degree in language studies from Moscow State University. The late Mikhail Suslov's daughter worked in a Slavic institute. One of the best-known of all Kremlin scions was A. I. Adzhubei, who ran the newspaper *Izvestia* while his father-in-law, Nikita Khrushchev, ran the country. He often accompanied Khrushchev abroad. His public position inspired the proverb, *nye imyei sto rublei, a zhenis kak Adzhubei,* which does not rhyme in English, but means, roughly, that it is not worth worrying about having a hundred rubles if you can marry as Adzhubei did.

The main route to privilege in the Soviet Union is through the Party and the Komsomol youth group. But education is now almost as important, and privileged parents try to make sure that their children have as much of it as possible. It is not easy, for the Rising Class, like the Western middle classes, besieges the same elite universities, institutes, and vocational centers for admission. There are simply not enough places to go around.

The Rising Class is alert to the value of education, especially in a society that traditionally values mathematics, chemistry, physics, and related fields. The average Urban and Rural Class child plods along in his nearest neighborhood school, scoring "threes" or less on the Soviet national grading scale of one to five for tests and examinations. He lacks the talent to be spotted by Party or government scouts always anxious to push the brightest children into special schools. He plays some sport—soccer, basketball; perhaps he boxes or skates. He may leave school after eight years rather than the standard ten years (Soviet children enter first grade at the age of seven) and work in a factory or on a farm; he is unlikely to possess the influence to avoid national military service. He might take night courses at a vocational institute or trade union–sponsored school, or he might not. He will have taken some routine courses in a foreign language, probably English, but his teachers will not have been abroad, and he won't have learned much. He emerges from high school with basic reading, writing, and arithmetic skills, with large doses of Party propaganda, and with a deep ignorance of the outside world.

One woman I knew had this kind of standard schooling, then attended an institute run by the state meat-and-milk-production industry. Having left high school after eight years, she spent four years at the meat-and-milk institute, graduating with an engineering diploma in refrigerating systems. However, she showed herself a cut above the ordinary Urban Class by pursuing even more education, this time at the prestigious Baumansky Engineering Institute in Moscow.

One dividing line between average and Rising Class parents is whether or not they try to find private tutors as their children complete high school and prepare for all-important university (or institute) entrance examinations. One friend of ours, a scientist, earned a lot of money by tutoring fifteen-and sixteen-year-olds for examinations into Moscow State University (MGU), Leningrad University, the Moscow Physics and Engineering Institute, and the Moscow Physics and Technical Institute.

His eager pupils came not only from big cities, but also from the deepest countryside. One peasant woman, brought to him by a family friend, came with a fifteen-year-old son lurking behind her long skirts. The mother wanted her boy to enter a prominent Moscow institute. When our friend agreed to teach him, she turned aside, took a wad of currency from the top of one of her stockings, and handed him 500 rubles, more than five months' wages on her state farm. That was in August: the boy came for tutoring at the next half-term holiday, in November, and in every vacation period after that, studying for several hours each day. In true peasant style, he never failed to bring gifts with him. "On the first day he brought two honking geese, all the way from his farm south of Moscow," our friend recalled. "And he had 200 eggs in a basket, and a large amount of cherries . . . I had to ask him to go and kill the geese, which he did immediately, on the stairs of our apartment building . . . My family certainly ate well while I taught that boy."

The boy passed his exams and entered the institute. Three years later, transformed into a confident young man with a mustache and the title of Komsomol secretary of the scientific institute where he was working, he appeared again at our friend's door. With him was his mother with another 500 rubles in her stocking, and the boy's younger brother hiding shyly behind her skirts. The tutoring, and transforming, process began all over again. "Social mobility," said our friend. "That is how the Urban Rising Class is born." Similar stories can be told in most big cities, our friends believe.

Since the most desirable jobs are those outside the Soviet Union, the higher levels of the Rising Class urgently seek language study. Émigré writer Elena Klepkova recalls twenty-two students fighting for each opening in the English Department at Leningrad State University ten years ago. The ratio was the same for other departments such as Scandinavian languages, where almost all graduates ended up as officials in such desirable capitals as Oslo, Copenhagen, Stockholm, and Helsinki.

One sunny August day, Dan Fisher of the *Los Angeles Times* and I pushed open the wooden door of a Moscow University law-school building on the right-hand side of Herzen Street on the way down the hill to the Kremlin. Inside, 400 high school graduates were competing for forty first-year places. The system, however, was weighted in favor of those graduate students who had spent two years in the armed services or in a job; for them, an additional 138 full-time law-school places were set aside for only 140 applicants.

The more prestigious the university or institute, the higher the degree of *klass* required to enter. At Moscow and Leningrad state universities influence is used all the time—though the percentage of truly incompetent students admitted is small in such difficult fields as mathematics. It is much easier to use influence to gain admission to the equivalent of "humanities" or "liberal arts" programs.

"It's done with a telephone call," a Moscow friend told me. "A member of the Academy of Sciences will call the rector of MGU (Moscow State University) and say he has a nephew who is a good boy and deserves a place. Provided the boy is not a complete fool, the place is assured."

"Party clout is easier to exert in the humanities than medicine or science," confirmed another, "because the skills needed are more general, less immediately measurable. In any case, the children of the highest elite don't need to work hard. Their roles in life are untouchable, as long as their fathers don't fall from office."

In Republic capitals or large cities it is common for ambitious blue-collar workers to trade favors to ensure their children's entry into local higher education. "A maintenance foreman will offer to paint the iron gates of an institute," one young man explained, "and the rector will jump at the offer. To have those gates painted through regular channels might take years. Two days later, his telephone will ring, and it will be the foreman, asking if his son, or a relative's son, can be enrolled in a certain faculty." He paused. "And it will be done. It is not so common in Leningrad or Moscow, but it certainly happens everywhere else."

Party officials can simply order a pupil into a university, or keep him out if they consider him unreliable. The agitprop chief of a Moscow *raikom*, a city district Party committee, once told prominent biologist Alexander Goldfarb that Jewish dissidents were causing too much trouble, even obtaining publicity on Voice of America shortwave radio broadcasts. The official added, "Look at Mikhail Ogursky [a cyberneticist turned dissident]. We took his daughter into university because, if we hadn't, he would have raised a stink abroad and claimed discrimination."

Comments Dr. Goldfarb: "It is clear that they can take who they want to take, and refuse who they want to refuse. In my opinion, it's not who they take that is the problem. Instead, it's that they reject Jews and others. The Party permits only a certain quota of Jewish undergraduates at any given time."[2]

Desperation leads to underhand deals. One young man paid a bribe of 3,000 rubles to ensure enrollment in a pharmaceutical college in a city in the Ukraine, but gave himself up to police when he learned that he was expected to pay fifty rubles more to college officials for every exam he wanted to pass. He was pardoned, but the two officials who had extorted the bribes went to jail.

Party connections are still the best way in to many academic institutions, particularly the two elite language and leadership institutes. One is the five-year Institute of Foreign Languages, or INYAZ, which trains diplomats, interpreters, translators, and trade officials who will work abroad and at home. The school is also believed to produce Soviet spies. It pays strict attention to courses on Marxism–Leninism, and any suspect background is usually enough to bar a potential student. Jews are generally excluded, but some friends I spoke with insisted that if a Jew was brilliant enough, and if his parents' Party record was ideologically clean, he might get in.

The other institute, the Moscow Institute for International Relations, or MIMO, is even further up the *klass* scale. "No Jews at all," reported one Muscovite source who knew the place well. "Only the sons and daughters of the Party elite." INYAZ trains those who will deal with foreigners or who will work abroad; MIMO trains those who will direct them. The two institutes are rivals. The main criterion at INYAZ is language skill; political reliability is the paramount virtue at MIMO. INYAZ graduates are the diplomatic elite who resent the extra status MIMO claims for itself. In turn, the ambitious Central Committee graduates of MIMO, who largely form the ruling elite, are known to envy the frequent opportunities for travel to the West that come more readily to INYAZ graduates.

Both schools are centers of Russian, as well as Soviet, chauvinism. One of their aims is to ensure the dominance of the Russian Slav in the Party hierarchy over other Soviet nationalities. Jews and some other non-Russians may excel in difficult disciplines such as physics, chemistry, math, and medicine, but Russian Slavs insist on retaining political power in their own hands.

One mark of a parent's status in the Soviet Union is whether he can keep his child out of compulsory military service. One such parent was Nikolai Smerdov (not his real name), a tall man with an iron-gray mustache, high in the ranks of the Writers Union. He had two sons, both of whom wanted to study acting. That meant trying to enroll them in a special Moscow drama institute against a flood of other competing applicants. Nikolai spoke to his influential friends, but one of his boys failed his entrance examination badly. Suddenly, a deferment was lost and two years' service in the army loomed ahead.

Nikolai spent weeks doing and promising favors, finally reaching the point where, in a supreme exercise of *klass,* he found himself talking on the telephone to the minister of defense. Briefly, he put his case for exemption: brilliant boy, sensitive soul, the need to concentrate on his studies, his own Party standing. The minister listened and then cut in:

"But, Nikolai, military service is an *honor,* don't you think? Is it not an honor to serve the Motherland?"

Nikolai spluttered. He could hardly argue the point with a full member of the Politburo who had himself had a distinguished career in World War II. But he continued to put his case, and soon the two men agreed on a *klass* compromise. The son would enter the army, but in a privileged way, assigned to a film-making unit where he would learn the art of making documentary propaganda. Realizing it was the best deal he could get in the circumstances, Nikolai thanked the minister profusely and hung up.

National service in the Soviet army and air force is for two years; in the navy it is three. In the ranks, conditions are spartan in the extreme. The food is unexciting and the pay only four rubles a month. Soldiers are granted only ten days' leave in two years; even that is often canceled for minor breaches of the rules. Wearing civilian clothes and drinking in public is forbidden. When parents travel to a camp to take their sons jeans, or if parents take sons out for a drink, the Soviet press denounces such behavior as lax.

Only a signal lack of status sends a boy into the enlisted ranks. *Klass* means higher education, where exemption is common until studies are completed, and courses are offered leading to the privileged status of an officer in the reserves. Efim Slavinsky, now a Russian-language broadcaster in London for the BBC, studied English, and graduated from Leningrad University as a translator with the reserve rank of second lieutenant, without ever going to an army summer camp. Only once did he visit a firing range, where he averted his eyes as he fired a burst from an automatic rifle. Engineering and science students, whose skills are more urgently needed by the military and the Party, undergo much more training. After graduating they must report for regular refresher camps.

Slavinsky's brother won *klass* by possessing a special skill for which the military is always searching: the ability to play soccer. He was a professional from the Ukraine. Returning to Kiev from a game, he found himself pinned between two draft officials on a train. He did nothing but play soccer for the next two years. He signed on for another tour, earning a handsome 400 rubles a month. Twice he was sent abroad, once to

Hungary and once to Burma, to play exhibition games. Finally he retired to coach a civilian factory team.

Despite steady Party indoctrination, ambitious Soviet people are not overly attracted to military service. To a big-city father with *klass*, the military is regarded as more punishment than reward for his child. The Soviet Union has sixteen military schools, and the main reason an elite city family sends a son to one of them is discipline. "I don't know what to do with my boy," complained a Moscow Party official. "All that Voice of America and rock and roll. I'll send him to a military school." As in the United States many (63 percent) of those who want to stay in the military were themselves the children of officers.[3]

For the children of the elite, privilege starts early in life. One way to glimpse some of it was to drive south along the inner, or Boulevard, ring road of Moscow, across Gorky Street to the stretch of a boulevard called Tverskoi, and turn right onto Malaya Bronnaya Street. It is a narrow thoroughfare in a fashionable area, and it teemed with *klass* along its left-hand side.

The second building was arresting. It was made of the same special, honey-colored bricks used by the upper reaches of the Party for their own elite apartment blocks. Two stories high, it was set well back from the road. In the playground were modern jungle gyms. My wife Margaret passed it on her way to Alexei Tolstoy Street at 8:30 several mornings each week, and she saw lines of black Volga and Chaika government cars turn into the driveway. They let out youngsters between four and six years old, well dressed, well scrubbed, and neat. There were no parents, just drivers in front and the children behind.

It was a *detsky sad*, or kindergarten, for the elite. Most Soviet children of that age walk to school with a parent or relative; these rode in cars. Ordinary children walk home again; these privileged youngsters waited for cars to pick them up.

Ordinary children grow up with untended playgrounds and standard-sized rooms; these sat in oversized classrooms with large windows. They were surrounded by *klass* cleanliness and neatness rather than by Soviet dirt and damp.

If you drove further along Malaya Bronnaya, another honey-brick building came into view on the left, as neat as the *detsky sad*: a *yasli*, or day nursery, for the privileged.

Klass can also provide better education as the child grows older. Some parents gained special privilege for their children in Moscow through an exclusive club organized for children from six to fourteen at Moscow State University. The energetic wife of a mathematics professor persuaded the triangular power structure of the University (the local Party branch, the Young Communist League, and the trade-union committee) to permit classes for rhythmic exercises, then for English, music appreciation, painting, drawing, and story-telling.

Parents paid about fifteen rubles per child per month, some 10 percent of an average worker's monthly salary. Preschool children attended during the week; older ones between 11 A.M. and 4 P.M. on weekends. So much did Moscow parents want this touch of sophistication for their children that they sacrificed much of their weekends to take the youngsters across town. Unfortunately for the children, the school finally closed when several teachers emigrated.

Most pupils attend their free neighborhood schools, but since Stalin's death, the Party has allowed a series of special schools to spring up in Moscow, Leningrad, Kiev, and elsewhere. In Leningrad, a high school specializing in English was set up on Chernyshov Street, and the city's elite were soon competing to send their children there. English classes began in the second grade, and students were required to speak English even in the corridors. "Scientists, of course, sent their children," remembers Elena Klepikova, who grew up in Leningrad, "and theatrical people, writers, and others who could see the benefits of speaking English."

Some Party watchdogs complained, and the special schools

became a political issue. Why was so much effort being expended to benefit elite groups? What about the children of the workers, in whose name the Party ruled? A number of blue-collar pupils were allowed into the special schools in *prosloiki* (streams), but as the years went by, working-class parents of such children became more and more dissatisfied. Their children became more intellectual, more assertive at home, less blindly obedient to "Papa Lenin" and the Party's dogmas. When some children began to question basic Party ideas, the Leningrad Party decided to act. It closed some schools and restricted others to pupils in their immediate neighborhoods. The remaining special schools were permitted to take only 20 percent of their pupils from other parts of the city.

Eventually, all English-language schools were closed except the one on Chernyshov Street, and that was suddenly moved from the city center to a new neighborhood on the outskirts called Novostroika, which was far more difficult to reach. Pupils already enrolled were still allowed to attend; and friends recall many an elite set of parents struggling twice a day to accompany their children across the city and back. The parents preferred the battle to the ordinariness of their own neighborhood schools. The quality of teaching at Novostroika gradually declined, but it still remained above average.

A few other special schools were left intact. When Elena Klepikova married and had a child of her own, he went to a French-speaking school before the family emigrated in 1977. In Moscow, School No. 22 taught English, and sometimes invited the children of the foreign community who attended the Anglo-American School on Lenin Prospect to its concerts. Other special schools in Moscow taught German, French, and Spanish, while still others had mathematics and the sciences as their main subjects. They were prime targets for ambitious parents with *klass*.

During his administration, Nikita Khrushchev was particularly concerned with establishing special math schools. When he ran into Party opposition, he waited, then allowed older children to attend them. Those established by the former leader in Moscow, Leningrad, and Kiev are still noted for their excellence. Children of Party members are given preference, but for children over twelve, talent is the main criterion for admission. Even Party members find it difficult to persuade principals to keep pupils if the children cannot do the work.

One of the most famous mathematics schools also happened to be one of the few boarding schools in the country, situated at Akademgorodok outside Novosibirsk, four hours by jet east of Moscow. Set up in 1963, it took in the winners of country-wide math Olympiads, and standards were extremely high.

There was also a network of special schools in art, ballet, and music for the gifted: there were about sixteen for ballet alone, of which the Bolshoi and Kirov schools were most renowned. In these special schools, students spend up to ten years combining academic classes with their chosen skills. When they graduate, they can be sent to perform or to teach anywhere in the country. Talent is vital but connections can provide introductions and advantage.

The Bolshoi School, officially known as the Moscow Academic Choreographic Institute, was founded in 1773. For a world-famous institution, it is deceptively drab on the outside, a nondescript three-story building with a flat roof near the embankment. Only a single statue of a dancer in the bedraggled courtyard indicates its purpose. Inside, pianos bang and instructors count the time: "*raz, dva, tri, chetyre*"— "1,2,3,4"—in twenty well-equipped studios, as students stretch to surpass their own limits of artistry and physical fitness in classes that run for an hour and forty minutes each without a break.[4]

So great is the honor of entering that about 1,000 nine-year-olds audition for the ninety places that fall vacant each year. The children are given rigorous physical examinations. Grim-faced, often rude, teachers accept only those with a certain kind and shape of elastic Bolshoi physique. Anxious mothers and grandmothers must wait outside in the hall. As usual, *klass* counts. Children of other performing artists, of dancers, and of Bolshoi teachers are given preference. It also helps to be a Russian Slav. Non-Slavs comprise almost 48 percent of the Russian population, but they account for a mere 25 percent of Bolshoi pupils.

Children do not enter the school until they are ten years of age. For eight years after that they study from nine A.M. to six P.M. six days a week, and longer when taking part in performances. Academic classes are formal, and discipline is rigid. The school canteen is well stocked with better meat and vegetables than ordinary children see. Dancers need good food, and they get it, along with sun-lamp treatment for extra vitamins. Pupils listen avidly to Western pop music in their dormitories before lights-out, obtaining tapes from foreign students, or from members of the Company back from tours abroad.

Another chance to turn talent into privilege comes at a school that offers a lucrative career including worldwide travel: the Moscow School of Circus and Variety Acts, where an unpretentious façade conceals a central performing ring with exercise- and classrooms surrounding it. So many parents want their children to be jugglers, acrobats, high-wire performers, and magicians that forty young people compete for every first-year vacancy. Total enrollment is kept down to 384. Pupils enter between the age of eleven and twelve and graduate six or seven years later, ready to be assigned to any of the seventy-four city circuses around the country.

Since Stalin's death, Party officials have argued about granting privilege to talented youngsters. In theory, the Party is opposed to separating skilled children from less bright ones. Party doctrine is that environment is much more important than innate ability and that children must be graded only by age and general attainment. These assumptions, however, are open to question, just as they are in the West, and in practice they are contradicted by the system of special and privileged schools.

Life for the young is not all schoolwork. *Klass* also plays its part in the Soviet when it is time to relax. A few privileged young people can vacation abroad, or at elite camps. Or they can go with their parents or in groups to resorts on the Black Sea or the Baltic coast, using tickets and rooms arranged by the Party or by trade-union clubs.

One afternoon I discovered another favorite pastime for sophisticated youngsters: watching Western movies in English. I drove down to the Kotelnicheskaya Embankment in Moscow, turned off near one of the seven skyscrapers built in Stalin's time, and parked near an elaborate but now crumbling movie-theater façade bearing the name Illuzion. For most of the week the cinema showed ordinary Soviet films, but on Tuesday afternoons it offered black-and-white British and Hollywood movies. Many were seized from Hitler's personal archives; others are illegally copied from Western negatives. I had to telephone in advance for a ticket. I walked through a drab hall, turned right, and found myself back in an ornate, fading lobby. The wallpaper was purple. One wall was covered with ancient black-and-white publicity stills of Clark Gable, Spencer Tracy, and Humphrey Bogart, and dozens more. Around me crowded elite Soviet teenagers in Western jeans and scarves.

We all sat in our overcoats because of the cold. The film was *The Citadel*, from the novel by A. J. Cronin made just before the war. It is considered ideologically sound because the hero, played by Robert Donat, is a doctor who gives up ministering to the wealthy to return to his early ideals, caring for the poor. Rosalind Russell, Ralph Richardson, and a very young Rex Harrison moved through splendid Mayfair scenes. Later, when I asked a young woman if she had enjoyed it, she sighed and said, "Even in 1939 you lived better than we do today."

The children of the privileged threw parties in their parents' apartments or in their own. Young people also gathered at one of the two Moscow night spots, Soviet versions of the discothèque. One was called *Sinyaya Ptitsa* (Blue Bird) and the other *Metelitsa* (Little Snowstorm). I am indebted to Alan Phelps of Reuters, a younger and more fashionable man than I, for an account of an evening at the Little Snowstorm.

"There's no sign on the door, of course," Alan told me, "and on Saturday nights after 8 P.M. the doors are bolted by uniformed guards. I suppose it is Moscow's answer to the Hard Rock Cafe in London or the Danceteria in New York. It's actually a café that has bent the rules a bit by patching up a 'Disco Express' from bits and pieces of home hi-fi equipment played at medium volume, in a room with bright overhead lights and no dark corners. A projector shows slides of Western rock stars and there are a few colored spotlights.

"Between the music numbers there are long silences, and the place obviously has to play local material as well as the imported stuff everyone wants to hear. Fleetwood Mac and Deep Purple come early in the evening, so that fans who really want to hear them must turn up at 5 P.M. Later, when the place is full, there's more Soviet and European rock. The doors shut at 11 P.M. and there's no bar, just Soviet champagne and ice cream. A bottle and four ice creams cost me fourteen rubles (at the time, $21), so it isn't really cheap, either."

In Metelitsa, in Sinyaya Ptitsa, and in parties elsewhere, two songs in particular brought everyone to their feet. One was "Money, Money, Money," the irony of which was not lost on the elite, and the other was "Rah Rah Rasputin," a Boney M hit. It, too, was an ironic status symbol: golden Russian youth gyrating to a spoof of a tsarist figure by a black group singing in English. Sinyaya Ptitsa, on Pushkin Street, was trendier than Metelitsa, and looked more like a nightclub, with dim lighting, cocktails, and a three-ruble cover charge. The *zolotaya molodyozh* wore American jeans and Italian boots.

Friends told us that some drugs were being used by students at Moscow State University and at other institutes. It seemed mainly to take the form of marijuana smuggled in from Central Asian republics in the south. A criminal gang smuggled hashish to Siberian cities from Tashkent in Central Asia in the mid-1960s. Heroin was said to be available on the black market, though little information was available on how much, or how widely it was spreading.

It would have been difficult to traffic in drugs in the Soviet Union. Customs and border checks were rigorous, and penalties severe. In the mid-1970s, an international ring tried to open a "Moscow Connection" through jet planes from Bangkok and Singapore to Amsterdam and Paris via Sheremetyevo Airport, but dogs sniffed out heroin in transit baggage and three young Americans were jailed.

One of the first newspaper articles I wrote from Moscow in 1976 was from a dingy courtroom in which several Americans were tried and sentenced to several years on drug charges. Such proceedings were usually closed, but officials clearly wanted the news of the sentence to be spread as a warning to other drug runners. Little was heard of the Moscow Connection in the following years and it was assumed to have been stopped by Soviet airport precautions.

Vodka is another matter. It is available to all, and its consumption is enormous, even among the young. It is the traditional Russian refuge from boredom and uniformity. A typical complaint came from a teenager in the Ural Mountains town of Nizhnii Tagil, near Sverdlovsk. "The program in our circus doesn't change for the whole month," he wrote to the *Literary Gazette*. "The same thing happens in the theater. The number of cafés is not enough, and we don't have the money to go to them anyway. The Palace of Sports has been under construction for the past five years. Popular ensembles, singers, and artistes don't often come here."

The Party had become sufficiently worried about vodka to allow the press to publish accounts of excessive drinking among teenagers, especially during the winter months. Articles in the *Literary Gazette* have described groups of bored young people, gathering in doorways and apartment-house courtyards, drinking, smoking, and shouting abuse at passersby.

The Western world has plenty of its own problems, yet it does offer young people more opportunity to direct their own lives. One Russian official I spoke with saw it differently. "What a waste," he said flatly over lunch in Washington, D.C., "what a waste in America when a young engineer drops his studies and plays a rock guitar."

"We call it freedom," I ventured.

"No," he said, shaking his head, "a waste."

I thought of him later while walking the streets of drab Soviet cities—the same environment the diplomat is happy to leave behind for his postings in the West.

A love of jeans, rock music, and art films, coupled with skepticism about Marxist ideals, is becoming ingrained in Soviet Top Class and Rising Class youth for the first time. So far it is only a social phenomenon. As this Soviet generation grows into leadership positions it could have wider ramifications.

CHAPTER 9

WOMEN:
THE STATUSLESS SEX

On the surface, and in a number of professions, women's liberation has long since arrived in the Soviet Union. No longer are women virtually barred from higher education. Tsarist-era proverbs such as "The harder you beat a woman, the tastier the cabbage soup," and "A woman has no soul, only vapor"[1] are now heard more in jest than in earnest. Legal equality is a fact. So is equal pay for equal work.

And yet . . .

Tanya was a graduate of a language institute in Moscow, short and comfortably plump in typical Russian style. She was familiar with the Party's claims and counted herself as a fervent patriot, but she was also quick to point out the shortcomings of the daily life of a Soviet Rising Class woman. She made male heads turn with her blue eyes and vivacious manner, but she has lived a sad life. Like many Soviet women, she married young; every Saturday she traveled for six hours to visit her husband at military camp during his two-year army service.

When her husband returned from the army, Tanya gave birth to a son, Volodya, and shared three tiny, cramped rooms with her strong-willed mother, who disapproved of her husband and of her. It was a situation known to millions of Soviet women: the husband, self-absorbed, loud, and offensive when half-drunk; a parent living in the same small space; personal conflicts galore. Tanya's husband began to ignore her, even in bed. To have an intimate moment or conversation was impossible with her mother and child listening to every whisper. Finally her husband walked out. Her mother offered no sympathy: "I told you so," was all she snapped.

As Volodya grew, Tanya's life became more miserable. Her mother lived in one of the rooms and her son spread out his possessions in another. Tanya was left with a couch in the connecting center room, which was more of a corridor than a room. She had no privacy. Her mother watched the television set in the center room every night until the programs ended; she refused to take the set into her own room. Her son, lacking discipline, made endless demands.

Tanya's job was her only escape from her family. It was a source of friendship, gossip, and identity, even minor privilege. Assigned to a foreign company, a month's wages a year were paid to her in hard-currency coupons which she used to buy a winter coat and a pair of imported boots. But by Western standards, Tanya was anything but a dedicated worker; she was usually too preoccupied with her personal problems.

Each morning she got Volodya ready for school, fussing over him, alternately scolding and spoiling him. A shortage of school buildings forces many Soviet children to attend half-day sessions six days a week, and Tanya's son went to classes only in the mornings. To keep millions of such children occupied for the rest of the day, schools offer "extended time" in the afternoons during which pupils eat, do homework, or go for walks. But Tanya's day was longer and Tanya's mother worked in the cashier's office of a Moscow theater until late. Volodya had to let himself in to an empty house with his own latchkey.

His grandmother felt she was twice as capable as her daughter and rarely hesitated to tell her so, often in front of the boy. She doted on Volodya and spoiled him. Tanya was usually too tired to stand up to her mother. She had to cook the evening meal, serve it, and wash up the plates as part of the "second shift" that extends her working week to well over eighty hours. No one ever offered to help. Her mother retired to her room and slammed the door until it was time for television. Her son had learned at least one lesson from his father: he considered housework demeaning to a man.

Tanya's housekeeping chores were drudgery. The shops in Moscow she had to frequent were crowded and dirty. She walked for mile after dispiriting mile. There are still few clean, modern supermarkets, no special sales, no comfortable department stores, no coffee shops to relax in. She knew that neat, pleasant, wood-paneled coffee bars existed in the Baltic capitals of Riga, Tallinn, and Vilnius, but she did not live there, and had only visited the area once.

There are virtually no advertisements. Almost everything Tanya bought was sold uncut, unpacked, and unwashed. Shopping in one of the farmers' markets for meat, fruit, and vegetables was possible but expensive. At the state stores, she was constantly forced to buy items she did not want in order to obtain those she did: scrag ends of meat put in with a passable piece so the meat store could achieve its overall sales quota for the month; cheap perfume she could not abide as part of the price for Western lipstick; a ticket for a boring outdoor lecture included with one to a politically daring play at the avant-garde Taganka Theater. She fumed, but dared not refuse the unwanted goods or services.

Prices for staples are low, but anything of quality costs a small fortune. It was useless for her to seek a shirt, a pair of shoes, or a hat in the first ten days of any month, for warehouse deliveries did not arrive until later. They might come in the second ten days, or they might not come at all. If they did, shop assistants immediately appropriated the best items for themselves. The only hope Tanya had of buying decent clothing was to get to know one of the girls behind the counter. The most productive shopping was when salespeople bring out their best items to meet the Plan, in the last ten days.

If they are not of the elite, Soviet women spend most of their lives mapping such strategies. When my wife, Margaret, gave Tanya copies of American and British home and garden magazines she would frown, sit down, and start leafing through the pages slowly and methodically. At first she did not believe that the items shown were available to all. Eventually, disbelief turned into grudging astonishment, then a kind of helplessness. "It must be wonderful for you," she told Margaret, "but of course, it can never happen here."

She was ingenious at adapting what she saw to her own life. One of Tanya's friends copied dress styles straight from the page without intervening patterns. Others took hints from advertisements on how to make best use of tables, chairs, or lamps to decorate a corner of a room.

The most ordinary tasks in the West were exhausting for Tanya. The saga of her son's school uniform was typical. Like millions of other high school boys, Volodya had to wear a uniform of dark blue jacket and trousers with metal buttons, but Tanya could not simply buy such a uniform in the nearest clothing store. She first had to present a special voucher specifying the size required. The voucher was necessary to make sure that the crush of out-of-towners flocking into the capital did not buy up the uniforms allotted to Muscovites.

Tanya knew of only one store in all of Moscow that sold the uniforms: Detsky Mir (Children's World), on Karl Marx Prospect close to the Kremlin and the KGB headquarters at the Lubyanka. During her lunch hour one day in August, expecting an hour's wait, Tanya encountered such a giant, shoving crowd that she had to return to work empty-handed. The day before school reopened, she went back again at 7:30 A.M., half an hour before opening time hoping to dash in and out before work, only to find 5,000 people standing six abreast in lines marshaled behind gray metal barricades by police. Inside, Detsky Mir had suddenly decided to stop selling uniforms on the third floor and had scattered different sizes on different floors. Hours later, upset at being late for work but unable to leave the line to telephone and almost overcome by heat and noise, Tanya reached a cashier's cage and pushed twenty rubles under the grille.

"Voucher," demanded the overworked cashier. Tanya began to panic. She had left it at home.

"See the supervisor . . ."

In the final part of the saga, Tanya found some consolation in sisterhood and sympathy, a mutual recognition among women that life is hard and Soviet men often impossible. Tanya burst into tears as she told the woman supervisor what had happened. To her relief, the supervisor said she could buy the uniform, providing she left her internal passport containing her precious Moscow residence stamp as proof she would return with her voucher. A few minutes later, an even more sympathetic sales assistant patted her hand and told her it was all right. She did not have to bring the voucher back. She could take the uniform and go.

Like all women who shop, Tanya never left home or the office without carrying a bag made of plastic, string, or cloth. One nickname for the bags is *avos'ka*, "the little maybe bag." For seven months of the year, appalling weather dogged her as she trudged from shop to shop, lined up for trolleybuses, took Metro trains. She did not even dream of owning a car. Her trade union lacked status and she would have to wait ten years even if she applied.

Tanya estimated she carried at least twenty kilograms in her two main carrying bags almost every day, and was accustomed to balancing such awkward items as glass jars of pickles, even a string bag into which an assistant had dumped a dozen unwrapped eggs. Tanya had to shop mainly in her lunch hour. Convenience foods were virtually unknown, though one frozen-food store did open in Moscow at the end of the 1970s. Tanya used to say that she could find anything she wanted if she looked long enough, but she rarely had time enough to do more than buy the basics: meat, bread, milk, butter, eggs.

She did have a refrigerator, like 80 percent of Soviet families—an improvement over 11 percent in 1965. The refrigerator took up valuable space against the short kitchen wall because no niche was provided in standard apartments. Her clothes washing machine consisted of a tiny, noisy, manually operated metal drum in a small plastic box, the kind owned by most families. Although many Rising Class women have a vacuum cleaner, she did not own one. Like almost everyone in the Soviet Union below the Top Class, she had no dishwasher, no floor polisher, no exhaust fan, no microwave oven, few paper towels, no mixer. Only a small number of families in Soviet society possess such items or have seen them while abroad.

Since there are few attractive restaurants in most of the USSR, families have some of their happiest moments sharing food around the kitchen table, drinking, eating, and talking, emotions spilling, passionate views colliding. I once asked Tanya what she planned to do on International Women's Day, which is a public holiday. Would her brother and his wife and his child be visiting her apartment as usual to celebrate the status of women?

"No!" came the immediate reply. "No. If he comes I have to stand in lines at the shop again, cook, clear away, and do the dishes. No one offers to help. My sister-in-law doesn't like me. My brother eats too much and drinks too much. No. I am celebrating Women's Day by staying at home and resting. No guests." It was an illuminating comment on the state of women's liberation in Russia in the 1980s.

Irina, an older woman, was quite different from Tanya, though a member of the same Rising Class. She was an intellectual, a voracious reader in Russian and in English. She had a heart attack not long ago and she worked at home, in a three-room apartment she shared with her husband, her teenage daughter, and an unmarried man to whom she rented one of her rooms. Irina could not tolerate lines and felt that shopping in Moscow was an insult to human dignity. Instead, she traded her translations, books, and contacts for food and for secondhand clothes. She paid a woman from a village outside Moscow city limits, a small, bent figure in a head scarf, to clean for her once a week.

"This is my sister's skirt," she explained proudly, "and my friend's blouse, and another friend's old slippers." She was constantly on the telephone hatching plans to find food and clothes. Once she became involved with a friend, a writer, in a long argument about whether or not potatoes were on sale in their region of the city. Irina said they were not, but the friend said she needed to look harder. "There we were," she marveled later, "two intellectual women, spending a long time arguing, not about Tolstoy or Chekhov or Gogol, but about potatoes. I am sure Western intellectuals don't spend time on such things. But that's our society and our system for you."

Irina was more critical of the Party than Tanya, and fought hard in her idiosyncratic way for the liberation that the Kremlin claims she already enjoys. A highly intelligent linguist, she drew parallels with Russian history and episodes in Russian literature to explain Soviet ineptitudes. She made do with a paucity of space and household equipment that would astonish any Western feminist. Her life's dream was to visit England, but she was resigned to the prospect that the dream would never come true.

The presence of a grandmother living at the home, the legendary ultracapable *babushka*, is the secret weapon of survival for some Soviet women. It made Lyuda's life more tolerable than Tanya's. Lyuda worked in an office all day, a hearty country girl filled with rural superstitions, gossip, good humor, emotion, and a deep, if understandable, ignorance of the outside world.

Without her mother to raise, feed, and care for her two small children before and after school hours, she would have had to exchange her job for a lower-paying one with flexible hours. Instead, Lyuda was able to spend several nights a week shopping and eating with friends, while her mother stood in line for food, cooked, cleaned, went to the bank, and washed the clothes. Lyuda's husband did not lift a finger in the home. She admitted that life would be tedious indeed without her mother's help, especially since her husband had the traditional Russian thirst for vodka.

Yet Lyuda's mother, the helpful, live-in *babushka* who once made domestic life possible for many a working woman, was a gradually fading phenomenon. One recent survey showed that 85 percent of all younger couples now lived apart from their parents. This put new pressures on marriage as wives tried to combine their dual roles of worker and housekeeper. It also added to the demand for more day-care centers and kindergartens—which the state tries, but fails, to meet.

Sex can be one casualty of the hard lot of Soviet women of all classes. When they drop into bed after seventeen nonstop hours they are seldom in the mood for romance. Urban Class husbands, regularly filled with vodka, insist that they fulfill all the obligations of marriage, on demand.

"I'll kill myself," Natasha said time and time again, clenching her fists in anger. But she was too sensible for that. Tall and attractive, Natasha was born in one of the Central Asian Republics, though her appearance was Russian. She had dark hair, a talent for languages, an intellectual's appetite for reading, and an intense curiosity about what life was like *tam*—"there," meaning in the West, especially the United States. She admitted that her husband was basically a "good man." She had been expecting his child when they married, and realized he could have left her then.

In crowded apartments, privacy is a luxury few can afford. Those couples who have reliable contraception can lead normal sex lives, but the evidence suggests that women are too often treated as objects rather than partners, and that the fear of pregnancy and abortion without anesthesia inhibits others.

There is considerable promiscuity in the Soviet Union, and what one Moscow friend called a private "preoccupation" with sex, even though public attitudes are still prudish. One doctor in the Ukrainian city of Vinnitsa whose patients came to him with their sexual problems said that sex therapy is nonexistent in the Soviet Union but much needed. He estimated that a higher percentage of women are frigid than the 18 percent the Soviet bureaucracy concedes, and he concluded that Soviet women lead lives of "sexual misery."[2]

At the same time, another Rising Class woman, Vera, told me that 80 percent of her friends were unfaithful. American students on exchange programs found a casual attitude toward sex among Soviet students, who quickly became drunk and uninhibited during parties that went on for hours, sometimes for days. But none of our older women friends felt their own sexual lives were adequate or fulfilling.

A large percentage of pregnancies in the Soviet are unwanted, a situation that could be alleviated if contraceptives were as freely available as in other countries—but they are not. Only one size of diaphragm was sold in Moscow stores, and many women were ignorant of the pill or fearful of its possible side effects. Intrauterine devices were popular with women but hard to find in some cities; where available, as in Moscow, they were of poor quality. In addition, Soviet men disliked using the less-than-sophisticated contraceptives available to them. Women's magazines did not write frankly about sex or birth control: such subjects were banished from view along with pornography.

The contraceptive method most often used is abortion, on a scale that would astound Westerners and shock the American "right to life" movement. Lyuda had had five. Six abortions for one woman were commonplace, and some women have had as many as twenty-four. Abortion was made legal in 1955, and by 1980, 16 million legal abortions had been performed.

Today the state is supposed neither to encourage nor discourage them, but Lyuda and other friends reported that the official attitude toward abortion had changed. The Party was alarmed at the way the birthrate had been falling in recent years. Only 25 percent of all Soviet families had three or more children in 1978, compared to 38 percent in 1966, and serious labor shortages were being forecast for the late 1980s. To turn the birthrate around, women asking for abortions at their local polyclinics in northern and western cities were often referred to government officials who tried, usually unsuccessfully, to persuade women to have their babies. Another method used to discourage abortions was to perform them in state clinics without anesthesia. Women who wanted anesthesia had either to find a sympathetic doctor or pay a bribe of up to 300 rubles.

The standard fee for an unofficial abortion was fifty rubles (at the time, $75), or one-third of an average monthly wage. Official abortions are free, but the treatment is far better if the woman pays. Lyuda had no hesitation in seeking her five abortions, though divorced Tanya decided to have her second baby even though she was not married to the father. She thought it might persuade him to propose. It did not, and she soon found herself with a new set of problems, from a contemptuous mother to an angry older son.

The extent of the stigma attached to abortion varies. In some cases it is little, but many women still want to keep their abortion secret and will go to great lengths to find doctors to perform the operation privately. However, even the difficulties and pain of abortions don't seem to reduce the amount of sexual activity. Meanwhile, the Party tries to tackle the falling birthrate in other ways. One is to offer cash bonuses for extra children, though families remain small everywhere except in the Central Asian Republics.

The birthrate incentives are not working, particularly in Moscow, Leningrad, and the more sophisticated cities of western Russia. Lyuda and Natasha simply dismissed the idea of another child, and would have gone through still more abortions if necessary. Even in Central Asia, where newspapers carry lists of Hero Mothers (ten or more children) every month, high birthrates are beginning to fall under the pressure of several factors, including increased immigration from European Russia and a less fervent spirit of Islam than in nearby Afghanistan, Pakistan, and Iran.

The Soviet system makes it difficult, though by no means impossible, for women to be feminine and attractive. One day, we went shopping with Tanya to the Siren cosmetics store on Kalinin Prospect in Moscow, the showcase street of the entire country. There I witnessed what even Rising Class Soviet women must contend with every day.

It looked inviting from a distance: glass display counters, bottles of perfume, and tubes of lipstick arrayed on shelves; assistants in white aprons serving, and shoppers milling. From an Intourist bus or from the sidewalk, all seemed normal, like much of the Soviet façade. "Such lovely buildings," said one wealthy American woman after visiting Leningrad for three days. She was almost offended when I told her that behind those imperial building fronts ten families shared the same kitchen and bath.

On the first floor of the Siren store, women were asking bored sales assistants the usual questions.

"Lipstick—do you have lipstick?"

"When will you have it?"

"Why don't you have any?"

The assistants shrugged. As everyone well knew, they had taken the best lipsticks for themselves as soon as each batch reached the store. That was their *klass* privilege. There are no incentives to be pleasant and there is no bonus to be earned by making an extra sale. Customers hunted for mascara, eye shadow, and face powder instead.

The assistants in the Siren store were selling Red Moscow and Red Flower perfume costing up to twelve rubles, or one and a half day's pay, for the largest size. Four kinds of face cream were also on sale: Yantar (Amber), Aloye (Aloe), Tetr (Theater), and Vita. Women examined them with varying degrees of distaste. "One of these will have to do," said Tanya at length. "But not Siren or Lily of the Valley. They're as coarse as tooth powder." At another, smaller, store on the main ring road, one item was being snapped up: brown plastic compacts bearing the brand name Elena, a joint venture between Moscow and Paris. Each compact cost eight rubles, a full day's wage for many women workers. Only one, dark, shade of powder was available.

An average Urban or Rural Class woman can buy basic cosmetics: face powder, lipstick, even mascara; but the Rising Class buys better quality, and the Top Class buys abroad or obtains them from returning friends or foreign visitors. An average woman buys Russian face power; a Rising Class woman buys Polish brands; a Top Class woman might use Elizabeth Arden. Another difference is availability. The average woman can buy French cosmetics rarely, whenever a batch suddenly appears on sale, but Rising and Top Classes can obtain better brands much more regularly.

Any good cosmetic is treasured. One friend showed me an American lipstick she had used so sparingly that some remained after three years. Women with *klass* regularly ask returning travelers to bring cosmetics from Helsinki, Vienna, Bonn, or London. Some of the best-received gifts we gave to our Soviet women friends were small eye-shadow boxes with brushes that can be found in British chain stores for only a few pennies.

"Why has our women's joy turned into a big problem?" asked a woman from Irkutsk in a letter to the monthly magazine *Rabotnitsa (Working Woman.)* "Is it harmful to paint one's lips?" asked a women from Novosibirsk with sarcasm. "If not, how can it be explained that lipstick is not on sale now?" *Rabotnitsa* sent a reporter to the administrative board of the perfumery-trade section of the ministry of trade, where deputy chief E. I. Bodrikova conceded that shortages did indeed exist. In one recent year, she said, only half the lipstick called for in the Plan had been made, as well as only one third of the mascara and one eighth of the eye shadow.

Why? Well, factories in Tashkent and in Krasnodar were being rebuilt, it seemed. As for lipstick, there appeared to be a shortage of tubes into which to insert them. *Rabotnitsa* was skeptical and even Bodrikova admitted that the tube shortage sounded "unconvincing." *Rabotnitsa* then unearthed another official, one V. A. Lazko, who promised that lipstick production would soon jump by 15 million pieces a year—not a figure to go very far among 140 million women. Warming to his task, official Lazko promised 10 million more bottles of nail polish; more lipstick, powder, and polish would be available through a joint agreement with Paris. *Rabotnitsa* remained unimpressed. "Who can tell us," it wrote sternly, "if the demand for cosmetics will be satisfied?"

Tanya read the article, and liked it, but finally produced another of her expressive shrugs. "Nothing," she predicted, "will really be done."

The same type of shortages prevent women from buying underwear and personal hygiene items. Tampons are almost unknown, and on the rare occasions when babies' disposable diapers go on sale, women rush to buy them for their own hygienic use. Ballerinas at the Bolshoi take three or more days off each month as a matter of routine when they have their menstrual periods. With tiny, dirty bathrooms, no privacy, crowded rooms used for living by day and sleeping by night, nowhere to lay out toiletries, little to buy that is feminine and attractive, women below the very top *klass* know few of the luxuries that Western women take for granted. The Soviet Union is a hard, masculine country. To be a woman there is generally a hard and demanding task.

When Svetlana Savitskaya, the second woman ever to fly into space, was launched with two male astronauts in a Soyuz T-5 capsule in August 1982, she was hailed by the Soviet press as another example of the liberation of Soviet women. A less official version of the trip soon circulated through the Moscow gossip mill: the next day, when Soyuz T-5 linked up with the Salyut 7 space station, the astronauts who had been in space since May eagerly greeted Svetlana with an apron. They pointed at the galley and said, "Now you can cook for us . . ."

The Soviet Union has long held itself up as a model for women's liberation movements. With more than 90 percent of women holding full-time jobs, it is certainly a country where women have won a considerable measure of economic freedom. Yet for all but a few, Lenin's creation is only a partial female liberation. Soviet women have failed to win social equality in a land where traditional Russian sexism is still overwhelming. There are exceptions, of course, and attitudes are beginning to change among young people and the intelligentsia. But Soviet society is still behind the United States and Western Europe in the emancipation of females at home.

The attitude of most Urban, Rural, and Rising Class Russian men reflects their rural origins. They expect their wives to stay out of the way, to shop, clean, and cook, to bear and look after the children, and to fulfill their conjugal duties on demand. In the tradition of a thousand years of Russian history, the man drinks enormous quantities of 90-proof vodka or illegal home brews (samogon) and is often drunk and abusive at home. He spends most nights with his male friends rather than with his wife and children. Wives, on the other hand, are expected to be sober, modest, virtuous, and uncomplaining.

Many women dislike the system, but with Slavic fatalism they make the best of it. The Party reserves for itself the sole right to determine the conditions under which Soviet men and women may live and it moves quickly against any dissenting movement, including female power. Women's liberation as a cause has no place in the Soviet Union, except in the dreams of a few. In the Soviet Union today, women are more useful than equal. Of the status and privilege dispersed by the Party, women receive considerably less than men.

As in so many other fields, Soviet society is a mixture of Western and Eastern attitudes. The Western side shows in a woman being able to rise to a full professorship; the Eastern side comes into play when she returns to her apartment to drudgery, toil, and dirt.

If you question the average Urban and Rural Class male about his attitude toward women, he is often incredulous. Just as his grandfather did, he considers it his right to spend his free time drinking with the other men, and to use his apartment mainly as a place to eat, sleep, and watch television. Men do no cleaning, no cooking, and little shopping. Sons learn from their fathers' indifference. In another socially conservative society, Britain, a recent survey of 1,082 people over the age of eighteen revealed that only 2 percent of husbands performed housework. Only 6 percent claimed to help with the cooking. Such a survey would show less than one percent in both categories in the Soviet Union.

On the surface, Soviet achievements for women look good. The state has brought legal equality to women along with the principle of equal pay for equal labor. A woman's working life can be personally and financially rewarding. Almost three quarters of all doctors and teachers, as well as one third of the engineers, half of all students in universities and institutes, and 60 percent of vocational and technical students in and beyond high school are women. Soviet hotels, museums, theaters, apartment houses, and construction and repair enterprises would close without the women who manage, supervise, and clean them. The chief of Moscow's Metro construction team and one third of the chief engineers on the gigantic Bratsk Dam were women. The wife of one of our émigré friends in London is a mechanical engineer and designer specializing in industrial refrigeration. (She was unable to find a job in the United Kingdom, partly because her English is not perfect, but partly, she believes, because of a British bias against women in her profession.)

It all seems to be a picture of enlightened recognition of the part that 140 million Soviet women—53.4 percent of the population—can play in a modern society.[3] It might not satisfy the feminist firebrand of the early Bolshevik days, Alexandra Kollontai, who campaigned against any inequality between the sexes and considered the family to be an outmoded, bourgeois institution. But to feminists in the United States and Europe there seems much in the Soviet record to study and admire.

Yet the official Soviet picture is far from complete. Tanya would not be greatly comforted by that record. Nor would Natasha, Vera, Lyuda, or Irina. Although they are generally proud of what their country has achieved, each feels a sense of being personally oppressed by the nation, rather than liberated. They each have some Rising Class status, but lack sufficient *klass* to make their harsh lives easier.

They are victims of the "second shift," which requires that before and after their full-time work, they do all the cooking and cleaning of a regular housewife, without the labor-saving conveniences of the Western world.

"Maybe we should free women from their freedom," commented a male letter-writer to a Soviet newspaper as he complained about working women who neglected their duties at home. Tanya, Natasha, Lyuda, and Irina indignantly rejected charges of sloth, but reference to their supposed "freedom" brought a wry smile; they could not really choose their own destiny. In private, they protested that both their State and their men took them for granted, but they had no channels through which to make those protests heard. Soviet propaganda claimed that they were better off than women in the West, but they doubted it.

In the British survey, more than 60 percent of those questioned agreed that the most important ingredient of a good marriage was the ability of husband and wife to talk freely to each other about their feelings. In the Soviet Union, many women would like such conversations, but do not expect to have them. The situation is somewhat better among the big-city intelligentsia, but even in these circles I observed men who had stopped making their homes the center of their lives despite the demands of their professionally qualified wives that they show more concern for their families.

In one way, the Soviet society we glimpsed seemed remarkably like its Western counterparts. One husband was having an affair with a younger woman attracted to him by the *klass* he had amassed through his creative art. A blue-collar woman spent her time with girlfriends and in flirtations with the occasional male while her husband had drifted into another way of life with a more sophisticated group. A divorced intellectual woman paid lip service to the need for equality but was pathetically, touchingly eager to flatter any presentable man in the hope of marrying again. Deep down she believed what she had always been taught, that the man was the boss. Without a man, she felt insecure, incomplete.

Almost all Soviet women work full time, but they often work for men, just as they do in the West. Even women teachers and doctors, who make up about three quarters of both professions, find themselves reporting to male hospital and school directors. The occasional woman does become head of an Academy of Sciences research institute, and in the 1960s, a woman headed the prestigious Moscow Institute of Physical Engineering. But women scientists and engineers often work under men, just as women bureaucrats work for male Party bosses.

Women hold little political power in the USSR. Only one woman has sat on the ruling Party Politburo in recent decades: Ekaterina Furtseva, a former Moscow Party worker who was a Politburo member from 1957 to 1961 and minister of cultural affairs. She was appointed and later ejected by Nikita Khrushchev, and no woman has since risen to a similar height. Women do not sit on the powerful secretariat of the Central Committee of the Party; none ranks high in Party committees in the republic capitals around the country.

Twenty-five percent of the Party membership at large is female, and 33 percent of the 1,500 deputies of the Supreme Soviet, or "legislature," are women, but the deputies hold no real power. They are selected by the Party amid stage-managed hoopla and transported to Moscow twice a year to ratify decisions already made by the Politburo and Central Committee Secretariat. Only 3 to 4 percent of the Central Committee are women. The idea of a Soviet Margaret Thatcher or Golda Meir is remote.

Less than one percent of the members of the Academy of Sciences are women, and there are no women among Soviet admirals or generals.[4] One American military attaché in Moscow said he had spotted only one significant female officer, a lieutenant-colonel in the ground forces, in several months. Women do much better in the trade unions, but Soviet labor unions have little power. They are merely conveyor belts on which Party discipline and rewards reach the work force, and which carry back reports on workers' mood and complaints. Typically, when a woman's name becomes a household word, she is either in a traditional role—ballerina, singer, actress— or she is a token in a male-dominated field.

It would be wrong to suggest that every educated woman in the USSR feels herself the victim of discrimination. We had intellectual friends, in some ways typical of the emerging Soviet bourgeoisie with *klass*, who insisted that as education increases and sensibilities change, women would feel a greater sense of respect. Some children of the intellectual elite claimed their attitude toward female liberation was closer to that of the United States than to Britain. The government has even permitted a noted sociologist, Viktor Perevedentsev, to write in the weekly *Literary Gazette* on women's behalf, urging that boys be taught at school how to help in the home, and arguing that cleaning and cooking do not demean genuine masculinity. It should be much easier, he said, for husbands, wives, and children to go on vacations together. Perhaps most important, he deplored the fact that so many women end a day's work only to face the "second shift" of housework and cooking at home.

When I spoke with Perevedentsev at his Institute, I was struck by his gentle manner.[5] Did he himself, I inquired, help his wife with the cleaning? He looked up, surprised at the personal nature of the question. "Yes," he said after a pause, then plunged back into his statistics. His superior was monitoring the interview. When he heard Perevedentsev answer "Yes," he laughed, then made it clear that Perevedentsev was the exception rather than the rule. "He does help at home, he does!" he said, finding it highly amusing, even odd.

The emergence of an elite in Soviet cities has also produced a class of women who do not work.

These are women at the very pinnacle of Soviet life, able to enjoy the Western phenomenon of being a nonworking woman caring for a family. Often of very simple, rural background, they are the wives of members of the Politburo or of the Central Committee Secretariat, of senior ministers, top KGB and police officials, and senior diplomats. Their husbands have climbed the ladder to power over many years. They themselves stay out of sight, Mrs. Chernenko and Mrs. Ustinov among them. The only Politburo wife to appear in public with a degree of regularity has been Lidiya Gromyko, who, for instance, accompanied her husband on his closely watched visit to the United States to see Ronald Reagan and Walter Mondale in September 1984. Even more unusual for a Kremlin wife, she was caught by news cameras waving goodbye with her husband at the door of his official Ilyushin jet just before returning to Moscow. That was very much the exception to the usual rule, however. Gromyko was so secure in his job, and was reportedly so close to his wife, that he could apparently make his own rules.

Women of the Top Class are found mainly in Moscow, with some in Leningrad and Kiev. Their men now run the country while the women sit at home or in the dacha or by the Black Sea or in Yalta. They want for no material comforts, and in their own bourgeois ways they seem to enjoy their privilege: large apartments cared for by state-supplied domestics; official limousines on call; food brought to the door from the secret delivery network called the "Distribution." Though their names or faces hardly ever appear in the press or on television, they are the products of a system of sharply differentiated *klass*.

Among the ranks of the leading professionals—scientists, diplomats, artists, writers, managers, musicians—women also live well. If they have reached this station through their husband's career, they may elect to stay home and not work. Or, if they are professional themselves, they may have maids—*dom rabotnitsi*—who come to cook and clean several times a week. They are free from the anguish of the "second shift," which forces most Soviet women to stand in lines for an hour or more to shop, then spend several hours preparing the food and washing up afterward, before they can go to bed—exhausted.

Privileged women have developed a number of ingenious shortcuts to take the common drudgery out of Soviet life. Nina Glazunov, wife of the celebrated painter Ilya Glazunov, orders ready-cooked meals from the kitchen staff at the well-known journalists' club, the Dom Zhurnalista. The rear entrance of the club is across the street from the front door of her own apartment block. Nina knows the staff and is able to maintain good relations by bringing them gifts from her trips abroad. Other women eat their main meal of the day at their husbands' offices or factory restaurants. Wives can also order semiprepared food from special *zakaz* stores, where meals can be ordered in advance.

As in the West, the divorce rate has been rising steadily. By 1981, the national divorce rate had already reached 332 per

1,000, one in every three marriages, but in Moscow, Kiev, Riga, and other big cities, the rate was closer to one divorce for every two marriages, about the same as the United States as a whole.[6]

In many cases, women petition for divorce on the grounds that their husbands are chronically drunk and abusive. One study in Kiev showed that 61 percent of all divorce applications came from women, with almost half citing heavy drinking by their men. In many cases, the men have already left home and the women are petitioning for child-support payments, which are rigidly enforced in the Soviet Union.

Incessant drinking by men is less acceptable to younger generations of Soviet women, who are better educated and more ambitious than their mothers; they are more ready to file for divorce than their parents were. "Women are rebelling against inequality and, of course, they are right to do so," Mr. Perevedentsev explains.

The number of one-parent families like Tanya's has risen to 9 million, fairly close to the figure for the United States. Tanya's husband, who has remarried twice, pays her less than thirty rubles a month in alimony, and shows no interest in their son. One reason Tanya decided to have her second child out of wedlock was because she was lonely; women like her feel trapped by the lack of opportunities to meet new friends.

She had a typical early life, staying in her own circle of high school, then Institute, friends. When we knew her she socialized at her office, trade union, and apartment meetings, but apart from a few discothèques for young people, and hotel restaurants where "drunken men never leave a girl alone," she knew no effective way to meet eligible men. One man asked her to join a local dancing group, but she stopped seeing him when she suspected that his intentions included more than dancing.

By 1980, Leningrad, Novosibirsk, Riga, Rostov-on-Don, and some other Soviet cities had opened one or two social clubs for people over thirty. Even publicly staid Moscow was considering one. In Riga, the press highlighted the club routine: weekly groups that met to discuss poetry, music, sports, flower arranging, mechanics. But this minor aid does not solve a gnawing Soviet problem: so many unmarried people are lonely that even the Academy of Sciences acknowledges the situation.

A 1978 study suggested greater use of computers to analyze traits and compatibility for single people. Even the staid *Literary Gazette* began a bold experiment by Soviet standards. They published two lonely-hearts notices, carefully edited for qualities the Party deems acceptable:

> Single man, aged 48, height 166 cm [5′ 5″], education in the humanities, homebody, would like to meet blond woman under 35 who loves the theater and symphonic music. Moscow. No. 1.

> Divorced woman, aged 32, height 162 cm [5′ 3″], has six-year-old child, construction technician, wants to meet a man who loves sports, is cheerful, and does not drink. Voronezh. No. 2.

Note the woman's preference for a vodka-free companion, and the description of the man as a "homebody." Those were the characteristics the Party (officially) favors. Within one year, *Literaturka* said it had received 10,000 letters urging a permanent get-acquainted service for young people, but the weekly was still cautious about the project. It had managed to match only two letter-writers. A woman in Siberia, whose son wrote a letter entitled, "I want a father," could find no one suitable in 1,200 replies.

One man, showing the Russian spirit of improvisation, wrote in to thank the weekly for all its efforts even though they had failed. He had posted his own get-acquainted notices on local bulletin boards and was happy to report that at the time of writing he had gone out on eighty-six dates. That was hardly what *Literaturka* was searching for, and the idea was dropped.

The strongest support for a dating service came from people like Tanya, who were aged between twenty-five and forty, divorced, with a child. With divorce rates high and fewer than half those divorced marrying again, the need to help women like Tanya to find new husbands and friends was urgent indeed.

Work can be boring, but for many a Soviet Rising Class woman it can be salvation as well. Millions of women sigh with relief as they burst through the doors of their offices and factories, leaving behind the difficulties of family and personal lives. Tanya was usually late after dropping Volodya at his bus stop, but once at her desk, her routine was the same as it was for millions of others west and east of the Ural Mountains. Off came her outer clothes and she settled down to gossip with her colleague at the next desk while they repaired their faces from the rigors of the long trip from home. When this ritual was included in a feature film called *Sluzhebny Roman (Office Love Story)* by director Eldar Ryazanov, the mainly female audience in our local movie theater reacted with delight as they recognized themselves.

Office and factory are places to talk to friends. They are bases from which to run out at mid-morning for thirty minutes of shopping for milk and eggs. By unspoken custom, more serious and lengthy shopping is left for the lunch break. Not that family worries can be completely left behind. Tanya's son telephoned every day after classes had ended and before his "extended day" began. Her mother called the office regularly to report on her latest shopping expedition. Lyuda's mother complained by phone each afternoon that her grandchildren were being disobedient again, or that she could find no meat in the shops, or that some other domestic disaster had struck.

A preoccupation of working mothers is making sure children are safe and have something to eat when they get home from school. When all else failed, Tanya took twelve-year-old Volodya to her office with her during his school vacations, making profuse apologies to her superiors. The boy sat in a corner, compiling lists of hockey teams and scores, talking to no one but his mother. His mother could not really concentrate on her work and tried to slip home early. It was better in the summer, when Volodya attended a Pioneer Camp in the countryside. He went for several weeks. Tanya, like many mothers, could not take her own vacation at the same time. She was entitled to twenty days of recreation a year, but she had to take the specific month assigned to her.

Natasha had the same problem: her husband was less senior in his job than she and could seldom lay claim to the favored month, August. Hotels and resorts are set up to handle groups of workers, not families with children, so many women vacation on their own, just as many men go away with their own friends. It is a practice that strikes hard at family life, particularly sexual fidelity, and many Soviets deplore it. Some liked it as a change of scene; others saw the chance for summer liaisons.

Natasha once told Margaret that she would like nothing better than to stay home rather than work. "What time you must have to read and be by yourself," she sighed, refusing to believe that three small children could take up all of a woman's time. Yet it was a romantic ideal of her own. Most Soviet women preferred to work than to stay home in typically cramped apartments.

Tanya, Natasha, Lyuda, and Irina were all white-collar employees, but many millions of Soviet urban and rural women still work with their hands. An enormous, powerful woman drove the steamroller that resurfaced the main Moscow ring road near our apartment, while other women helped on the road crew. Only women appeared in spattered work trousers and jackets to paint and refloor our apartment. It was female faces who peered through the second-floor windows of our apartment one Christmas Day as crews climbed scaffolding to paint the exterior of the building. Women drive cotton combines, tractors, and heavy lorries without the benefit of power steering or power brakes.

In 1965, about 60 percent of the women working at one ore-enrichment plant in eastern Siberia were involved in what they called "hard physical labor." At another plant, women made up 70.4 percent of steel erectors and concrete workers, 55 percent of "transport workers," 95.6 percent of crane operators, and 97.1 percent of motor mechanics.[7] Elderly women chip ice and sweep streets at 5 A.M. in the bleakest of weather. I talked to one woman in the Caucasus who tended 2,400 cattle in indoor pens, twice the usual number allotted to good workers.

One in every three construction workers is a woman, carrying bricks and mixing cement in subzero temperatures. A British executive who spent two years installing British machinery in a Moscow truck plant told me that "the best workers in a factory are usually women. They carry large loads, they don't complain, they don't malinger, they don't keep stopping to smoke and to talk. They work more neatly and accurately than men, and some are almost as strong and as tough."

The Party needs these women workers, but it wonders how to push up birthrates while keeping them on the job. One answer in 1980 was to ban women from 460 occupations, including unusually heavy or dangerous work in building, chemicals, and metals. After January 1, 1981, women were not supposed to drive vehicles carrying more than fourteen passengers, or do certain types of arduous repair work.[8] The specific aim was to make life easier for women, and to boost the birthrate and therefore the labor force within twenty years. But decisions in faraway Moscow are often shaded by local officials struggling to reach production targets; it will be surprising if women are not heavily involved in backbreaking work for decades to come.

Away from Moscow, out in the capitals of the republics all the way down to Afghanistan and eastward almost to Japan, trusted local women can rise to varying governmental heights and achieve a modicum of *klass*. They do not have the power of men, and they share the same household burdens of all Soviet women, but their condition is a vast improvement over the semifeudal Islamic world of poverty their grandmothers knew. For them, the 1917 Revolution was a step forward.

In Alma-Ata, the attractive capital of gigantic Kazakhstan, a republic large enough to hold much of Western Europe, Manura Akhmetova talked shyly but firmly for an hour in her capacity as a deputy education minister. One of six children born on a remote farm, she supervised 3 million children in 9,000 secondary schools, and cared for the domestic needs of a husband who worked at an Institute of Philosophy, an eighteen-year-old son studying physics, and a seventeen-year-old studying biology.

More than 1,000 miles to the southwest, in the intense heat of Ashkhabad, capital of Turkmenia, bordering on Iran and Afghanistan, Amangul Berdiniyazova served an elaborate tea on her office desk as she described her duties as one of the city's deputy mayors in charge of public health, women's and cultural affairs, and sports and trade. The daughter of a silk weaver, she was proud of a country and a system that had allowed her to move from a distant village to sit at a desk beneath a large official portrait of Vladimir Ilyich Lenin.

Our guide in Alma-Ata was a striking Tatar woman in her early twenties, who had already led a group of Kazakhs on a tour of Cyprus, Turkey, Egypt, and Greece. On a state farm of 17,000 acres outside Dushanbe, the capital of Tadzhikstan, demure Oybibi Holova, a trained agronomist at twenty-two, wore the traditional red silk dress of a Tadzhik woman over long, narrow trousers shot with purple, green, and black. Sitting cross-legged beside her at a fine meal of kebab and watermelon in the warm dusk was Rahima Hafizova, about the same age, leader of the state farm's Komsomol brigade. These women are more emancipated, and live in a more comfortable environment, than Moslem women across the border in Iran and Afghanistan. On the other hand, in smaller Soviet settlements on the other side of the spectacular Tadzhik mountains, women remain subservient to Islamic tradition, and are used as pawns by rapacious fathers who haggle for the *kalym*, or bride price. But millions of women in Soviet Central Asia have homes with electricity and running water, and the chance of a career. Ninety percent of Ashkhabad's health clinics are headed by a woman, and 73 percent of Kazakh schoolteachers are female. Many of them applaud the Soviet state for this kind of progress, and would not think of returning to the old ways.

The lives of Tanya, Lyuda, Irina, and Natasha were difficult, but it would be wrong to suggest that they did not have their share of happy times. They were all strong-minded and volatile. They were not easily put off by the problems they had faced all their lives. They had warm and close friendships, and shared joys and a more communal, emotional existence than Western women. They hugged and touched more, and cried more easily as well. They knew that people in other countries lived better than they did, and most of their days were spent hunting for the *klass* that made the difference between ease and discomfort. But they survived. They worked harder than their men, and drank less; they had little political power, but did not aspire to it. Their society forgave a man's faults, particularly drunkenness and adultery, more easily than a woman's, but it was the only society they knew.

It is women who hold family units together in the Soviet against the opposing forces of confined living space, red tape, and vodka. Sociologist Viktor Perevedentsev wanted the Party to recognize this to a greater degree. "There can be families without men," he said, "but not without women."

We knew older Soviet women who dismissed the complaints of Tanya's generation as a sign of being spoiled. "I remember before the last war," one veteran recalled, "we lived in wooden shacks with no electricity or running water. Some of us lived in those places until the 1950s. Conditions today are much better." In one shop an elderly woman remonstrated: "These young women complain too much. What's wrong with standing in line anyway? Get up early! Get to the store an hour before opening time! Stand in line and you'll get what you need!" One middle-aged woman with a history of illness said she preferred the communal apartments where as many as ten families share the same kitchen and bath. She was comforted by the knowledge that there was always someone close by if she ever felt unwell.

Many women, ignorant about conditions in other countries, accept that at least part of the Party's propaganda about the West must be true: that America and Europe are plagued by drugs, crime, unemployment, and moral degeneracy. Women can still be fervent patriots even as they blame the Party for food shortages.

Despite their stoic patriotism, however, the majority of Soviet women, compared to men, remain the statusless sex. "I am a quiet person," observes émigré Marina Voikhanskaya, "but the only time I cannot remain quiet in England is when someone tells me how wonderful women's liberation must be in Russia. Then I become agitated. I cannot push the words back down my throat." Women were largely statusless under the tsars; since then they have made much legal but only limited social progress toward the equality with men that the Party would have us believe Lenin created overnight in 1917.

CHAPTER 10

SOVIET MEDICINE:
A MATTER OF PRIVILEGE

At three o'clock one Monday afternoon in Moscow, my office telephone rang. During the next few hours I was to witness Soviet health care functioning close up, an experience that underscored the vital importance of privilege and *klass* in every aspect of Soviet health.

The caller was Boris, a thickset man in his thirties. He was not an open dissident, but was chafed by the restrictions of Soviet existence, and curious about the outside world. He was well connected in intellectual circles and not afraid to seek out Westerners as friends. The night he called his wife was in the hospital and his daughter was staying with his mother-in-law. He had taken advantage of the situation to move furniture from his former apartment to a new, larger one he was subleasing from a man who had been sent abroad for a year, but on the previous Friday he had stepped on a nail. He tried to continue working but the foot worsened over the weekend and on Sunday he had lost consciousness from the pain. When he telephoned his local polyclinic, he was told that its two ambulances were busy.

"Can you walk?" the duty nurse had asked.

"Barely."

"Then come in at 5 P.M. tomorrow."

In great pain and only able to hobble, Boris played his *klass* card. He telephoned me, a foreigner with an office car. Could I help him? Stopping work on an article with a deadline for that evening, I drove to a massive intersection in a new area on the outskirts of Moscow; after repeated delays and incorrect directions, I finally found Boris, white with pain, leaning on a homemade crutch.

"Shouldn't we go straight to the hospital?" I asked.

"No, no," he insisted. "You must first have a paper from the polyclinic before the hospital will take you."

"It might be dangerous if people see you in my car with its U.S. correspondent's white plates. Couldn't anyone at work help you?"

"No, no, only two people I know have cars, and they are both out of town."

"Does your office have a car?"

"Yes, but not for me."

The polyclinic was a block away, a standard, nondescript five-story Moscow building, pieced carelessly together from prefabricated concrete slabs, set in a straggly, untended lot. We pushed open the glass doors, passed a man and a woman in white coats behind a counter to the right, crossed a small lobby, and lined up behind half a dozen people at a glass window. Boris leaned heavily on his crutch.

After a ten-minute wait, it was his turn. He pushed his internal passport across the counter, showing his permit to live in Moscow and in the local district. One of the two elderly, grim-faced women behind the glass looked at his papers but could find no record of him in the files.

"Where do you live? No. 53? You're in the wrong place. Go to your own polyclinic." She turned away.

Boris was desperate. "But I telephoned you. Look, you can even see my apartment, over there . . . well, where is my polyclinic then?"

The woman shrugged. "You have no place here."

The man at the counter we had just passed was more sympathetic.

"You're in the long apartment building, the new one, on

the far side of the square? Let's see . . . oh yes. The dividing line between polyclinic areas goes right down the center of your building. Go back and tell her you actually live in No. 52, on the other side."

Boris had to wait another ten minutes in line. The woman railed at him and flapped papers about, but eventually gave him the all-important piece of paper.

"*Kabinyet* [office] 42," she snapped.

"Where is it?"

"Third floor. And I wouldn't be surprised if the doctor won't see you."

Boris did not even ask if there were any elevators. The building had been constructed during the Khrushchev era, when five-story structures were built without such costly extras. Slowly Boris pulled himself up the stairs, cursing. Like the building, the stairs were filthy, but Boris was better off than heart patients who sometimes have to negotiate the five flights to see doctors on the top floor.

Reaching the third floor, we decided to turn right along the corridor, which ran the width of the building. It turned out to be the right way. It would have been a long walk back from the far end. Several people were waiting on seats outside the door to Room 42. Boris ignored them, pulled open the door and went inside, asserting his determination to see the doctor quickly.

The nurse was astonished: "Go back outside into the corridor," she commanded. Boris assumed the attitude of privilege and refused. She shrugged. Ten minutes later the doctor, a man, appeared. Five minutes after that, Boris returned to the corridor, now even whiter in complexion.

"They have to operate, tonight," he said. "But both their ambulance cars are still busy." I said I would drive him. After another ten minutes, the nurse came out and silently handed Boris a single slip of paper. On it was written a bus route and stop, and the name of the nearest hospital that had a free bed. It seemed a long way away.

I drove Boris back to his apartment building, helped him through the courtyard and up two flights of stairs so that he could pack and telephone his in-laws with a message for his wife. We stopped one more time because he said he could go nowhere without his favorite Uppmann cigars, manufactured in Cuba.

Thirty minutes later, searching for the hospital in a heavy rainstorm, we were hopelessly lost. I asked a *skoraya pomoshch* (an ambulance, literally "quick help") driver for directions. He was surprised that I was so far out of the way. We drove on through the thunderstorm for another half an hour before we skidded through the gate of the hospital complex. Around the corner of one building, the road narrowed into a muddy footpath. Swinging around, I began to inquire at every building. Eventually we had to leave the car and walk one last stretch of uneven ground to a tall building that looked like a set of offices. Boris hobbled more and more slowly.

One of two elderly nursing aides in white coats pointed down the corridor to the left: "Room 73." We started on a long walk over the unwashed floor, thick with dust. We finally reached Room 73, where a small, apathetic group of patients was gathered. They seemed surprised, but heartened, by our show of determination. Out came a young nurse, blond, about twenty-two, tired and strained, wearing a long white coat unbuttoned over a blouse and a pair of flared jeans with flowers embroidered down each leg.

"Number 32," she said and led the way back along the corridor we had just traversed. Boris was moving with much more difficulty now, beads of perspiration on his forehead. We pushed open the door to Number 32, and he sat down heavily. I looked around at a medical scene from a half century ago: an old table and chairs, ancient instruments on a rusting tin tray, and through a connecting doorway a pair of gnarled bare feet protruding from a blanket at the end of a cot. I shivered. Boris, accustomed to it all, produced his *spravka* (polyclinic document) and insisted I leave: "They have to take me," he said. "I'll be all right now."

Once I had found the car it took me forty-five minutes to reach the center of Moscow again, still in the rain, driving in the dark on roads with no direction signs, feeling dispirited at the red tape and upset that I had not been able to do more.

The operation took place that night. The next day Boris got up and stood in line for a public phone to call me. He was in a ward with twenty beds, no partitions, no privacy, no radio, and only *kasha* (porridge) and occasionally some fish to eat. For the next eight days, he fought an infection caused, he believed, by insufficiently sterilized instruments, an alarmingly common occurrence in Soviet hospitals. However, the operation itself had gone well and eventually the foot healed.

Soviet health care for the average citizen suffers from the same shortage of funds and clumsy central planning endemic to the rest of the economy. There are not enough ambulances. Telephone lines to the hospital are always busy. On the plus side, Boris did have his operation and, in time, he did recover. Nor did he have to pay anything, and he was able to get reimbursement for his time off from his trade union.

Boris had received no-frills care. The surgery had been performed with only a local anesthetic; general anesthetics are used only in major operations. American physician Dr. William Knaus, an expert on Soviet medicine, believes that, considering the state of medical art in the USSR, it is probably better that way. "Putting anyone under is a risk," he told me, "and the Soviets don't have the same kind of monitoring equipment that we do."

Boris was not without *klass;* relatively few Soviet citizens, after all, live in Moscow and know a foreigner well enough to ask for use of his car.

But the possession of even more *klass* can improve health care even more dramatically. *Klass* can mean superior health care and medicine on a level never seen by ordinary Urban and Rural Classes.

The disparity, in fact, is startling. When a typical citizen such as Boris falls ill, he goes to his local polyclinic, where he might wait for hours to be treated by weary, harassed doctors with only minutes available for each patient. If he is seriously ill, he can be sent to a hospital such as the Pervaya Gorodskaya Bolnitsa, the First City Hospital in Moscow, where beds often line the corridors and the lack of hygiene can be fatal. Most hospitals hold twenty to forty beds in small wards without partitions or privacy of any sort. The state budget per patient for all services including food is less than fifty kopeks a day, reducing meals to minimum quality.

For the elite, however, all is different.

When one scientist's wife fell ill in Moscow, she was working on a graduate degree in an institute under the aegis of the Academy of Sciences. Her father-in-law was a noted professor. On the strength of that combined *klass*, she was able to enter the special Academy Hospital behind the Univermag Moskva on Leninsky Prospect, beyond Gagarin Square. She was placed in a special ward with only three other women, and her diet included meat every day. The hospital spent four times as much on each patient as ordinary establishments did.

The next step up in health care is a private room and specialized attention, reserved for higher levels of the elite. When the professor himself fell ill, he went to the same hospital, where he qualified for a room of his own. It was small, with a bed and a table, and he had to use the public bathroom on the same floor, but it provided precious privacy nonetheless. If he had been a full Academician, he would have been entitled to a suite on a separate floor of the same hospital with telephone and a television set, and a private bathroom as well.

The highest grade of medical care in the USSR is given at the Kremlyovka, a medical-hospital complex operated by the fourth department of the ministry of health. It is available only to members of the Politburo, the Central Committee Secretariat, the Presidium of the Academy, the Council of Ministers, and other Kremlin workers. Physical examinations of deputy ministers and people of lesser rank are carried out in private cubicles. Ministers themselves use special rooms fitted with carpets, bookcases, leather couches, and heavy red drapes. Politburo members who need hospital care stay in their own suites, are served the finest food, and are cared for by the best medical specialists in the country.

The advantage for those with *klass* is not only the quality of the doctors attached to the hospital, but the comfort, the service, the availability of medicines that other hospitals lack, and the consultation of specialists. The Academy hospital has a special dispensary department on the floor above the regular reception room downstairs. It boasts a comfortable waiting area, with armchairs and magazines, and its own pharmacy.

One of the extra comforts *klass* brings is better hospital food. Five times as much money per day is spent on each patient in the Academy of Sciences hospitals, for example, than in ordinary establishments. The diet in the Academy's Moscow hospital included meat every day. The best food, of course, is served at the Kremlyovka, especially in its main hospital behind the Lenin Library, a stone's throw from the red walls of the Kremlin itself.

The Bolshoi Ballet and Opera Company is one of dozens of cultural organizations that maintain their own medical system, including a polyclinic, its own doctors, hospital, and assured supplies of high-quality food. If a dancer needs special care, or an abortion, the Bolshoi's own doctors arrange it quickly and quietly. Workers in high-priority industries (computers, munitions, chemicals, plastics, mineral fertilizers) also have their own networks of clinics and hospitals. One is reserved for railroad workers; another for oil and gas drillers and support teams.

Klass provides access to medical technology not available

to the general public. A Soviet friend affiliated with the Leningrad Writers Union visited the union's dental clinic, bracing himself for a painful session. Soviet dentists routinely extract teeth for conditions that would be repaired in the West. But at the union dental department, he was pleasantly surprised to find that his woman dentist was using a new, superfast drill from Hungary that caused hardly any pain at all. The dentist was particularly proud, since only three clinics in Leningrad had received the new machines: the Sverdlov Hospital reserved for the Party elite; the clinic for the Academy of Sciences, and the one at the Writers Union.

At higher levels of status, even better non-Soviet medical technology is available. When a Soviet endocrinologist was called in to consult in the case of a government minister who had diabetes, he was surprised that he had the use of a German-made electromyelogram, a machine used to test nerve conduction, and a slit lamp for examining eyes. Neither device was available to him even in his faculty position at Moscow's prestigious Second Medical Institute.

Even foreign medical consultation can be sought when the patient is important enough. In 1972, when the head of the USSR Academy of Sciences, Mstislav Keldysh, became dangerously ill, the minister of health himself, Boris Petrovsky, asked an American friend, the famed surgeon Michael DeBakey of Houston, Texas, for help. DeBakey flew to the Soviet Union to consult, and finally operated in Moscow early in 1973, prolonging Keldysh's life by several years.

In February 1979, Dr. Warren Zapol of the Massachusetts General Hospital, an expert on acute respiratory failure, flew to Moscow to treat the oldest daughter of Dr. Vladimir Burakovsky, head of the Bakulev Cardiovascular Institute, with a new antibiotic unavailable in the USSR. Intravenous-feeding solution was flown in from America by Aeroflot three times a week.

Even emergency care can be excellent in the Soviet Union—if the patient is deemed important. One Australian diplomat I knew, John Godfrey, broke his wrist in two places after slipping on ice. To avoid Soviet medicine, resident Westerners normally prefer to fly to Helsinki; but in this case the doctors at the British and American embassies agreed that the wrist needed to be operated on at once. It was late on a Saturday afternoon and the diplomat was rushed to the Botkin Hospital, where a separate wing is set aside for VIPs and foreigners.

Since Godfrey also had a history of heart trouble, an EKG was needed. "I was embarrassed," he told me later. "An old man was on the EKG machine when I came in. They just pulled him off the machine to allow me to go on. There was a long line but they handled me right away. I was taken straight upstairs to the prep room. They operated there and then, and within a few months, I was able to write with my right hand again. It was a marvelous job." He paid full tribute to the skill of the doctors and was grateful that he was not charged.

While in the hospital, Godfrey noticed some details of Soviet care that surprised him. In the prep room stood what looked like a metal hat stand with a forest of arms, from which hung not hats but miniature clothespins. From the pins fluttered minute pieces of X-ray film. Every now and then, an assistant would unpeg a small square of film and hold it up to the light. When he produced his own full-sized wrist X ray, taken at the American embassy clinic, it caused a sensation. White-robed women crowded around. "How easy it is to read!" marveled one. "Where did you get it?"

When the diplomat explained it to the nurse, she replied, with admiration in her voice: "Well, why are you here? If they can do an X ray like that, surely they can set your wrist as well."

Later, Godfrey ran into two other aspects of Soviet health care from which not even his *klass* could shield him: roughness and red tape. After the operation, he found himself being wheeled on a stretcher into the freezing night air, apparently en route to his ward in a separate building. He was dressed in

a pair of shorts and covered with a single sheet. As he gasped
with cold, the stretcher wheels hit some ice and jolted him
off. Fortunately he was thrown to the left and was able to
break his fall with his good wrist.

The old man pushing the stretcher was unconcerned. "*By-
vaet*," he grinned ("It happens"), and helped him up. As they
reached the door of the next building, the stretcher snapped
up into a closed, U-shaped position, so that the diplomat's
nose was suddenly threatened by his knees. The old man
grinned again and straightened out both stretcher and patient.
He then pushed on through the door, only to be stopped by an
officious nurse.

"Documents?"

The old man said he had none. It was an emergency, he
explained. They began to argue. The diplomat lay there, cold,
his wrist aching. His arm had not been shaved and itched
murderously against its plaster cast as he struggled to regain
his bearings after his fall and concertina squeeze. Finally the
nurse grudgingly admitted that a man clad only in shorts and
a sheet, with one arm encased in fresh plaster, lying on a
stretcher, being pushed by an aged orderly from a building in
which she knew operations were performed, might indeed be
an emergency patient. It was all highly irregular. She sniffed,
and let them in.

The Soviet system works best when the patient's *klass* is
considerable, and if the powers-that-be want to impress him.
A trade-union leader visiting Moscow, another Australian,
found that he was having difficulty reading and decided to
have his eyes checked. Moscow wanted to cultivate him,
since he headed the pro-Soviet wing of the Australian Communist Party. Doctors ordered him to hospital and prescribed
a series of laser-beam operations. The technique was also
available in Sydney, but in Moscow it could be done immediately, without a tiring journey home, and it was free.

Over the next weeks, the labor leader had eight separate
laser-beam treatments, and he credits them with saving his

reading sight. He paid only two rubles and fifty kopeks for a new pair of glasses. He had a bed in a VIP hospital, excellent food, and regular deliveries of Australian newspapers and union publications. When I interviewed him he was buoyant, and said the entire experience showed the "superiority of Soviet medical care."

The Soviet health system is enormous and available to all. In theory, it provides excellent care. Almost one million doctors, one fourth of all physicians in the world, administer 3 million hospital beds. There is a polyclinic in every neighborhood, and one in every large factory as well. Every year, the average Soviet citizen makes use of his health service eighteen times. Sixty million people are admitted to hospital annually. Any citizen can telephone his polyclinic and a doctor must see him, on the same day if he calls before 10 A.M. and on the next day if he does not. In Moscow alone, 2,000 emergency-care doctors and 5,000 *feldshers* (assistant doctors) stand by in 800 ambulances driven by a pool of 2,400 drivers.[1]

The Soviet Union has sophisticated specialized medicine. The vast Cancer Research Center of the Academy of Medical Sciences covers several blocks near the main road leading from Moscow to Domodedovo domestic airport. The center has 1,000 beds, a staff of 4,000, and $128 million worth of Western equipment paid for by workers who contributed a day's pay to charity.

There are 250 specialized cancer hospitals in the country, and a modern research institute for organ transplants north of Moscow. The Bakulev Institute of Cardiovascular Surgery, which performs forty operations a week in nine operating theaters, is led by internationally famed surgeon Vladimir Burakovsky. The Soviet Union is noted for pioneer work in ophthalmology, among other fields. Perhaps most important to the consumer, Soviet health care is provided *byezplatno* (free of charge).

Achievements like these cannot be ignored, yet the official picture does not tell the whole truth. It omits the reality encountered by the bulk of Soviet citizens. It highlights the superior aspects of Soviet medicine, but leaves the rest in shadow. Above all, it fails to make the essential point: truly good medical care is available mainly to the privileged.

Says Dr. William Knaus: "As a national program aimed at conserving scarce resources while providing basic services, it is a qualified success." But he adds: "From the perspective of a patient in need of special attention or individual emphasis, [the Soviet system] is frequently a failure."[2] To avoid this failure, and gain a modicum of comfort, dignity, and excellence in care, the Soviet patient often needs to call on his social position. He needs *klass* to avoid the regimentation experienced by Boris and to force the medical system to focus on him individually as a patient. Unless one has status in the USSR, medical care can be bureaucratic and erratic.

The majority of Soviet doctors are not as well trained or as well paid as their American counterparts. A typical American medical student devotes ten to fourteen years after high school to intensive study, while a Soviet *srednyi vrach* (ordinary doctor) spends seven. After graduation, professional status for most doctors is low. In fact, most earn an average of 180 rubles a month, the same level as a semiskilled factory worker. Seventy percent are women, filling jobs regarded by the Party as routine. Soviet physicians feel less personally responsible for diagnosis and treatment of patients than do doctors in the West. The system has its rules and doctors follow them. "Despite her training and title, she is not an independent professional but a paid employee working for the world's largest employer of physicians—the Soviet government," says Dr. Knaus.[3]

The Soviet system seems designed to process the maximum number of patients with the maximum amount of red tape. A Soviet patient is more likely to be sent to the hospital than are patients in Western countries—for several reasons. Apartments are small and crowded, and it is often impossible to allot an entire room to someone who is in bed all day. Furthermore, hospital care is free and hospitals are eager to fill every bed. Their state funds are based not on the quality of the care but on the number of people they treat. In that sense, hospitals are like the factories that turn out shoes no one wants to buy: the higher the production, the larger the bonuses.

Another failure of the system is that patients rarely see the same doctor twice. In the polyclinic, patients see whomever is on duty, and doctors are frequently moved from one clinic to another. As a Moscow health economist says: "No one is taking care of the entire patient. . . . Why, we found one woman in Moscow who had been to see twenty different doctors in a total of seventy-three times in one year."

The state says that it spends 18 billion rubles a year on medical care, but if we disregard expenditures for such items as physical therapy, vacation sanitoriums, and construction costs, the total is reduced to 10 billion rubles spent on actual medical care, or less than $40 per person. In the United States, the figure is $956 per person. Real (adjusted for inflation) U.S. spending for medical care rose 233 percent between 1960 and 1980, whereas Soviet spending went up by just 50 percent. The United States spends 9 percent of its gross national product on health; the USSR spends 2 percent.

While the Party correctly claims that Soviet health care is *byezplatno*, or free, the Rising Class is learning that it is often better to pay for illegal private medical care than to risk the uneven performance of the official system. One longtime Leningrad citizen told me he paid 400 rubles, *na levo*, to have a distinguished surgeon operate on his wife.

At the very top level, it is not necessary to buy private surgery because the physicians who operate on political leaders are the nation's best. But at the Rising Class level—particularly among scientists, engineers, and members of the intelligentsia—only personal contact can ensure that a talented surgeon will do the operation. In such cases, the patient or a member of his family will call the doctor, who will then examine the patient at his hospital and make all the arrangements. The fee will range from 200 to 500 rubles.

A musician in the Moscow Philharmonic Orchestra found a way to get excellent care when he broke the crown on his back tooth. He wanted the best possible treatment, which he knew he could get only from a private dental practice. A neighbor who was a professor at Moscow State University passed on the telephone number of a dentist working at the Moscow Polyclinic for Old Bolsheviks, veterans of the 1917 Revolution who receive privileged medical care.

The musician telephoned the dentist at home the same evening. Without hesitation, the dentist told him to appear at the polyclinic at one o'clock the next day. Normally, the musician would have to go to the polyclinic near his home and fill out various forms. In this case, he simply asked for the dentist, who came to the lobby to meet him. "Sign this man in," the dentist told the reception clerk. Without a word, she did.

The musician went upstairs, where treatment began. He wanted a new gold crown instead of the steel ones commonly used by Soviet dentists. His aunt had just died, and according to Russian custom, the hospital had removed her gold crowns and sent them on to her closest relative. He had brought one in with him. The dentist sent it off to the laboratory, where a technician who often did private work for the dentist fashioned a new crown out of the gold. The musician was pleased and paid fifty rubles to the dentist, who kept thirty and gave his technician the other twenty.

Physicians also conduct private practices on the side. If someone believes that a particular doctor is good, he will contact him and arrange for the medical care to take place outside the polyclinic, either at the doctor's apartment or the patient's. The fees are moderate, but, to underpaid Soviet physicians, this private medical practice is the difference between mere survival and a decent living.

The Soviet habit of bribery invades Soviet hospitals. Bed-sheets are changed only when hospital aides, usually elderly women, can get around to it, and if they are paid extra. Many a friend has confirmed the same story: of having to pay nurses and assistants on duty between one and three rubles every time they wanted a bedsheet changed or a back scrubbed. Ten rubles is often needed to persuade a nurse to bring a pain-killing drug or a sedative.

Even the government newspaper *Izvestia* was struck by the story of the man from Odessa who entered the hospital for an appendectomy fortified with a pocketful of one-ruble bills. As long as he kept dispensing them to nurses and aides, all went well. He was taken promptly to the operating theater and was able to recuperate in comfort after surgery. His bed linen was changed regularly, his back scrubbed, his pain eased with drugs, until his supply of rubles ran out. Suddenly, everything changed. Drugs were not available, thermometers disap-peared, even his bedpan was missing. Only when he managed to get a message to his wife to bring a fresh supply of rubles did conditions return to "normal." *Izvestia* may have been exaggerating to make a point, but the experience of bribing hospital staff is so common that readers could nod in instant sympathy.

The care in the outpatient polyclinics is often no better, Russians complain. "Everyone hates the polyclinics," an émi-gré from Vilnius told me flatly. They are legendary for their long lines and overcrowding. Anatoly Tulainov, my office translator, who died while I was in Moscow, once described why he avoided his local clinic even though he was fre-quently ill with ulcers.

"You see," he said in his quiet, precise voice, "you can't go in on Mondays, because the place is filled with the overflow from the weekend. The local clinics are closed on weekends and people have to go to the one that stays open elsewhere in the district. But often they don't want the bother of making the journey, so they wait until Monday. Tuesday is no good:

still crowded from the weekend. Wednesday is out of the question: people come in to start their treatment before the weekend ahead. Thursday is too difficult: the crowds are thicker. Friday? Well, Friday is hopeless, of course. The clinic is always packed the day before the weekend or public holidays."

He thought for a moment.

"Once I had a temperature of one hundred and three degrees," he said, "and I waited at the polyclinic for hours. Finally a nurse said, 'All those with temperatures of a hundred and two or less, come over here. Those with a hundred and three and above stay there. We'll take the hundred and threes and above first.'"

A woman friend described the care given to pregnant women. When she went to the polyclinic for her first maternity care she was asked, "Keeping it, or getting rid of it?" Women intending to keep their babies are directed one way, and those wanting abortions are told to move in the other direction.

The Soviet system does, however, have one advantage over much of Western medicine. Even though they are undertrained and underpaid, Soviet doctors still make house calls, an almost vanished tradition in America. Doctors making the calls use public transportation. One doctor freely conceded that up to 50 percent of apartment calls in the USSR were unnecessary—doctors were often called only to provide the document needed to ensure sick pay for days off. If a man has a hangover, the doctor writes "cold" on his trade-union slip. Although a doctor might have only seven minutes to spend with each patient, the house call adds warmth to an otherwise impersonal system.

Has the 1917 Revolution improved general health care? Yes. But statistics also show that the Soviet health-care system in the 1980s is in a state of crisis.

The life expectancy of Soviet men has dropped almost four years since 1965, to 61.9 years, while most nationalities are living longer than ever. By 1980 the average Soviet life span, for both men and women, was down to 68.5 years (men 63, women 74) below the level of thirty years ago, and several years less than life expectancy in America and other Western nations. Soviet men now have shorter life expectancies than Cubans, Jamaicans, or Albanians.

Infant-mortality figures, too, are alarming. They had risen by one-third between 1970 and 1974, a startling increase that undoubtedly explains why the Kremlin stopped publishing the figures after 1974. An American expert on Soviet demographic trends, Murray Feshbach, has estimated the true figure as approximately 40 per 1,000. By contrast, infant mortality in the United States, though not the world's lowest, has been falling steadily, to twelve deaths per 1,000 births. The Feshbach estimate is on par with such less-developed nations as Panama and Trinidad.[4]

A Soviet official has conceded an infant-mortality rate of about 28 per 1,000, double the United States rate, since 1978, but claims that the rise is due to better reporting methods.

Both Feshbach and British expert Christopher Davis dismiss this explanation and suggest a range of other reasons: poor-quality baby food and infant formula; uterine damage caused by the large number of abortions undergone by Soviet women (an average of six for every woman of childbearing age); repeated influenza epidemics; environmental pollution. Also involved, though in a less measurable way, is alcoholism.

In a land of chronic shortages, one item that never runs out is vodka, nicknamed the "green snake." In fact, alcoholism, in the USSR and the Ukraine particularly, is an enormous, unsolved health problem: a national undertow of misery and oblivion, retarding progress, splitting families, slowing production. A Russian quip asks: "What is alcoholism?" The answer is: "An intermediate stage between socialism and communism." One Western analyst has estimated that Soviet people drink more distilled spirits per head than any other people in the world.

To possess *klass* does not mean that one drinks less. Topmost Party, government, KGB, and police elites are men of rural, blue-collar backgrounds, raised in an atmosphere of heavy and continual drinking and accustomed to celebrating every occasion with vodka. It is only the intellectual and scientific classes, the most "Western" of the Soviet people, who are learning to drink modestly, to sip slowly instead of tilting back their heads and rushing toward oblivion.

For those with status, drinking means that one does not have to go to the local beer bar, or split a one-liter bottle of vodka among three people, as is commonly done. The elite classes drink at home or in their union clubs, where vodka is viewed as a mark of masculine status and as a sign of hospitality. As a nondrinker, I would offer toasts to Soviet hosts or guests in mineral water or *sok* (juice), and sometimes eyebrows would be raised. It became necessary to explain that in the West a growing number of people no longer feel they have to drink or smoke to enjoy themselves.

More and more Soviet women and young people now appear to be drinking heavily. A *Pravda* article reported that chronic alcoholism among Soviet young people was concentrated in the 15–17 age bracket. Ninety percent of all Soviet alcoholics started drinking before they turned sixteen. The press, in periodic efforts to sound the alarm, prints letters saying that as much as one-third of combined family income in the USSR is used to buy vodka.

All across the country, studies by an All-Union Institute looking into the causes of crime discovered that one murder in every three, two rapes out of five, one motor accident in three, and virtually every aggravated assault was due to drunkenness.

The phenomenon is hardly new. A thousand years ago, Prince Vladimir of Kiev is supposed to have said that Russians could not do without their drink. In 1839, the visiting French Marquis de Custine commented that "the greatest of the pleasures of these people is drunkenness, in other words, oblivion. . . . Poor people! They have to dream to be happy. . . ."[5] Ballet dancer Valery Panov, who defected to the West, wrote that, "without travel, jazz, and a million forms of recreation available in other countries, vodka was the only refuge. Whole villages sometimes went on monumental binges."[6]

Dissidents Anatoly Shcharansky and Vladimir Slepak were tossed into a "drying-out" tank for fifteen days in an effort to stop their public protests in late 1977. They were astonished at the drunks they saw and the stories they heard in prison. When let out, they talked to me and to David Shipler of *The New York Times*. Said Shcharansky: "I really had no idea how big a role vodka plays in everyday life. Of course, everyone drinks, but . . . most of the men in that tank had been committed by their wives, who had called police after the husbands arrived home drunk. . . . Others were turned in by mothers-in-law or neighbors. We had about sixty in my cell during my fifteen days." Some of the men arrested were blue-collar workers, but they possessed a modicum of *klass*. Their photos had been put up on honor boards in their factories, and they were in line for extra bonuses. They were frightened at being arrested, knowing that police would inform their trade-union committees. Their photographs could be taken down and their bonuses frozen. Other men were fatalistic: they had little to lose, and getting drunk was the price they paid for drinking. Still others were defiant, stating that a man was not a man unless he drank. He did not stop just because his wife had turned him in.

The state tries to hide the extent of the national drinking problem, but émigré Vladimir Solovyov in New York has done a thorough job of documenting its extent, especially at the bottom end of the social classes. Despite its effect on their health, Soviet men apparently will drink almost anything: formalin used to preserve bodies in morgues; eau de cologne; the drug valerian; varnish; a glue called "B-F"; denatured alcohol; methyl (wood) alcohol. In a Leningrad shop, Solovyov saw a young man order twenty liters of "skull and crossbones" (denatured alcohol). Queried about the amount, the man said that he was "going to a wedding." But he added reassuringly, "It's for the men; the weaker sex will drink vodka."[7]

Generations of Soviets have drunk themselves under the table with *sivukha*, a badly distilled vodka, and a grape brandy called *chacha*. In addition, Russians, particularly country people, drink a home brew. Known as *samogon* (literally, "self-distilled") or *kerosinka*, it consists of water, yeast, and sugar, flavored with anything from oat straw to sugar beet. It is part of a do-it-yourself tradition that goes back to the era of Soviet prohibition, which existed until 1925. As in the United States, prohibition was widely ignored. Even today, jail sentences of up to three years and fines are simply shrugged off, and smoke from stills curls up into many a night sky.

Drinking is a problem in the armed forces as well, particularly in the ranks. A former tank officer discovered that members of his company were drinking secretly, but steadily, during the 1968 invasion of Czechoslovakia. It took considerable effort before he discovered the hiding place for the alcohol: the capacious engine radiators of armored troop carriers. The men drank each evening by sliding beneath the engines and pretending to carry out routine maintenance.[8]

Party campaigns against drinking have little impact. The Party needs the taxes from alcohol; if it reduced the volume of vodka on legal sale, people would only brew more of their own. In any case, the root causes of drinking would be untouched—tradition; boredom; difficult living conditions from which oblivion is a welcome escape; a firm belief that drinking and drunkenness are essential aspects of masculinity and a requirement for all social gatherings. At this writing, the

Soviet medical system, with its million doctors, was doing little to alleviate this enormous health problem.

Alcoholism is only one of the many medical problems that have made life expectancy in the Soviet the lowest in the civilized world. "Observers have referred to the Soviet medical system as either an enormous success or a colossal failure," sums up Dr. Knaus. "It truly is both."[9]

Some changes have come about, but it remains true that women are considered to lack *klass* in the USSR, and the professions they dominate—including medicine—are also held in low repute by the authorities. Partly because of the impact of the U.S.–Soviet medical exchange agreement and increased contacts with Western Europe since 1970, more men are now specializing in medicine. They are bringing the profession more prestige and attention.

As I look back, I think of the contrasts of Soviet socialized medicine—of the insensitive treatment of Boris, and of the huge cancer-research hospital in Moscow; of the luxury of the Kremlyovka medical complex in contrast to the situation of the patients in other hospitals who have to pay a semiliterate old woman a ruble every time they want a clean bedsheet or a wash.

I think of two successive issues of *Pravda* that seemed to me to sum up the unevenness of Soviet medicine, and the need for *klass* to ensure better care. One of the two editions carried an account of two research scientists, who conducted thousands of tests to discover polymers that could be made into thin celluloid-type strips containing medication. The strips were to release their medicine in tiny measured quantities within the body over an extended period. It was ultramodern, another triumph for the Party and Soviet health care.

The previous day, *Pravda* had published an article of exactly the same length but very different in tone. In it, a specialist in dentures made the ritual verbal bow to the system, but went on to complain that dentists who wanted to make good dentures were also forced to take into account other tasks "in no way connected with the patient's needs." Dentists had to see a certain number of patients each day. The more they saw, the more the polyclinic was able to claim extra budget allowances under the Plan.

The result, he said, was more attention to the Plan and less to the patient. "It is much simpler for the orthopedic stomatologist to fulfill his financial plan and assignment in terms of dental work units if he orients himself towards the simplest sort of prostheses that do not require a substantial outlay of time or money. . . . But easily produced, nondurable dentures quickly wear out and . . . a vicious circle is created: the number of dental prostheses being produced increases, but the lines at the dentists' offices do not get any shorter."

Basic Soviet medical care is available without charge to every Soviet citizen. The Party is proud of progress since 1917, which is considerable. The problem for the Rising Class is to cut through the state bureaucracy to secure better physicians, better hospital facilities, better polyclinics.

It requires *klass*.

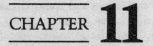

THE UNDERSIDE OF *KLASS:* THE "BLACK" ECONOMY

Much of Soviet humor has a sardonic, ironic biting edge. One story circulating in Moscow when I lived there had an Aeroflot flight taking off from Tbilisi airport in Soviet Georgia. It was barely in the air when a hijacker with a gun ordered the pilot to change course for Paris. Soon afterward, a burly Georgian jumped from his seat with a knife, overpowered the hijacker, and told the pilot, "To Moscow, as planned." When the plane landed, the KGB took the hijacker away and held a ceremony on the tarmac to praise the Georgian's heroism. As the crowd dispersed, KGB agents cornered the Georgian.

"Come on," one agent said. "Why did you really tell the pilot to fly to Moscow?"

The Georgian spread his hands. "Well," he replied, "what would I have done in Paris with 100 kilograms of oranges?"

The story amuses Russians because Georgians are legendary for the ingenious ways in which they exploit shortages, bottlenecks, and red tape to extract *klass* privilege by black-market means. What they do is part of a much larger "second," "parallel," or "black" economy throughout the USSR. It exists because the state-run centralized Soviet economy simply cannot produce or deliver the goods and services that most people want. Slowly rising living standards and expectations make the black economy an ever-present, ever-tempting way for the Urban and Rural Classes to win themselves some of the *klass* privileges that the state itself provides the Top Class, the Military Officer Class, and the upper rungs of the Rising Class.

The Soviet Union forbids purchase and resale for private gain. The use of crafts and trades for private income is illegal. All exchange transactions with foreigners are against the law. Owning foreign currency in the Soviet Union is usually a punishable offense (though it is not a crime in Poland and other Eastern bloc countries).

Many activities that are considered normal, even praiseworthy, in the West are classed as crimes in the USSR. Some, of course, would also be considered criminal in the West; but much of the second Soviet economy is actually the exchange of goods at their true market value.

Barter is a growth industry. One Moscow actress supplied hard-to-get theater tickets to a skilled dentist who worked after hours on her daughter's teeth. A filmmaker who needed regular fresh fruit and meat for an ailing relative asked a friend to introduce him to another friend who worked in a food store. He paid not in rubles but in tickets to private screenings of late-run Western movies.

A scientist who worked in an Academy of Sciences Institute wanted a Western outboard motor for his dinghy. He offered a speculator some rare books he had collected. The speculator, in turn, used some of the books and a few bottles of French cognac to extract a secondhand motor from an under-the-counter dealer with contacts in a trade-union boating club in another city.

One professional man I knew used his home stereo equipment to record bootleg tapes of other records, then bartered the tapes for items he needed, including Western shoes. This form of Soviet back-scratching is familiar to anyone who has already lived in the middle East; Moscow in winter was quickly summed up by one visiting correspondent from the Arab world as "Cairo with slush." Newcomers who do not customarily use barter as an everyday tool find adjusting more difficult.

The purchase of private services is usually illegal. The government owns both the equipment and the worker's time. Since people are usually impatient to get an apartment painted or a car repaired, and the government is too inefficient to do it, bribery and the second economy are called into play. Workers do the jobs *na levo* (on the side), and all parties—except the state—are pleased.

Lyuba, a Moscow friend, did what many others do when they need a room decorated. She spotted a pair of painters working in the next building and arranged for them to come to her own apartment after hours. The following day the workers, both women, came to look at the room. The day after that, they arrived at about 6 P.M., bringing paint, brushes, ladders, and drop cloths, and finished the work in a few hours. Lyuba did not have to ask where the supplies came from; she knew they were "borrowed" from the government job next door. Lyuba paid sixty rubles, delighted at the service and the speed. The two painters had thirty rubles each to spend. Everyone was happy—and everyone had broken the law.

One day my eye stopped at a story in *Izvestia*'s weekly supplement *Nedelya* (*The Week*), an account that helped to explain why private initiative is so popular in the USSR. The supplement had asked a reporter to redo his own large apartment without offering any bribes to government officials or workers. He was to rely entirely on the legal services of the state. He failed miserably, and quickly. On the very first day, he wrote, he was forced to lay newspapers on the floor and to carry out piles of dirt made by the workers, then to sign a paper attesting that the workers themselves had done it. When he was told that no linoleum was available for the kitchen, he resorted to time-honored methods. He offered a bribe and it suddenly appeared. In all, he spent 420 rubles, but only 100 rubles went toward materials. The rest was for bribes. In any case, the linoleum began to lift from the floor two days later, about the same time that his wallpaper began to peel.

Since transport is one of the state's most poorly organized services, taxi and truck drivers can, and do, earn a great deal on the side. Taxi drivers make deals to deliver packages and carry furniture, especially if their Volga automobiles are station-wagon models. Strictly illegal, this type of *na levo* work exists on a wide scale. When our clothes and belongings arrived in Moscow by rail from Leningrad, the crews of two trucks we hired stopped work in the midst of loading and demanded double the price we had agreed to pay.

Villages in the Caucasus send their menfolk flying to the cold cities of the north with knitted winter garments to sell at high prices. The wool is not their own: it is stolen from the backs of the state sheep. Only the small private plots that supply the expensive (and legal) farmers' markets with food are legal.

Like *na levo* activity, stealing from the state is endemic. One young university student who needed extra money for food took a job as an attendant at a parking lot. Since most Soviet car owners are afraid to drive in harsh winter conditions, they buy space in parking lots for several months and put their vehicles up on blocks. "We charged thirty-five kopeks a day for space," the student said. "Often owners would come back a day or a week late, sometimes more. I would charge them overtime, and put that money into my own pocket. No one but I knew exactly when they had returned."

The student told himself he was doing no harm. He took home about five extra rubles for every twenty-four-hour shift he worked, although he could have been sent to a labor camp for three years if he had been caught. He looked surprised when I asked if he felt any guilt. "No, why should I?" he asked. Like millions of other Soviet citizens, he simply did not believe that stealing from the state was a crime. Only taking from an individual was wrong.

"You know what we say," he said, laughing. " 'We pretend to work, and the state pretends to pay us.' "

Stealing from the state can be as small a transgression as seamen taking home rolls of toilet paper from their ships. "There was a time," a Leningrad intellectual told me, "when people like myself could buy toilet paper easily because most Russians had never heard of it. Now many more think it is fashionable, and the demand is so great you can hardly find it any more." Or the theft can be as substantial as the operations of what the *Literary Gazette* has called "underground millionaires," who run at least 1,000 illegal factory chains with profits adding up to about $5 billion a year.

Fraud can sometimes be elaborate. In one case piles of paperwork attested that a large factory for repairing truck engines had been built in the Great Russian republic over a period of years. In fact, all that existed was a hole in the ground guarded by an elderly man carrying an ancient blunderbuss. The satirical magazine *Krokodil* devoted almost an entire issue to that episode, explaining how hundreds of thousands of rubles had been paid out in government bonuses and fees for construction work done only on paper.

And there are always the shops. Some of the devices used to cheat the state wholesale delivery network are complicated. Word spread around Moscow in the late 1970s that the "caviar caper" was back in business. Unsuspecting buyers at a Moscow store had taken home cans marked SMOKED HERRING, only to find them packed with the finest black caviar. The discoveries set off a chain of inquiries that eventually led to the resignation of the fisheries minister himself. Caviar, it turned out, was being shipped abroad in the "smoked herring" cans, and Western contacts were repacking the contents, labeling them BEST CAVIAR, and selling them at high prices. A share of the profits went into bank accounts in Switzerland controlled by officials in the Soviet ministry.

The government owns and sells all gasoline, but one speculator found a way to compete. Gogi Chanturia regularly flew from the southern city of Poti to Moscow, where he visited gasoline pumps at truck depots, offering rubles to truck drivers in exchange for state gasoline coupons. Chanturia would fly back to Poti and sell those coupons at much higher prices to the operators of gasoline stations. The operators were delighted. They, too, knew how to cheat the state. When cars drove up they would charge cash for gasoline, put the cash in their own pockets, and turn in Chanturia's coupons at the end of the month to prove that they had "sold" gas in the approved way.

In a single day, Chanturia once bought coupons in Moscow for 2,400 liters of gas, about 600 gallons. When police caught up with him, he had coupons in his suitcase for 117,000 liters, worth more than 20,000 rubles, or ten years of an average monthly salary. He was sentenced to five years in a labor camp for *spekulyatsia*.

A meat-packing plant worker in Vladimir made so much money from another scheme that he was able to buy a two-tone Mercedes sedan before he was caught. He saw to it that carcasses were improperly frozen, losing less weight than prescribed by law. He wrote on his log that the freezing had been carried out to the legal limit, then sold the excess meat on the black market and pocketed the money.

Operating a hotel for the state can be a gold mine, but for the director, not the state. In the Ukraine, one hotel chief regularly hung out a NO VACANCY sign as soon as she came on duty. All day long, a stream of desperate travelers would file into her office, begging for a room. If they offered large enough bribes, the director would register them as "disabled war veterans," which automatically entitled them to a room. Unfortunately, one guest handed over his bribe in full view of the staff. Police were informed, and they found the director's kitchen stuffed with the fruits of her labors: cognac, caviar, smoked meat, coffee.

At first, I thought that at the top levels of *klass*, Soviet individuals did not need to make money by bribery or extortion. But this is not always true. The higher a man's position, the more others rush to please him, often by bringing him a form of tribute known as *prinosheniya,* anticipatory bribes aimed at building goodwill in the hope of benefits to come.

There was something feudal about the sight of trucks driving up to the apartment buildings of local Party, government, and police officials in a small town on the White Sea in the Arkhangelsk district, bringing *prinosheniya* of fresh and smoked fish, livestock carcasses, potatoes, and hay for the officials' own privately-owned cattle. The officials were receiving tribute just as the tsar's local officials took it from peasants hundreds of years before. One retired Moscow lawyer became indignant, and fired off letters of complaint to local and national Party offices. The only result was that a relative whose home he was sharing was called in and told he would be fired from his job unless the older man left the area at once. To keep the peace, the lawyer went.[1]

A large restaurant on Gorky Street in Moscow provided free lunches and dinners for local Party and government leaders, for the fire chief, the public health inspector, and the local police, and even for officials of the special police department assigned to combat embezzlement from the state, an office known by its initials OBKhSS.

In their turn, top people must also take care of those who run their special food and clothes shops and perform other vital services. One privileged young man, who shopped several times a week at a special food store in Moscow, was usually served by the same woman seated behind a small desk. "We had to make sure we kept on her right side," he recalls. "Yes, of course, we tipped her. Bribed her, if you like. Something from abroad was best—makeup or a scarf—anything Western. If you didn't hand over something, you might find that, although your father was entitled to every kind of privilege, some of the food you had ordered somehow wasn't available that week."

Bribery is endemic in the Soviet Union and shows no sign of abating. It is often the only way to move the lethargic Soviet bureaucracy. While I was in Moscow, an American television network tried for six months to obtain an apartment for its Moscow correspondent and his family. The government agency that serviced foreigners kept promising them an apartment; meanwhile the correspondent and his wife were forced to live in an uncomfortable Moscow hotel. Eventually, he and an editor from New York obtained an appointment with the agency chief. During the conversation, the Soviet official mentioned that he had become keen on golf while stationed abroad. How, he wondered out loud, could he obtain an indoor putting machine for his office?

The Americans decided it was worth a try. The editor telexed New York and ordered a putting machine put onto the next flight to Moscow. A day later it was at Sheremetyevo Airport. A day after that it had been delivered to the chief, with a graceful note. The long-promised apartment suddenly materialized.

Law-enforcement officials are in good positions to extort bribes. One in the Kuibyshev district in Moscow took payments ranging from 25,000 to 100,000 rubles to quash cases against black marketeers in the local court. He was finally punished, but the young official who caught him became a marked man for doing so. He was himself arrested and jailed a year later.

Corruption is even more entrenched in the three Caucasus republics, in the five in Central Asia, and in Moldavia on the Romanian border. In Azerbaijan, the prosecutor of the Shemaha district was jailed for fifteen years for extorting so many bribes that, as a local newspaper put it, "his suites of rooms in Shemaha and in Baku were adorned with paintings and thirty-four rugs (and) entire bolts of crêpe de chine. . . . His homes contained as much crystal as a large store." The director of a motor vehicle inspection station received so many bribes for passing cars as safe that he was able to pay

100,000 rubles for his family to obtain an apartment much larger than usual.

Bribes are routinely extorted by people who deal with the public. The director of a special science high school in the Siberian city of Tomsk, for instance, solicited bribes in return for admissions, as *Izvestia* reported. She took anything from "mink coats to pails of berries."

Extortion methods used by officials vary: some are crude, others subtle. "I wonder where people get these Japanese watches from?" one official asked a citizen seeking a favor— and who had just such a watch on his wrist. The petitioner took the watch off and made the official a gift of it, there and then.

In some cases, bribery and other illegal deals are necessary just to keep the legal socialist economy in motion. "Capitalist" arrangements are often made to cut through bottlenecks. In Azerbaijan and Georgia, managers who have already obtained requisition forms for raw materials must sometimes bribe the officials who authorize the actual shipments; bottles of champagne, and in at least one case, a set of kitchen equipment, have been used.

Private deals made for profit can help the sluggish economy. Officials in charge of a Moscow auto-repair garage bribed the ministry in charge of spare parts in order to receive more than their allotted quota. In turn, the garage officials took bribes from their skilled mechanics to allow them to conduct private car repairs after hours. The garage officials used their power to sign requisition slips for carburetors and transmissions in return for theater tickets and fresh food from taxi and truck operators who were desperate to keep their vehicles running.

The Soviet system teaches its citizens to make the best use of whatever they have for extra income. A farmer near a big city can grow fruit, vegetables, or flowers on his private plot of land, travel to town once a week, and sell his wares at one of the sanctioned farmers' markets. Prices are supposed to be restricted, but ceilings are often ignored. When Margaret was told that the price of tomatoes was an astronomical five rubles per kilogram, she pointed to a sign stating the legal limit. The elderly woman behind the makeshift wooden counter merely flailed the air with her hands and shook her head; such legalisms were not for her. If we wanted to buy, we had to pay. She was a "capitalist," except that the tools, the fertilizer, and much of the time used to grow the tomatoes in the first place all came from the state.

Farmers sell whatever they can put their hands on: laurel leaves for jam; mandarins; accommodations for vacationers if they live near the Black Sea or the Baltic coast. A woman known as Aunt Taya illustrated the lengths to which some people will go to exploit state shortages. She had inherited a house in the city of Gorky not far from the Red Etna rolled-steel plant, and soon figured out how to take advantage of a lag in local construction. The plant union had not received a single new apartment for a year.

One of her outbuildings became a virtual hotel. Taya rented a tiny cubicle to a twenty-eight-year-old widow with a seven-year-old daughter, an adjoining space to a working family with three small boys, a third space to another family, and a fourth to a couple expecting a child. All shared the same kitchen and bath. Radiator pipes had burst in one of the rooms and had not been repaired for months. The rent per cubicle was thirty-five rubles a month, far more than state rents for better two-room apartments with their own kitchen and bath.

The widow wrote to *Pravda* to complain, and the newspaper sent a reporter to investigate. Aunt Taya's son-in-law, a member of the Party, told him that the local housing shortage was so bad that she could ask for even more rent if she wanted it. The widow located a nicer room nearby, and was willing to pay the rent of forty rubles a month, but the owner demanded three years' rent in advance, and she could not find the 1,440 rubles required. *Pravda* discovered that the steel plant was helping its employees only by providing a limited number of dormitory-style beds in a hostel. Countless people suffer in the same way, and fortunes are made by exploiting them.

Even pets play a part in extracting *klass* income. Friends of ours combed their big dogs with great care during molting season and sold the hairs, not only to those who knitted or wove them into cloth for men's and women's clothes, but also to others who made pads and sold them as traditional "cures" for backache.

Foreign currency is worth so much on the black market that underground trade in it thrives. One of the first enterprising currency dealers after World War II was Jan Rokotov, who paid three to nine times the official exchange rate in rubles to American and British tourists for their dollars and pounds, then resold the bills on the black market at twelve times the official rate. Rokotov did much of his horse trading in the restaurant of the National Hotel in Moscow, across Karl Marx Prospect from Red Square, until he was caught and shot. The National was the hotel in which Lenin lived before moving into a Kremlin apartment in 1918.

On the lower end of the currency scale, an émigré scientist told me of an experience that illustrates the complexities of Soviet currency rules and the arbitrariness of the police in enforcing them. A friend in the United States sent him $70, which arrived at the state bank. He converted the dollars into fifty certificate rubles, and paid twenty in state tax. At the time, the certificates came in several grades, with those exchanged for dollars at the top, and those for Eastern European and third-world currencies at the bottom.

The scientist made his way to a hard-currency store to buy a pair of imported shoes for twenty "certificates." He felt a tug at his sleeve. It was a man he had never seen before. "I want a folding umbrella," the man told him nervously, "but the only certificates I have were exchanged for Hungarian money. For an umbrella I need your kind of certificates. For shoes, you can use any kind. How about if I pay part of your bill for the shoes, and you buy the umbrella for me with your certificates?" It was a typical Soviet scene, men trying to extract the maximum advantage from a tangle of red tape.

The scientist hesitated: penalties for currency dealings were severe. He asked the cashier if it would be all right; she shrugged and said she had no objection. The deal was done. But almost as soon as the two men left the store, plainclothes police detained them and informed them that they had no right to use their certificates for anyone but themselves. The police fined the scientist ten rubles (he is certain it went straight into their own pockets) and let him keep the shoes. This time, they said, they would not write to his employer. They confiscated the other man's umbrella and let him off with a warning. The final scorecard: the scientist, one pair of shoes less ten rubles; the second man, nothing; the police, ten rubles and a valuable folding umbrella.

The West itself is far from perfect. It, too, has huge black markets.[2] It still has not found the right balance between too much government and too little. The Soviet Union, however, insists that it has found all the answers to the human condition without religion and capitalism. It claims a moral right to spread its system to other countries, though the gap between what it promises and what it delivers is so wide that many a Soviet citizen learns cynicism at an early age.

The Party is well aware of the growing world of bribery and *na levo.* The late Yuri Andropov solemnly announced new campaigns against corruption in high places. The director of Soviet circuses, a man of considerable *klass,* was found to have taken bribes in return for approving permissions for his performers and other personnel to travel abroad. In his apartment police found more than one million dollars' worth of diamonds. The chief of a famous food store on Gorky Street was arrested and finally shot for corruption. Few Soviet people I know expect serious, or lasting, reform. Bribery and corruption have been part of Russian life for many hundreds of years. They will not be rooted out by sporadic campaigns. Indeed, the passion for underground dealings is another line of continuity with the tsarist past going back to the founding of the Kievan state one thousand years ago. The tsar constantly complained that he was too poor to pay fixed salaries to local officials, and expected them to live off the land. After sending the tsar the taxes demanded, they were permitted to keep anything else that they could raise. Peter the Great and the Empress Catherine tried to reform the system, but were unsuccessful.

I have not tried to estimate the size of the underground economy in the Soviet Union, but illegal Soviet buying and stealing exists on an enormous scale and penetrates almost every area of society. It is a way of life.

It all comes back to the goals of the Party. The state creates a shortage of good jeans, for instance, by giving their manufacture low priority. The Soviet product I knew was made of soft denim and lacked stylish Western cut. As long as that continues, Soviet sailors will smuggle in American jeans and denim tops made by Lee and Wrangler, and earn the equivalent of two months' salary for each outfit. Enterprising individuals will continue to make money by sewing U.S. and West German labels into inferior Soviet jeans, and persuading youngsters to pay 100 rubles per pair.

Since the state forbids religious motifs outside churches, there will always be operators like the young man caught in Moscow with a suitcase containing ninety-nine T-shirts, each with a picture of Jesus painted on the front. According to the newspaper, *Evening Moscow,* the "young man with a big suitcase" was sentenced to jail with other members of his black market group.[3]

The thirst for *klass* in the middle ranges of Soviet society grows steadily. More consumer goods open up new opportunities and markets for more speculating in a system that pushes people to operate outside the law. That is not to say there are not honest Communists (and non-Communists) in the USSR. There are. Virtually every Soviet citizen I met in my four and a half years, however, accepted a certain amount of extralegal activity as a fundamental part of life, whether or not they engaged it in themselves. Everyone knew someone who did, and Margaret and I suspected that people we knew were more deeply involved in the second economy than they cared to admit to outsiders.

The status and privilege that help to make up *klass* remain essential to every Soviet citizen who hopes to assert at least some measure of individuality. If he cannot obtain it through Party-defined means, he will look for it any way he can.

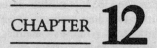
THE ROOTS OF *KLASS:* NATIONALITY

I t isn't just a person's job, or the size of his apartment, or the cut of his clothes, or whether he owns a private car that stamps him with *klass* in the Soviet Union today. His nationality also has a lot to do with his social position.

The Soviet Union is made up of 130 or so separate nationalities, dominated politically by the Great Russian Slavs who have been centered around Moscow for 1,000 years. The Russians, in fact, control the last great empire left on earth, forged by centuries of armed invasion, and spanning 4,000 miles from Minsk to Vladivostok. The tsars annexed the Central Asian khanates a century and a half ago, and each still represents a separate republic in the Union of Soviet Socialist Republics, which number fifteen in all. During and since World War II, Russians have kept the Ukraine under close KGB control; they have virtually annexed Eastern Europe, absorbed the Baltic states, neutralized Finland, and turned Mongolia into what almost amounts to a sixteenth republic as a buffer zone against the Chinese. Moscow, the capital of the Russian republic, the biggest of all, is shoring up the eastern flanks of its Russian heartland by building a second Siberian railroad to the north of the existing Trans-Siberian, which is now deemed to run much too close to the Chinese hordes to the south.

Clearly, to have the nationality "Russian" stamped in one's

internal passport in the USSR is a *klass* asset of considerable value. There is little love lost between the Russians and the nationalities they control. What, I wondered, did Russians actually think of the other races in their empire, and what did the ruled think of the rulers?

One clue to the Russian attitude was a remark overheard at Moscow State University, a center of Soviet scholarship: "How would you know?" snapped one student to another. "You're not even European!"

"Oh, yes," said one Muscovite friend, a Slavic intellectual and linguist, "Ukrainians are Slavs, hard workers, and pretty reliable. They are dirty, too, you know, and not too bright, but they are good people." I soon discovered that Russians rarely give unadulterated praise to any other nation, not even to other Slavs.

"Look at it in terms of power," commented another Moscow intellectual. "Several of the Politburo members are Ukrainian (including Party chief of the Ukraine, Vladimir Shcherbitsky, and Premier Nikolai Tikhonov). The Russians dominate, but the Ukraine is much too important to ignore. Look at its coal mines, and the food it grows."

The Ukraine, whose very name means "borderland," and which has suffered so many invasions and partitions over the years that its people have been called the "Irish of Eastern Europe," contains 49 million people. It is the largest unfree nation in Europe. Rich in thick, black soil, and the only place where the USSR can grow high-quality wheat, the Ukraine's 233,000 square miles—almost three times as large as the United Kingdom—are vital to Soviet survival. A mere 3 percent of the land mass of the Soviet empire, the Ukraine nonetheless produces one fifth of all Soviet grain, two thirds of its sugar beets, one third of its coal, half of its iron ore, and one fifth of its electricity. It adds up to economic power, and it demands a measure of Soviet respect.

Slavic Belorussia is much smaller, 9.5 million people, and has been more thoroughly penetrated by Russian language and customs than the still nationalistic Ukraine. "Well," continued my intellectual friend in 1980, "when you've talked about the Ukraine and the Belorussians, you've virtually run out of non-Russian nationalities with real power. If you're a Lithuanian, a Latvian, or an Estonian, you can forget about breaking into the very top circle. Except for [the late] Arvid Pelshe [a former Politburo member], of course, but he's an Old Bolshevik, and actually more Russian than Latvian.

"One Kazakh sits on the Politburo, Dinmukhamed Kunaev, an old colleague of Leonid Brezhnev's. An Uzbek, an Azerbaijani, and a Georgian are nonvoting Politburo members. Every secretary of the Central Committee is a Russian except for Mikhail Zimyanin, and he's Belorussian."

The rest of the nationalities? "No real status, no power. Russians don't like them, don't trust them."

Some other stereotypes of non-Russians, gathered from Russian friends and acquaintances include these from one Moscow intellectual:

"Ukrainians are reliable. Belorussians are about the same as Russians. The Baltic people are foreigners. They don't want Russians in their countries; they don't like us, and we don't like them.

"Central Asians? You mean Kirghizis and so on? Russians don't really like people who look different. We don't think too much of Central Asians. Slanted eyes. They look like Chinese or Mongols, and you know what the Mongols did to us for 200 years from the thirteenth century, occupying and torturing.

"Georgians? Clever people. Good wine. They chase women a lot, especially Russian girls with blond hair and blue eyes.

"Armenians? Extremely clever, intelligent.

"Azerbaijanis? They'd buy and sell their mothers.

"Moldavians? I don't know much about them. They make wine, don't they? Yes, they do, and they grow fruit."

From a Leningrad intellectual:

"Armenians are particularly intelligent. Georgians have

good business sense, they buy and sell on the black market. I met a Russian in Tashkent who spat out his hatred of the Uzbeks he had lived among for many years, but I think he was just giving back some of the dislike that Uzbeks have for Russians.

"Estonians don't like Russians, it's true, but they do appreciate anyone, Russians included, if they try to speak their precious language, even if they get the tenses wrong."

Another Leningrad professional, a woman with particularly strong prejudices, commented:

"Ukrainians are seen as cunning, sly, and dirty. Moldavians—well, almost gypsies, aren't they, on the border with Romania, and they make all that wine.

"Azerbaijanis are not very bright, but they aren't dumb, either.

"Armenians? Everyone knows how intelligent they are, more intelligent than Jews even. We have a saying which means, roughly, that in business or commerce, what Armenians have done, not even Jews could do better.

"Georgians are artistic and good architects, even if they are also lazy, black marketeers, and womanizers. Kazakhs, Uzbeks, Kirghizis, Tadjiks, Turkmen: they're all slow and below average. Not mentally retarded, you know, but not like us."

A Russian from Kiev gave me his views:

"Russians have got to watch the Ukrainians carefully. There are so many of them and they are crucial to the country.

"Russians are rather envious of the Baltic states for their European culture and *kultura*. When we say *kultura*, you know, it means something a little different from the English word 'culture': it also includes everyday bearing and politeness, saying 'thank you' and 'please' and so on. The Balts are civilized in that way, much more than Russians.

"Azerbaijanis are famous for being corrupt. Georgians are crooks. Armenians are superintelligent . . ."

In turn, the people of the minority nationalities have their own views of Russians, very few of which are flattering. The Baltic nationalities of Estonia, Latvia, and Lithuania deeply resent the Russians for reoccupying their countries after World War II and for trying to impose Russian ways and language on them.

Ukrainians combine acceptance and hard work with a dogged, frustrated nationalist ambition, fueled by some 3 million expatriates in the United States, Canada, Western Europe, South America, and Australia. A Ukrainian dissident and nationalist movement since 1970 has produced such figures as Yury Badzyo, Mykola Rudenko, Ivan Dzyuba, Ivan Svitliony, Vasyl Stus, Army general Pyotr Grigorenko, Valentin Moroz, and coal-miner trade-union activist Vladimir Khlebanov.

Georgians and Armenians tend to regard the Russians as usurpers, even though without Soviet military power both Christian nations would be vulnerable to pressure from Islamic Turkey, which waged war and tried to commit genocide against Armenia before 1917. This does not eliminate nationalist movements in both republics, however, and it encourages a strong and often successful drive toward economic and cultural self-assertiveness to compensate for the loss of political autonomy. Yerevan, the capital of Armenia, has links with Armenian expatriates in many countries who bring in the *klass* of clothes and other Western consumer items all year round.

Some analysts have argued that the Russians have an Achilles' heel in the tensions that exist between themselves and their subject nationalities. Russians, it is said, hold themselves to be "elder brothers" to all other races in the USSR, and to be *pervyi srednii ravnykh,* or "first among equals"; yet the actual number of Russians, compared with other races, keeps slipping. By 1979, Russians were only a bare majority in their own country (52.4 percent), down from 53.4 percent in 1970. By 1990, it is further said, slow Russian population growth, and far higher birthrates in Central Asia, will make

Russians an actual minority. The implication some outsiders draw is that this could weaken Russian control of the levers of power, especially in the armed forces, where almost one in three new recruits could be of Moslem ethnic origin by the year 2000.

This kind of thinking, however, contains much overly hopeful surmise. The facts are that Russians control Party, armed forces, police, and church. Each non-Russian republic has a Russian second-in-command who reports directly to Party and KGB back in Moscow. The Party is a good deal more flexible than outsiders might suppose in balancing and containing nationalistic fervor around their empire. They have shown a shrewd grasp of when to yield and when to stand firm.

Certainly it is true that ethnic patriotism and hostility to Russian Slavs bubbles and hisses beneath the ordered surface of Soviet life. It is also true that many a Russian I met felt aggrieved that his own race provided, as he saw it, political leadership, defense, and superpower status for the rest of the country, whose only response was to complain endlessly about Russian boorishness and to enjoy higher living standards for which Russians themselves could take at least some of the credit. Russians point out that their own Russian republic, which forms the top half of the country from west to east across eleven time zones, contains the core of the Soviet military-industrial complex. They also say that one reason life is difficult for them is that, while the bulk of the 137.5 million people in the Russian republic live west of the Ural mountains, most of their oil and gas lies to the east, and must be transported long distances, at great expense.

I see no immediate weakening of the Russian grip on the USSR, and none for the foreseeable future. Russians will continue to hold most of the political *klass* in the country, and to enjoy many of the consumer benefits such *klass* brings with it.

To have a Russian passport will continue to be an advantage in making a career in the Party or the military. Of all the military generals appointed between 1940 and 1970, 91 percent were Slavs. Of those, 70 percent were Russian. Eighty percent of general officers elected to the Supreme Soviet in the same period were Russians and 15 percent Ukrainian. Almost 80 percent of officers elected to the Party Central Committee between 1952 and 1976 were Russians. In a list of forty-two general officers mentioned by the Soviet press in 1975–76, forty were Slavs, one was Armenian, and one was of German origin. The lack of Latvian, Estonian, Lithuanian, Georgian, Armenian, Central Asian, or Jewish names was striking.

The two most prestigious cities of the Soviet empire, Moscow and Leningrad, lie in the Russian RSFSR. Moscow has the Kremlin and the political power; Leningrad (formerly St. Petersburg), is the site of imperial, intellectual, scientific, naval, and revolutionary traditions. One of the most important *klass* advantages for the Rising Class is the word MOSKVA on its resident permits, or *propiska*s. Moscow permits are carefully rationed; if they were not, people would pour into the city from everywhere else for its superior shops, theaters, museums, and its aura of being "the Center."

Young people constantly explore ways around the living restrictions, often by staying in friends' apartments in Moscow and Leningrad while looking for jobs. The law states that anyone moving away from his legal residence must register with the local police within three days, but the regulation is mostly honored in the breach. If a person has a skill in urgent demand, such as a construction trade, he or she can get a job, stay in the city illegally, and win a permanent Moscow *propiska* by living and working there for five years.

Not everyone prefers Moscow. The devotion of many Leningraders to their own city is proverbial. They love its distinctive architecture, its canals, its Dostoevskian air of brooding and intrigue, its summer "white nights" when the sun never sets. They know full well that the food and resources of the Baltic states are drained off to supply its own foreign tourists and government and social elites.

The dominance of the Russian Slav has shaped the history of both the tsarist and communist eras. Always poor, the Slav has lived on a vast, natural plain that has both beckoned invaders in and allowed expansionist Russians to move outward. The Russian loves space, and the *razmakh*, or sweep of the steppe. He is close to the American Westerner in his feeling for range and sky.

So fast did the Russian empire expand that between 1550 and 1700 the area controlled by Moscow multiplied many times over. Overall population growth followed; barely doubling between 1550 and 1750 (from 8 million to 17 million) it zoomed to 68 million by 1850, doubled again by 1900 to 126 million, and yet again by 1980 to 264 million. Growth rates have since slowed sharply in Russian cities, though they are still high in Central Asia.

The concept of Russian chauvinism is deeply imbedded, and has two main roots. The first is the sense of expansionism, of manifest destiny. It was Stalin, himself a Georgian, who used Great Russian chauvinism as the Soviet Union's battering ram to superpower status. By the end of the 1930s, he was declaring that the tsarist empire, while of course anathema to the Party, had at least brought the redeeming value of Russian thought to scores of "backward" peoples. Under Brezhnev the new phrase to describe Russian rule over other nationalities became "democratic centralism."

The second Russian nationalist root lies in the mystical fervor of the Slavophile, from the moral thundering of Alexander Solzhenitsyn to the work of the jailed Vladimir Osipov and the semihidden activities of a group called the All-Russian Society for the Preservation of Historical Monuments. This aspect of Russian nationalism is concerned with a search for pre-1917 Russian origins to set against Soviet modernity. It preaches individual freedom only within an established moral order. To a man like Solzhenitsyn, it means a theocracy with the Russian Orthodox Church at its head. In either case, it revolves around a sense of Russian superiority.

In the Soviet Union, Jewishness is also a "nationality," one that on the face of it lacks the usual Soviet *klass*. Anti-Semitism endures in the Russian soul just as it has for centuries. The legal barriers erected by the tsars, which restricted Jews to the Pale of Settlement (East Poland, the Ukraine, Lithuania, Bessarabia), have been removed, but in the last decade discrimination has increased to the point where it is often difficult for a sense of Jewish identity to survive Russian political, social, and cultural imperialism. Jews say it is increasingly difficult to obtain superior educations and good jobs. They are largely excluded from the police, the KGB, and the upper levels of the armed forces.

Many a Jew still overcomes discrimination and enters the upper levels of the Rising Class, however, through intellectual or creative achievement. Denied the chance to continue their pre-1917 roles as artisans and traders, Jews have become a significant part of the Soviet intelligentsia and scientific community.

"It's not so much a question of nationality, as it is of control, of whether an individual can be trusted by the Party," argued the non-Jewish dissident Vladimir Bukovsky when we talked in the living room of his Cambridge home in England. "For the Party, it's a matter of testing you. If you pass, you'll be promoted." He cited the examples of a Jewish general, Mikhail Milshtein, who has risen to be a senior member of the KGB, and Colonel-General David Dragunsky, of the Tank Corps. "It's the same with other nationalities," he went on. "The Party has no love for Latvia, but Arvid Pelshe was in the Politburo for decades."

Many Soviet Jews dismissed Milshtein and Dragunsky as token appointments, as "useful Jews." They also acknowledged that in other fields, Jews had attained more than token *klass*. Maya Plisetskaya was one of the best-known of all Bolshoi ballerinas. Arkady Raikin was the nation's leading stand-up comedian. Long before they applied to emigrate, Academician Benjamin Levich and geneticist David Goldfarb had world reputations and great *klass* privilege at home. Many a prominent Soviet scientist, surgeon, composer, musician, and actor was Jewish. In the 1930s and 1940s the Bing Crosby of the Soviet Union was the Jew Leonid Utyosov, praised by Stalin for raising the morale of Soviet troops.

Yet even successful Jews find life in the Soviet Union difficult. Prejudice and envy run deep. A Jew must perform superbly in the face of constant Party suspicion that he is not committed to Soviet ideals. Most Jewish families react to the prejudice by living a secular life without observing their religion.

Some members of the Jewish community enter "Russian" on their internal passports, but most insist on staying openly Jewish despite discrimination. "I was always fighting as a child," one doctor said of her childhood in Leningrad. "Other children would call me *zhid* and I would insult them back. I didn't know why they were so mean. They called me 'Sarah' to mock my Jewish name. My patronymic (middle name) is Izraelevna. To them, all Jews like us were *podonki*, scum.

"When I went down to the registry office after turning sixteen, to receive my first internal passport, one of the officials there, a woman, took pity on me. 'Oh,' she said, 'such a lovely girl. Wouldn't you like me to mark you down as Russian on your passport?' She knew I would have a lifetime of discrimination if she put *Evrei* (Jewish). I hadn't bribed her or anything. I thanked her and said no, I would take the nationality of my parents. She was upset, and wrote out my passport in a huff, without looking at me again. She thought I had insulted her Russian nationality." The doctor laughed. "Can you imagine me carrying a passport showing my middle name as Izraelevna and my nationality as Russian?"

In other countries, minorities can eventually assimilate, but in the USSR, nationality is a lifetime of identification. The stamp *Evrei* brands an individual. "It certainly affects those who are trusted and who rise through Party ranks" says Bukovsky. "You can be sure a man like Milshtein of the KGB had to prove his loyalty to a far greater degree than the Russians he works with."

Efim Slavinsky, a slightly built, gentle man, grew up as a Jewish child in the Ukraine in the 1940s and 1950s. "I always knew I was different, even though my mother tongue is Russian and I did not grow up speaking Yiddish or Hebrew," he said as we drank coffee in his London apartment with fellow émigrés from Leningrad and Vilnius. "A lot of Jewish families were afraid to celebrate Jewish Holy Days during Stalin's time, but my father and mother did celebrate Passover and Hanukkah. Out on the street I had to fight other children all the time when they called me *zhid* and other names. They didn't know why they did it. They picked it up from their parents."

Efim's parents told him nothing about the Old Testament, but they did stress that he was unique, that he was surrounded by gentiles, and that he was persecuted. He would have to live by his wits and study hard. They instilled in him a respect for the Jewish nation, which had given birth to "great people." His father, a milling-machine operator in a Kiev aircraft factory, did not tell him of Moses or Abraham, but of Karl Marx and Albert Einstein.

"All this time," Slavinsky said meditatively, "I was hearing at school that religion was the opium of the masses, used to keep people down. I didn't read a Bible until I was twenty-one, and even then I started with the New Testament, because that's what I came across first. To be Jewish, especially in the Ukraine, meant to come home at night and find that your father was not roaring drunk, as so many other fathers were. It meant an apartment quiet enough to enable one to do homework and study hard."

The tradition of study is still strong among Soviet Jews. Intellectual Jewish families in Moscow, Leningrad, Kiev, Odessa, and elsewhere still insist their children study intensively to gain every last scrap of *klass* that education can bring. Geneticist David Goldfarb hired an English tutor for his son, Alex, when he was young. "Much later," Alex told me, "my father said he wanted me to know English so that I would have it if I ever emigrated. I always knew English better than my schoolmates, and in fact I ended up doing their English homework for them." A young émigré from Vilnius also explained that her parents signed her up for the entrance exam for an elite school teaching English when she was aged five. Why were her parents so keen to give her a better education? She was surprised at the question. "They are Jewish," she replied. Also, the very fact of learning English is a status symbol.

As young Jewish students mature, they try to enter institutes and universities, where discrimination becomes more official. "Jews don't fit in," says one Jewish professional man. "The Party is always talking about the 'Friendship of the Peoples,' in the Soviet Union. To us, the 'Friendship of the Peoples' is when all the peoples stand shoulder to shoulder—to beat up the Jews."

David Goldfarb, a full professor at Moscow State University (MGU), had to intercede so that his daughter could enter medical school. Her excellent grades alone were insufficient. Alex Goldfarb, his son, had to make use of his father's *klass* to be admitted as a junior research fellow at a biology institute then affiliated with the Kurchatovsky Atomic Institute. His father called the director, Anatoly Alexandrov, later to become chairman of the Academy of Sciences itself, and his own professor also intervened.

Alexander Levich, whose father was a member of the Academy, saw the face of an interviewer at one institute fall when he produced his internal passport. The word *Evrei* was enough to ensure that the interview ended quickly. But when his prestigious father contacted the Institute's director, he was called back at once.

The policy of keeping Jews out of the top ranks of the professions is working. The number of Jews holding coveted membership in the Academy of Sciences is falling. It is greatest among older members in their seventies and eighties, lower among men in their sixties, and much lower among young men. In Moscow and Leningrad, Jews have to be exceptional to gain entry to departments of science and mathematics.

Some Jews may aspire to senior military rank, but few make it. Virtually none are admitted to the Military Institute for Foreign Languages, or to the Moscow Institute for International Relations (MIMO), which trains Party translators and diplomats, or to higher Party schools.

The desire to excel in science, writing, or the creative arts can be so frustrated that emigration seems the only way out. During the period of détente in the 1970s, upward of 250,000 Jews were allowed to leave the USSR, but after the trial and sentencing of Anatoly Shcharansky in the summer of 1978, the price of releasing dissidents rose. The Jewish population, as officially recorded by the national census, slid from 2,151,000 in 1970 to 1,811,000 in 1979, yet by 1984, with détente only a memory, emigration has slowed again.

Although the campaign against the Jews gathered momentum in the late 1970s as the Kremlin sought to reassert control over emigration, Soviet society was filled with conflicting currents. While Jews were being attacked, a Jewish author, Anatoly Rybakov, was permitted to publish a novel, *Heavy Sand*, whose heroes and heroines were Jewish. It was serialized in the conservative literary magazine *Oktyabr*. The story, of a family of shoemakers and craftsmen in the Ukraine between 1910 and 1942, which climaxed in the horror of the Nazi ghettoes, became an instant best-seller.

Generally, however, there is little support for Jewish culture. Jews cannot learn Hebrew or Yiddish in Soviet schools. Even in the so-called Jewish Autonomous District in far-off Birobidzhan in eastern Siberia, which was once supposed to become a Jewish homeland, only 8 percent of the small population are Jews, and a Russian Yiddish-language magazine has a circulation of only 10,000. In the former Jewish centers of Odessa and Vilnius, Yiddish theater has languished, and little remains of the proud tradition of the Moscow State Jewish Theater (GOSET) which Stalin closed in 1948.

Yet Yiddish was heard once more on a Moscow stage in 1979, when a Jewish Dramatic Ensemble performed Sholem Aleichem's *The Enchanted Tailor*. Working against great odds, a graduate of the Bolshoi Ballet School, Yuri Scherling, founded a Jewish Chamber Music Theater of fifty actors that same year. Officially the group had to be based in Birobidzhan, but in fact it staged its first production in Moscow, where it performed a rock opera called *Black Bridle for a White Mare*, a title taken from a Yiddish proverb which says "poverty suits a Jew like a black bridle for a white mare." These developments hardly signal a renaissance in Jewish culture in anti-Semitic, Slavic Russia, but they do testify to the resilience of Soviet Jewry.

Nor should it be assumed that all Russians are anti-Semitic. As a student in Leningrad, one Jewish girl, Tanya, went through a period of low grades. Her teacher, a gentile, called in her parents and locked the classroom door. "Look," she said, "don't you realize that Tanya must improve her grades? She can do better, and it's important that she must do better. She is a Jew, and she has to do extra well if she is to have a good career."

"Russians can be anti-Semitic in theory but still marry a Jew," says another Soviet citizen. "You wouldn't believe it, but I know people like that. The husband just doesn't think of his wife as Jewish."

Discrimination against Jews is rarely far from the surface, however. When Tanya won her Ph.D. in German language, she was constantly promised that the next staff vacancy in her institute would be hers. It never was. Her superiors shrugged and asked, "What can we do?" When her husband, an English translator, applied for a post by telephone, the official he talked to was friendly and invited him to "come on over." The institute needed an English translator badly. When her husband arrived, and the official saw his dark, Georgian-like face, the reception was even more friendly. But when he offered his internal passport, the mood cooled. The official suddenly remembered that the vacancy had been filled between the time of the first telephone call and his arrival at the institute.

In recent years, anti-Semitism has taken a reverse twist. When large-scale Jewish emigration began in the early 1970s, Jewish women found themselves approached by Russian gentile men asking for marriages of convenience so that the men could leave with them. By 1974, the going rate for a bride was 1,000 rubles, more than five months of an average salary.

"I would have married one particular man, to help him out," says one Jewish woman who emigrated soon afterward. "He was walking the streets looking for a Jewish wife. But when the authorities realized what was going on, they made a rule that a non-Jew had to be married to a Jew for two years before he or she could leave the country. It was too risky for me." Jewish marriages to gentiles who wanted to emigrate soon spawned an ironic catch-phrase: *"Evrei, eto nye roskosh, a sredstvo peredvizheniya"*—"Jews are not a luxury but a means of transportation."

Anti-Semitism can vary in degree with Soviet geography. In the late 1950s Leningrad was a relatively free city for Jewish advancement, while the Ukraine was noted for its anti-Jewish attitudes, as it had been since the seventeenth century. When Tanya's relatives from Kiev came to stay with her parents in Leningrad they asked how much had to be paid in bribes to university officials to get children admitted. The parents said they used no bribes to get Tanya into prestigious Leningrad University. The relatives grew angry, convinced the parents were trying to conceal the amount. For Jews in Kiev to enter the best schools, bribes were essential, and the relatives could not believe they were not needed elsewhere.

The Russian Soviet Federated Socialist Republic, the Ukraine, and Belorussia, which together constitute the three Slav republics, are the most anti-Semitic areas. The least amount of anti-Semitism exists in Georgia in the Caucasus, which is traditionally open and nonracial in attitude. But most Jews, some 81 percent, live in Great Russia, the Ukraine, and Belorussia, and only 1.5 percent, or 28,000, in relatively free Georgia. In Estonia, venom is reserved for the Russians who have occupied the country since World War II, and Jews are accepted as preferable to Slavs.

Moscow and Leningrad are still the centers of Jewish population, and what little Jewish tradition remains is there. Outside these cities, Jewishness is subverted by apathy and fear of the authorities.

A Georgian Jew, Nodar Djindjihashvili, a Doctor of Philosophy in his thirties, spent two years traveling 20,000 miles photographing people in the Soviet Union, including outlying Jewish settlements.[1] He was dispirited to find that only fifty-five of the 5,000 synagogues of tsarist times still operated. Hundreds of the former synagogues, along with thousands of churches, were being used as cinemas, factories, and warehouses, and a large central synagogue in Odessa was a storage depot for local Communist Party records. Only a small percentage of once-Jewish settlements still celebrated religious holidays, and even those services were held in secret. "What you find is nothing on the streets—and a mixture of ignorance, indifference, official propaganda, and faint hope in Jewish homes," Djindjihashvili reported. Some people he met were so afraid that he was denounced to local authorities as a "traitor" fifteen times.

On the scale of Soviet *klass*, the West is the Jew's strength as well as his weakness. Jews use their close connections with the West to capitalize on the Kremlin's sensitivity to outside criticism and its yearning to be accepted as respectable. Although Russians remain isolated and suspicious, and although Moscow has cast its lot with the Arabs against Israel, the Soviet Jew has won concessions because of his links with the West. Ceaseless broadcasts of his plight on the Voice of America, the BBC World Service, the German radio station Deutsche Welle, Radio Sweden, Dutch radio, and others, combined with publicity in American newspapers, has had a marked effect.

At the same time, the Jew has been used by Moscow as a pawn in the larger stratagem—trade with the U.S. and Western Europe. When détente was strong in the first half of the 1970s, the Kremlin let Jews emigrate as one way of placating Western opinion. Now that détente has cooled, the incentive is gone, and anti-Semitism has rarely been stronger against the Jewish Soviet "nationality."

The nationalities that are the most remote from Moscow and Leningrad, in distance as well as in ways of thinking, are in the so-called Islamic republics of the USSR. To be a native Central Asian from one of these republics is to have the lowest level of *klass*. By 1981 the Asian republics contained 31.5 million people, including Azerbaijan, and 46.2 million if Kazakhstan was counted. Kazakhstan is an area larger than Western Europe, covering one million square miles; Kazakhs in the north live on the same latitude as Moscow and those in the south are parallel with Madrid or Istanbul.

Apart from the Russians, do other nationalities in the USSR try to exert their own prerogatives, their own way of living, their own *klass*, despite Russian rule? Yes, they do, in several ways.

RELIGION

One freezing night in Vilnius, capital of Lithuania, three American colleagues and I found the entrance to a narrow courtyard. We crossed to a small staircase, mounted it, and knocked at a dilapidated door. An old woman answered, and for the next hour we caught a glimpse of the Roman Catholic faith that still burns in Baltic Lithuania. A colored photograph of Pope John Paul II hung on one wall, a wooden crucifix on the other. Each night the woman listened to a fifteen-minute shortwave broadcast in her own language from Radio Vatican. She was a hotel cook; her husband was in jail for distributing Catholic literature and she was desperately afraid he would die from the cold and the hard labor. She shivered with fright that we might have been seen entering her courtyard. Her only hope, her one sense of identity, came from her faith.

The next morning we attended early Mass amid the statuary of the 1684 Peter and Paul Church. People trekked through the cold and the dark in streams. Bibles and prayer books were in short supply and some in the congregation read from hand-lettered missals. Lithuanians had flocked to border regions near Poland to watch the installation of the Polish Pope on a live television hookup from Rome. A vigorous underground church trained its own priests, claiming that graduates from the official seminary in Kaunus were indoctrinated with Soviet ideals by the KGB.

Neighboring Estonia and Latvia also clung to their religious ideals, in this case Lutheran, partly as a way of asserting a degree of national independence.

In Azerbaijan and Central Asia, Moslem traditions are stronger than actual Islamic worship, but the nationalistic brotherhoods called *tarika* have tens of thousands of members, to the consternation of Party officials. In the northern Caucasus, an estimated half-million Muslims belong to the *tarika*s.

Mosques coexist uneasily with Marx, but compliant, Islamic leaders toe the Party line. Members of the Religious Board of the Trans-Caucasus in Baku earnestly explained in 1980 that they were delighted to see the Ayatollah Khomeini rise to power in neighboring Iran, but that, of course, no such resurgence of Islam was necessary in the USSR. "They in Iran had the revolution they dreamed of," said Allokshukur Pashaev, his beard black under a white turban, his dark blue cloak lined with a yellow band. "But we had our revolution in 1917 and we want nothing more." That, at least, is what an alert young male translator to his left told us he had said.

Accurately translated or not, Pashaev's words echoed what we sensed in our stay in Azerbaijan, and in various visits to Central Asia. The upsurge of Islam in Iran had evoked no audible public echo on the Soviet side of the border. If citizens were heartened, they kept it to themselves. Yet Moscow was still afraid of latent Moslem attitudes, and limited Tashkent, the fourth largest city in the Soviet Union, to a mere thirteen mosques for its 1.8 million people, and Baku, the fifth largest, to six for its 1.55 million.

Western scholars Alexander Benningsen and Chantal Lemercier-Quelquejay say that Moslem traditions remain strongest in the rural areas. Elders retain authority. Moslem women do not marry non-Moslem men. The culture is maintained. Russian women, on their part, will not marry Moslems because of what they see as the inferior status of women in Islam.

Religion as a badge of nationalism is also found in Armenia, where a champion athlete invited myself, David Shipler of *The New York Times*, and Kevin Ruane of the BBC to dinner in his apartment. Before we began, he glanced at me. "Your newspaper is Christian, no? All right, then—say grace." When I hesitated, he smiled.

"You are Christian," he said emphatically. "I am Communist, but I believe that religion is a good thing. It helps keep the peace, and it is the best protection against . . ." and he leaned on the next word, "barbarism." He was saying that Christianity was what distinguished Armenians from their hated neighbors, the Turks. "All my children were christened, and I was, too." He beamed. With that, I said grace.

Our host followed with grace in Armenian, and we began to eat.

We encountered more Christian nationalism a few days later when we made our way through the Tbilisi streets at night to the apartment of tall, dark, mustachioed Viktor Rtskhiladze. He had just been fired from his job as director of the Office for Preserving Historical Monuments in Georgia for protesting against the damage being done by artillery shells from an army test range to nearby sixth-century cave monasteries. He had also tried to stop soldiers from gouging gold out of priceless cave frescoes with their pocket knives. In his tiny apartment, he recited the Lord's Prayer in Georgian before we ate.

In Armenia, so many people have their children christened that 5,000 ceremonies were reported at the religious center of Echmiadzin in 1974 alone. Many were for children of Party members. Thousands more take the hairpin mountain road to the ancient stone church at Geghart to make ritual sacrifices of sheep.

BIRTHRATE

At 70 Azerbaijan Street in the historic old city of Shemaha in Azerbaijan, swarthy taxi driver Arif Guseinov lived behind head-high walls with his wife, in-laws, and three children. A glance about the courtyard revealed how much more pleasant conditions were there than for Russian families in the north. It also partially explained why Central Asian birthrates kept rising faster than Russian ones. The Guseinovs had six spacious rooms, a large garden, a dining room with orange curtains, a kitchen with a stove and a refrigerator, a telephone, a television set, a radio, and a separate bathhouse with its own shower. Chickens ran in the yard.

The 45 million or so people of Turkic-Moslem descent in the USSR live in sunny southern republics, in an environment that stimulates larger families. If these birthrates continue, by the year 2000 every third Soviet citizen could be of Moslem origin.

Central Asians use these growing numbers, and their unwillingness to intermarry with outsiders, to help retain their own separate cultural identities. They seldom emigrate to other parts of the country, a short-term strategy that keeps their communities cohesive, but they still feel threatened as more and more Russians are sent south to work. The Party continues to set up factories to take advantage of good weather and abundant local labor supplies.

In once-Catholic Lithuania, too, a high birthrate has helped keep Russian infiltration at bay. The Russians have made greater inroads into Lutheran Latvia and Estonia. Lithuania's population, now 3.4 million, grew at a rate almost one third faster than Russians in the decade leading up to 1979.

LANGUAGE

A shouting crowd of several thousand moved down Rustaveli Street, the main thoroughfare in the Georgian capital of Tbilisi, in the spring of 1978, in a highly unusual display of public defiance. People called up to others in apartment windows to join them in a protest against a new draft constitution for Georgia which had left out a clause affirming the status of Georgian as an official republic language.

Eyewitnesses told me later that the local Communist Party chief Eduard Shevardnadze appeared on a balcony and began to address the crowd below as "My children." The crowd shouted back, "We are not your children!" Shevardnadze turned and went inside. A short time later he reappeared, in a placating mood. The clause was reinstated in the draft. Other sources said that the Politburo in Moscow conceded only when the senior Russian army general in Tbilisi telephoned Moscow to warn of trouble. Armenian and Azerbaijani state-language clauses were quickly put back into the draft constitutions of their respective republics, before the people there had a chance to protest.

Language is an electric issue in Georgia. In 1976 Revaz Djaparidze used an address to the local Writers Union to attack the increasing use of Russian in Georgian higher education. All dissertations must still be submitted in both languages. Shevardnadze made some concessions in April 1979, ordering the Education Department to establish new Georgian-language departments, but the work was blunted by directives from Moscow to boost the level of Russian-language teaching in non-Russian areas of the country as a whole.

So deep does feeling about the mother tongue run in Georgia that 364 academics, writers, journalists, and others protested to Brezhnev and Shevardnadze at the end of 1980 against the policy of bilingualism and the exclusion of the Georgian language from the sciences. Georgians also demanded telephone directories in their own language and the right to use the language to send telegrams. Baltic states insist on eleven years of primary and secondary schooling instead of the usual ten years in Soviet schools, hoping to ensure that full time is given to teach local languages as well as the obligatory Russian.

Pride in non-Russian languages is growing right alongside Russification. A young university student confessed to John Morrison of Reuters when we were in Tbilisi: "Some years ago it was fashionable to speak Russian, and to use Russian words. Now it is quite the opposite. In fact, I blush whenever I find myself using Russian words instead of Georgian."

Historically, six and a half decades is a short time, but the Kremlin has so far succeeded in imposing political and economic control over its internal empire, even though it has not extinguished local national feeling.

It has done so in several ways. One is through the army, which serves as a vehicle for the Russification of other ethnic groups. All soldiers are taught Russian, and if they want to advance in the army they must be relatively fluent. The army makes the Soviet Union what one Moscow intellectual called "a self-occupied country." By keeping national contingents together, then stationing them in other parts of the giant nation, the Party makes sure that troops have little support among local populations, and little sympathy for them. Asians are often stationed in the Baltic states; Balts in Kazakhstan; Uzbeks in the Ukraine.

The Party installs a Russian KGB man as the second secretary of each republic. It is also helped by strategic factors. Georgia and Armenia fear that the Turks would menace them once more should they ever leave Soviet protection. It would be difficult for the Central Asian republics to exist on their own, even if they could exercise Article 72 of the Constitution and secede. The prospect is hardly imminent. The concept of nationalities breaking away exists only in theory.

Russians now outnumber Latvians in Riga, and are approaching the number of Estonians in Tallinn and Lithuanians in Vilnius. As Baltic governments-in-exile grow older, the dream of independence from Moscow fades, even though younger Balts try to keep hopes alive.

We had young friends in the Baltic states who quietly but adamantly rejected Russian culture and ideals. They told me Latvia would be the first to be flooded by Russian ways, while Lithuania would be the last. It is still possible for 10,000 people to demonstrate in public in Estonia, using a football match or a Christmas celebration as an excuse. Yet demography and time seem to tilt in the Russian's favor.

Minority sentiment has long seemed a logical Achilles' heel of the Soviet Union. When Nazi troops marched across western borders on June 22, 1941, they met little resistance in the early stages, partly because they confronted Ukrainians and others who resented Russian rule. Nazi Alfred Rosenberg, author of *The Myth of the Twentieth Century*, based his own plan to defeat Moscow on exploiting minority nationalities. He suggested that Hitler foment independence of subject nations around the borders of the Russian republic, isolating Moscow and making her vulnerable. At first Berlin chose the Caucasus as a testing ground and ordered its armies to sup-

port national movements that sprang up after the first Red
Army retreats. Kadi Bairamukhov set up a Karachay national
government and began to denationalize farms and to restore
religious ways. But German disagreements killed the Rosenberg plan. Hitler himself wanted to colonize all Soviet soil
wherever it lay. Eventually the Soviet minorities, appalled by
German atrocities, moved back to union with Moscow.[2]

The thought of Soviet minorities rising up in wrath always
intrigues outsiders. Some Western diplomats I knew in Moscow would while away long winter Saturday afternoons speculating that the subject peoples might turn to violence. On
June 29, 1978, a prison administrator shot and killed the minister of the interior and two subordinates in Baku, the capital
of Azerbaijan. A spokesman confirmed by telephone that
Lieutenant-General Arif Geidarov had been shot by a man
called Muratov, who had then shot himself. Despite his Azerbaijani name, Geidarov had worked for the Russian KGB for
twenty-five years. On December 4, 1980, someone shot and
killed the prime minister of Kirghizia as he lay asleep in a
sanitorium in Lake Issyk-Kul east of the republic's capital,
Frunze. An official of the Frunze Party newspaper blurted out
on the telephone to Richard Balmforth of Reuters that it had
been a "political murder," and a "provocation" on the eve of
the XXVI Party Congress in Moscow in February 1981.

Yet these were isolated incidents. It is a long way from
them to gaining political freedom from Moscow. A degree of
cultural, religious, and, in some places, even economic autonomy has been won in some republics. Yet Moscow can well
afford to grant these small freedoms. Its dilemma is that more
loosening might encourage the rest of the empire to protest
against the cement of force and fear.

Perhaps the largest potential threat to Russian hegemony is
the rising proportion of Moslem peoples in the USSR who
threaten Moscow's authority, not only in the Central Asian
republics, but in the armed forces themselves. One theory is
that large numbers of Moslem recruits in the ordinary ranks

have only a limited command of the Russian language and may decide not to fight in case of war. A former tank officer using the pseudonym of Viktor Suvorov has written that some Central Asian troops from "mountainous kishlaks and distant reindeer-breeding farms" were used in the invasion of Czechoslovakia. They knew a scant ten words of Russian, the commands for "get up," "lie down," "right," "left," "forward," "back," "run," "turn around," "fire," and "hurrah."[3] For that invasion, the words sufficed. Meanwhile the officers corps is, and will remain, firmly Russian.

Despite local sentiment, Russian remains the language of *klass*. Its use is spreading, especially as a second tongue. The 1979 census showed that non-Russians fluent in Russian as well as their own language had risen from 41.8 million in 1970 to 61.1 million. Eighty-two percent of citizens in general (and 62.1 percent of non-Russians) had Russian as a first or second language.

The nationalities may be restive but the non-Russian republics remain firmly within the Russian empire. This empire survived the onslaught of World War II and the Nazi invasion, and seems likely to continue through the current period. The best that the individual nationalities can hope for is to maintain some of their historic culture and to carve out as much individuality, privilege, and *klass* as they can within the overall limitations of Russian power.

CHAPTER 13

TRAVEL, SOVIET-CLASS

Olga, a quick, nervous, precise woman, was the talk of all her Kiev friends. Not only had she taken the *klass*-filled step of a brief trip to Eastern Europe, but on her return her suitcases were stuffed with such wondrous items as shoes, knitting wool, records, and books. She had also managed to save 500 rubles in the past year and her one desire was to use it to do something for her ten-year-old nephew, Boris. After some thought, she suggested three weeks of sunshine down on the Black Sea coast at the resort of Sukhumi, just along the coast from Sochi. The boy was thrilled; so was his mother who, in his absence, would have a break from her daily routine.

In the West, a holiday at the seashore is a fairly straightforward event. In the USSR, it is a task whose complexity and frustrations can rival those of space travel. As Olga told me the story of what happened, she also unfolded an object lesson in Soviet *klass*, and what the lack of enough of it can mean.

For a start, she could not simply pick up the telephone and order tickets from the Aeroflot airline or reserve a hotel room at Sukhumi. Air tickets must be bought in person, after hours of waiting. Hotel bookings are generally made by organizations, not individuals. In the Soviet Union's inadequate civilian telephone system, long-distance lines to the Black Sea coast are almost always busy, and in any case, there are so few hotels for ordinary citizens that a phone call would almost certainly be futile even if it did go through. Vacationers and other travelers routinely sleep in train stations and airports while looking for rooms. Hotel staffs wield such enormous authority that it takes bribes or excellent connections to do business with them.

Olga could buy her plane seats only ten days in advance, a general rule of travel in the Soviet Union. She could not confirm return dates before leaving Kiev, but had to purchase open-dated tickets. Once in Sukhumi she would have to battle crowds and lines again to obtain a return flight and seat number. She would have to pay in cash, for there are no credit cards. Travel in the Soviet Union, as she well knew, could only be expedited by one commodity—*klass*—or access to someone possessing it. Without at least some of it, Olga would not even have thought of traveling so far from home.

Fortunately, she had two *klass* benefits readily available to her. Her job, gained through language training at an institute, occasionally took her abroad and allowed her to earn a little more than average. In addition, her sister worked in a hotel that catered to tourists from Eastern Europe. The sister had sent some tourists to a hotel in Sukhumi and had gotten to know its officials. When the sister herself had taken a trip to Sukhumi the year before, the staff had found her a room—not for the three days that is the standard stay in most Soviet hotels, but for several weeks. So, Olga's sister sent messages to the hotel, confirming that her relatives were on their way, and she used her influence to order Aeroflot tickets, sparing Olga an exhausting day in line.

The superior way to travel is by trade-union *putyovka*, or pass, entitling a person to reserved tickets, a guaranteed room, and cut-rate prices. But demand is so great that only a small percentage of applicants receive the passes. Trade-union clubs for writers, composers, actors, ballet dancers, architects, and a host of other professions all have as part of their *klass* benefits special *otdyeli* (departments) with full-time staffs who buy tickets and arrange vacations for members. Often these are at the dachas and resorts built by the unions themselves, such as the excellent Writers Union resort in the Crimea.

More ordinary citizens such as Olga must fend for themselves. On the appointed day, Olga took an Aeroflot bus to the airport where she pulled Boris through dense, chaotic crowds. She found the departure gate and they walked across the tarmac (usually only officials and foreigners are ferried by buses). At the plane they mounted the ramp to the narrow cabin of a Tupolev 154 jet, whose Aeroflot odor (as I can attest) was a mixture of disinfectant, dirt, old vegetables, and unwashed bodies.

Two other people were occupying their seats. Olga and Boris waited, then obeyed a brusque stewardess and dropped into two others nearby. It was the error of harried Aeroflot clerks who often double-book as they scribble out mountains of tickets by hand. The seats on a 154 are so close together that when the man in front pushed his seat back to sleep, his hair almost touched Olga's face. Three hours later, the plane landed at Sukhumi. Since Aeroflot serves food only on flights lasting more than three hours, aunt and nephew missed lunch. Elated at having finally arrived, they went straight to the hotel, splurging on a taxi and marveling at the sharp, clear air, the sun, and the blue sea.

Once at the hotel, Olga quickly discovered a disconcerting aspect of *klass:* while some of it is transferable, some is not. A Central Committee functionary can avoid lines by slipping through the unmarked door of an elite shop to buy caviar or oranges, as can his wife and children. If a member of the Academy of Sciences can sidestep the twenty-bed wards of state hospitals and be treated in a private suite, so can other members of his family when they are ill. But if your sister has excellent contacts in a resort hotel, there is no guarantee that the hotel will treat you as it does her. They need her; they might not need you.

Olga found the hotel director and front-desk women unprepared to exert themselves. It was their busiest time, early

August. As usual, the director kept a quota of empty rooms for senior Party figures and military officers, even though his lobby was filled with people clamoring for beds, but Olga lacked the status to obtain one. The director did not want to alienate Olga's sister altogether, so he made excuses and ordered a plump, officious receptionist to hand Olga a piece of paper on which was written the name of a small hotel on the far side of the city.

Sighing, Olga grasped Boris firmly by the hand and hailed another taxi. The other hotel was much smaller, and not as clean, but the director did agree to give her a room. Olga unpacked, and for two days she and Boris walked by the sea, trying to unwind. On the third day, the director demanded the room back.

She wrung her hands. "But we're here for three weeks!"

"That is nothing to me. You must leave, now."

"But please, we have come so far, and the boy needs the sun . . ."

"What is that to me? Do as I tell you or I'll have the *militsia* (police) throw you out."

Running to a nearby store, Olga stood in line to buy cognac and chocolates. She hurried back and pressed them upon the director, begging him to relent. He did, but only for another three days. A pattern developed: every third day he would threaten to toss her into the street. Anxiously, her holiday mood evaporating, she would scour the shops for more bribes.

After two weeks, the director finally evicted them. Olga and Boris took a bus to a street lined with ramshackle private dachas and went from door to door. They found nothing that morning, but after lunch a woman who lived in the top half of a small two-story house agreed to rent them the back room of the ground floor for five rubles a night. It was typical Soviet vacation style: two iron cots, a battered wardrobe, and no bathroom, only a cold-water faucet in the yard. Olga was happy to have a roof of any kind.

"What I didn't realize," she told me later, "was how expensive a holiday can be. I spent the whole 500 rubles on the two of us for those three weeks. That's almost three months' salary. It wasn't just the bribes, though they cost a fair amount, but the food.

"Sukhumi is crowded in summer and everyone has to eat. The lines at the open-air places are very long. Georgians are always out to make money and they'll sell you anything. By the end of August no meat was available, only *kasha* (groats). After waiting for an hour for lunch one day, I heard two Georgians talking in the kitchen, and a man translated for me. One was saying that the next batch of *kasha* had spoiled because it had cooked too long. He asked if he should still serve it. 'Of course,' the other answered."

The final hurdle was confirming a trip back to Kiev. That took an entire day standing in line, with Boris bored and fretful. Olga obtained two seats, not on the flight she wanted, but on one two days later. She arrived home exhausted. Despite the hardships, she and Boris still retain bright memories of the sea.

Why not eat in hotel restaurants? She laughed. "Women and children don't go into restaurants alone in the Soviet Union generally, and in Georgia in particular," she replied. "You know the terrible amount of drinking in our country. Restaurants are filled with men who have had too much. Georgians are notorious for the way they chase after Russian women, and if you have blond hair, as I do, it is ten times worse."

More *klass* would have helped. Politburo members travel in special Aeroflot aircraft or in reserved trains, and stay either in former tsarist palaces or in more modern buildings such as the Party Chairman's retreat at Oreander in Yalta, or the marble-and-glass mansion with its own swimming pool at Pitsunda, south of Sochi on the Black Sea coast. Near Moscow, Politburo and Academicians' dachas are at Zhukovka and at Zavidovo, where the Volga and the Shosha Rivers meet, seventy miles northeast of the capital.

Members of the Party Central Committee have their own Party dachas and resorts, and their own limousines, flights, and trains to take them there. The Central Committee hotel in Kiev has chandeliers, soft carpets, unobtrusive service, and deluxe rooms. A similar hotel in Irkutsk has extensive grounds and a more varied menu than Siberian cities can usually offer. I myself stayed in the Central Committee hotel in Vilnius while on a foreign ministry trip with other foreign correspondents. By Western standards it was nothing out of the ordinary, but it was cleaner than the typical Soviet hotel, and its furnishings were more elaborate.

Party, government, military, scientific, cultural, and sporting elites travel by Aeroflot so often that ordinary civilians must endure constant lines and disappointments. The obstacles for the typical Soviet citizen are multiplied by foreigners who receive almost the same *klass* priority given to senior Soviet individuals.

I remember with embarrassment being taken with other foreign reporters to a tiny plane on the runway at Bukhara, in Uzbekistan, for a flight to Urgench. We had already waited for several hours and our official guides were upset at the delay, fearing it would be reflected in what we wrote and lead to rebukes for the guides. Not until we boarded the plane did we realize what had been done. Other people's coats and parcels were in the racks above the seats, and the plane had a lived-in, rumpled air. As we sat down, we heard a crowd of passengers arrive at the rear door. They began shouting, but stewardesses answered rudely, "Go back, go back," and began tossing parcels and coats onto the tarmac. The passengers had left the plane while in transit to Urgench and were astonished to find that they would not be flying on. One of the stewardesses summed up what happens to air travelers without *klass*: Staring down at the frustrated ex-passengers from the door of the plane she snapped, "Take the bus!"

During a nine-day trip to frozen Yakutia in northeastern Siberia a small group of Western correspondents, including myself, stayed in the decrepit Lena Hotel in Yakutsk. We took three separate flights to even more remote areas, returning to home base at Yakutsk each time. As foreigners with high *klass* priority, we walked straight to our planes through an airport filled shoulder-to-shoulder with people, many of whom had been waiting for days for flights. At 6:30 A.M., as we prepared to fly to the world's coldest continually inhabited valley (the Oymyakon, where temperatures have been recorded as low as minus ninety degrees Fahrenheit), Peter Hann of McGraw-Hill looked at the huge waiting area filled with sleeping, snoring bodies on couches, chairs, and on the floor. "Who says the Soviet Union doesn't have the best airports in the world?" he asked. "You don't see people using American airports like this."

Traveling ordinary Soviet-class is time-consuming and arduous. It remains today as the French nobleman, the Marquis de Custine, discovered it to be almost 150 years ago in tsarist Russia: "continuous and obstinate work." Olga's small quotient of *klass* made her trip to Sukhumi possible, but was not sufficient to make it comfortable.

Such Western niceties as travel brochures, travel agencies, competing airlines, clean trains, an adequate number of hotels, quality control in restaurants or hotel rooms are absent for most Soviet travelers. Hotels do not have switchboards. To find out if a particular individual is staying in a hotel, even in Moscow and Leningrad, you must be able to tell the reception desk the day he checked in. You cannot simply call him; the phone in each room is an outside line, with its own ordinary city number, and to reach a guest you must know what the number is.

A trip abroad is still the most sought-after *klass* symbol of all. I met Igor, a nuclear physicist, at Gate B-57 at the Frankfurt airport one bleak December day as we waited nine hours for an Aeroflot flight to Moscow. Snowstorms in Moscow had delayed the plane's arrival, and when Aeroflot provided us with luncheon vouchers, we sat together. He was anxious to know what the public-address system was announcing in English; I wanted to talk to a Russian privileged to be so far from home.

Igor, a dark slender man, had just spent several months in the apartment of a West German physicist near Hamburg. He was going home satisfied that the German lived no better than he did at home in the *klass*-filled academic community of Akademgorodok, near Novosibirsk in Siberia. His own apartment was apparently larger and better appointed than most in Moscow.

At times he surprised me. "Your system and mine," he said softly. "If I were to compare them, I would say that yours has certain advantages." He smiled.

"Yes," he went on, "your service industries are better than ours. Your hotels, buses, trains, and airplanes. They are geared to provide personal service, and you've had more experience at it than we have. We had war, you know, against the Nazis, and it takes time to recover from such a tragedy." I was to hear that same observation, or excuse, about World War II hundreds of times. "But our system is, on balance, better," Igor continued, back on more familiar ground. "We offer security, safety. Housing is cheap, basic food doesn't cost much, education and health care are free. You can't say the same."

He paused, preparing to launch a rhetorical point as a follow-up flourish. "Tell me," he asked, "why did you in the West give Sakharov the Nobel Prize for peace [in 1975]? If you want to honor him, give him the Nobel Prize for physics. Then we could argue the point on equal ground. But peace? Sakharov does not create peace. He creates argument, division, criticism of his own country. I don't understand."

Later, when our Aeroflot plane was grounded in Leningrad at 1 A.M. by another snowstorm, Igor used his considerable *klass* as a nuclear physicist to cut through the crowds and order a taxi when none was visible at the airport. He found us a place at the exclusive Astoria Hotel, securing not just a room but a vast corner suite with chandeliers and inlaid furniture as well as a hard-to-get ticket on a flight to Moscow the next day. He shook out a Soviet magic carpet for me and I appreciated it.

Igor had spent months on his own in Western Europe, a priceless privilege for any Soviet citizen. Only a stay in the United States held more privilege. One night I talked with another man, Sasha, who had spent three months traveling up and down the east coast of the United States attending an international youth conference and "looking around." He was one of a select few: in 1978, a year before Soviet troops entered Afghanistan and détente began to freeze, only 11,000 Soviet people traveled to the United States, 8,500 of them on official government business. A mere 2,500 Soviet citizens went privately or on group tours. That same year neighboring Poland, with a population almost nine times smaller, sent 30,000 citizens to the United States.

After the rigorous checks by the KGB, his trade union, and the Communist Youth League (Komsomol), Sasha exchanged his internal passport for a brand new red-covered external one valid only for one trip. When he reached the United States he followed the usual rules for Soviet travelers and deposited it with the nearest Soviet consul. He picked it up again just before flying home, where he exchanged it again for his internal passport. Soviet citizens may not keep permanent passports for foreign travel; they are issued a clean one each time they travel. It is one way of trying to prevent defections and generally to keep travelers on a tight rein.

Moscow hoards its foreign currency. Air fares for Sasha within the U.S. were paid by the Soviet embassy in Washington. So were his hotel bills, and he received only $500 in cash for each month of his stay. Even on that small allowance he saved enough dollars to go shopping in New York. "I ate only in the hotel," Sasha explained, "so that the meals would go on the hotel bill and the embassy would pay. I saved absolutely everything I could. What did I buy? Let's see: records and tapes, of course, and some clothes, and small gifts, and a tape recorder, and a typewriter."

Less prestigious than an individual journey but coveted nonetheless is the official trip abroad as part of a delegation. Party and government officials attend conferences and trade meetings; scientists travel to meet other scientists; ballet dancers, actors, filmmakers, athletes, and others also tour. Foreign currency is doled out sparingly, and travelers skimp on personal expenses so they can take home American goods.

The lowest level of foreign travel *klass* is a trip to a third-world country or one in Eastern Europe. On one collective farm, a young woman agronomist laughed when I asked her if she had been abroad. "No," she said, "but the woman who lives upstairs from me"—her eyes shone—"has been to Bulgaria!"

Gaining permission for any trip abroad is not easy. Even after the usual KGB and trade-union checks, the Party is anxious to see that its tourists create a good impression. One Russian told me of oral examinations that he and his friends had to take before a trip to Poland. "We went to libraries to look up information beforehand," he said, "but we didn't know what the questions would be." The panel consisted of five people. The first question: "What is the name of the head of the Polish government?" Next: "How far has socialism developed in Poland?" My friend passed, but a friend of his failed because he could not come up with the official name of the Polish Communist Party. He had to try again at a later time.

Those who travel to Eastern Europe include loyal and productive workers in steel plants and coal mines; oil and gas drillers from Siberia; translators and interpreters in Moscow. It took years for Galina, our maid, to secure permission for a two-week bus trip through Poland and East Germany. She came back astonished by Poland, a Communist country with crucifixes by its roadsides and people praying openly without official harassment. In East Germany, she was impressed by the shops, the good shoes and cameras available to anyone. Like most travelers the world over, however, she was glad to be home again with her husband and children. The outside world, even the Communist one, was interesting, but only in a remote sense. "I missed our dark bread," she said at one point in her breathless narrative, "and our friends, and my family. This is where I want to be."

I suspect that if the Kremlin did tomorrow what Nikita Khrushchev advocated in his memoirs—unlocked the workers' paradise and allowed Soviet people to travel freely abroad[1]—many would certainly take the opportunity to go and see the capitalist world, but most would eventually return. While many do want to emigrate, most Russians are attracted more by Western affluence and materialism than they are by capitalism itself, which strikes them from afar as chaotic and confusing.

"I know the West is not really like what they tell us," Abe Stolar mused one afternoon in Moscow. Stolar was born in Chicago but was taken to Moscow at the age of eleven when his émigré parents returned to the Soviet Union in the 1930s. "Now I want to go back," he said, "but even I hesitated for a while. When you hear anti-American propaganda every day of your life, you find yourself wondering if *some* of it might not be true."

Despite any ideological reservations about the West, Soviet citizens will use almost any method to travel from their country and see what it is like "over there." A friend's husband, who worked for a Western company in Moscow, was once permitted to drive the company's Volvo to Helsinki and bring back a new one. He stayed in a *pension* with other Russians, saving his money to bring back records, a high-fashion quilted winter coat for his wife, a leather jacket for himself, and ski gloves and hats for his children.

The most common method of external travel for ordinary citizens is reserved for "reliable" workers, often Party members, in large factories: cut-rate trade-union tickets. Margaret and I ran into a group of them around a swimming pool in Colombo, Sri Lanka, twenty-five Soviet oil workers from the Caspian Sea port of Astrakhan. We were on our midwinter break from Moscow, and the last thing we expected to see was a group of jovial, plump Russian men and women, in print dresses and open-necked shirts, chatting by the pool of the Ceylon Inns Hotel, looking like country cousins among the sleeker European tourists. Moscow allows some 6,000 Soviet tourists to visit Sri Lanka each year, sending them back and forth on near-empty Aeroflot jet flights run at an immense loss for political reasons to reward and encourage Sri Lanka in its role in the nonaligned movement.

One broad-faced worker, Ivan, pulled out a notebook to read me the details of their trip. They had flown from Moscow to New Delhi, with a side trip to Agra, where he had carefully drawn a pencil sketch of the Taj Mahal, then on to Madras and finally to Sri Lanka, where they were staying for four days. His ticket, he said, had cost him 500 rubles, more than two months' salary, and his trade union had put up the additional 2,000 rubles needed. He was enjoying Colombo, but he could not wait for the highlight of the tour: on his return he would exchange his foreign-currency allowance, less than $10 a day, for "certificate rubles" which he could spend in Moscow at the well-stocked special stores closed to the average citizen.

Traveling Soviet citizens go to great lengths to conserve foreign currency in order to exchange it back home. We stopped a day later at a pineapple plantation on the road from Colombo to Kandy, where we met the small, spluttering figure of owner Nihal Gunasena. While our children played with a fifteen-month-old gray monkey and pored over tables of brightly colored masks, shells, wooden elephants, and batiks, Mr. Gunasena launched into a description of the busloads of Russians who pulled up at his plantation several times a week.

"They have no money," he said, "but they all carry plastic

bags filled with Russian cigarettes and pencils, and sometimes wine, and those little wooden dolls that fit inside each other. They come up to the stall and offer me pencils for the souvenirs. I don't like to be rude, and sometimes I take the pencils, but I really don't want them, you know. We have pencils here. I am hesitating, you see, over the pencils, and another group of Russians is in the batiks. I run over there, and the first group is opening its plastic bags and scooping masks into them, and shells. I cry 'No, no,' and I run back, and the second group is alone with the batiks and I don't like that, and I run back . . . They set off round the property, and my goodness, they take the coconuts from the ground and put them in their plastic bags. They really should be paying, it's not much but they should pay. And that is not all, my word no.

"I built a special toilet for my customers, see it over there? It is brick, very fine. The Russians use it and when they go back to their bus I find all the toilet paper stolen! Why? They are a superpower, aren't they?"

We tried to explain that paper is in short supply in the Soviet Union, because so much is exported for hard currency, and huge amounts are used by the military. New consignments of toilet paper in the shops bring Muscovites into long lines hours before the stores open.

"They keep saying 'Dorogo, dorogo,'" Mr. Gunasena complained. "What is that?" As we gave him the translation ("expensive, expensive"), he brightened. "But wait until they find out what is the brand of toilet paper they are stealing," he cried joyfully. "It is Plum Blossom brand—from China!" He rocked with laughter.

If a Soviet citizen cannot find a trade-union-assisted trip such as Ivan's, he needs at the very least a considerable amount of money. Galya, a middle-aged Moscow friend, was once told she could have a week in Britain for 700 rubles. She earned barely 130 rubles a month, so the trip was out of the question. Bank loans for travel are not available.

Travel by air within the Soviet Union is an unusual experience requiring both stamina and a sense of humor for all but the top of the Top Class. Aeroflot flights can be delayed for hours, even days, without warning or explanation. Female ground staff are often rude and unhelpful as they file their nails and gossip in corners, ignoring questions thrown at them.

Westerners are accorded great *klass* privileges in the USSR whether tourists or residents, but they are by no means exempt from Aeroflot-itis. One of the first Americans I met in Moscow was the wife of the principal of the Anglo-American School, run by the State Department and Whitehall, which our three children were to attend. As we began to talk about travel, she advised me to take not only a book on my journeys but a tablecloth as well. A tablecloth?

"Yes," she said as though it was the most natural piece of advice in the world. "Then, when planes are delayed, you can spread it in the terminal and set out the food you'll also have brought with you, and enjoy a decent meal. You probably won't be able to buy anything. . . ."

But how long were planes delayed? I was, after all, still fresh from the Western world.

"Well, last week, when I went to Georgia, it wasn't too bad at Domodedovo (one of Moscow's domestic airports)," she replied.

My hopes rose.

"We took off only six hours late."

I was to think of her often as I waited hour after hour at Domodedovo over the next four and a half years. Sometimes Margaret would set off early for a trip to the south on a 10 A.M. Aeroflot flight, and call home at 4 P.M. "What's it like down there?" I would ask, about to congratulate her for getting a call through. "I'm still at Domodedovo," she would reply. "It should be any hour now."

Once, for a period of three days, no Ilyushin-62 jet at all took off from Domodedovo for the 4,000-mile leap to

Khabarovsk on the Far East coast. It was peak summer travel time and at least half a dozen round-trip flights were scheduled each day. After the first twenty-four hours, so many passengers had arrived at Domodedovo that they were camping outside under the trees, not daring to make the hour-long journey back to the city in case the planes suddenly started taking off. Repeated complaints drew only the response that the weather was bad in Khabarovsk. But when the nightly news came on the television set in the waiting area, the weather was announced as perfect at both ends of the journey.

Three days later, with 3,000 people waiting at Domodedovo, flights began once again, without explanation. When the weekly *Literary Gazette* began asking questions, it reported that deliveries of aircraft fuel to Khabarovsk had been mysteriously halted for three days. In the Western world, an airline would have to explain and apologize. But being Aeroflot means never having to say you are sorry.

Service aboard most Aeroflot planes is poor, a fact that most Soviet citizens take for granted. They are happy to have obtained any tickets at all. Stewardesses have little training or interest in their jobs. Once I was flying back to Moscow from Lvov, near the Polish border, after a week-long tour designed to show off new ways to make Russians work harder by offering incentive pay for quality as well as quantity. The flight was short, so no meal was served. I watched our two stewardesses sit down for take-off, and then stay in their seats for the entire flight. As I read over my notes on raising the output of Soviet workers, one stewardess took out some stockings to mend. The other one fell asleep.

The food served on Aeroflot to all manner of *klass* passengers is unattractive. It often consists of rubbery chicken, stale brown bread cut thick without butter, mineral water in dingy gray plastic cups, and lukewarm tea. I shall not soon forget the look on the face of Parisian Félix Bolo, then chief of the Agence France Presse bureau in Moscow, as he con-

templated an oddly shaped piece of chicken on his tray on our
flight together to Tashkent, in Uzbekistan. Shaking his head,
Félix turned his attention to a peeled peach that lay in a pale
liquid in a small dish. Simultaneously, he and I dug gray plastic forks at the peaches, which proved to be as hard as steel.
Like ball bearings, they spun in their syrup, spraying thick,
sugary juice over us. As I tried to wipe it off, I became aware
that I had lost all feeling in my left arm. I was in a left-hand
window seat, and the plane's insulation was so thin that the
wall was like the inside of a freezer chest. I put my sheepskin
coat between me and the window for the rest of the flight.

An American pilot I knew suffered more than minor discomfort on some flights. "I have shaken in my seat at times,"
he said after months of travel through the Soviet Union.
"Aeroflot doesn't usually report accidents unless foreigners
are involved, so it's hard to know how many there are. On
one takeoff from Kiev we were nose-high and almost stalled,
but we didn't land for another forty minutes. I have been in
planes flying in 'cross-control' (ailerons and rudder opposed to
each other) for thirty minutes at a time."

Only the airports at Kiev and the resort of Mineralnye Vody
had automatic approach control, the type used in the West, he
went on. This meant that in Moscow and all other cities, all
approach and separation intervals between planes were
worked out by hand twenty-four hours ahead of time. "It's
common to bounce on landings," he continued. "I'm sure
you've noticed that. The door frame fell out between fore and
aft compartments on one Tupolev 154 I was in, and the stewardess simply kicked it back into place." He cleared up something that had puzzled me: why Aeroflot pilots suddenly
zoom, then slow, as they come in to land, making the stom-
ach lurch. "They have to pass from one control sector to another at exactly the right second," he explained, "so they wait
until the last minute and put on power.

"Can you imagine," he continued, "a Western pilot showing up ninety minutes late for a night flight, as happened to

me at Vnukovo (an internal Moscow) airport, without explanation? A stewardess said to him as he walked up the aisle to the cockpit, 'People have been asking why they've waited so long.' The pilot replied, 'None of their business.'"

The best internal Aeroflot flight I took showed what *klass* Aeroflot could provide if it wanted to. The flight was from Domodedovo across the country to Khabarovsk in an Ilyushin 62-M. There was plenty of leg room. The food was good because, I suspected, correspondents from the United States, Canada, West Germany, France, Britain, Italy, Spain, and Japan were on board. We had red caviar; their brown bread wrapped in cellophane; butter; warm meat that did not assault the eye; fried potatoes; half an apple; a small packet marked "One-Apple Jam"; and a huge orange from Morocco. It was all served by two stewards in white chef's hats. As we ate at 36,000 feet above the Siberian plain, I looked down into the darkness punctuated by ghostly red flames burning off excess natural gas at the tops of invisible oil rigs.

The flight illustrated the immensity of the USSR and the sheer necessity of air travel. Flight 25 left Moscow at 9 P.M. on a Sunday in February, and landed 4,000 miles away seven and half hours later at 11:30 A.M. on Monday, local time. In tsarist days, the journey took months across a Siberia filled with so many exiles and prisoners that Maxim Gorky called it a "land of death and chains." In the same flying time, we could have reached Nova Scotia to the west, Singapore to the southeast, and Kenya due south. The return flight, against westerly winds, took nine hours.

Klass can make flying more convenient, but it is even more important on Soviet trains. While Aeroflot is mainly one class, except for overseas flights, train travel is divided into three: "soft," with two berths to a compartment; "hard," or four berths; and dormitory-style, open-plan carriages with bunks along each side, holding fifty-four passengers in clouds of cigarette smoke and a litter of paper, food, and vodka bottles.

I took trains as often as I could to meet as many Soviet people as I could. Western diplomats and military attachés did the same. Fortunately I was not prevented from looking out of the window; one group of military attachés was, by officials who at one stop covered the outside glass with white paint. When the attachés exploded with rage, the officials said calmly, "Disinfectant."

Train is the basic means of travel in the Soviet Union, where the age of the automobile has not yet fully arrived. Fares are low and trains are punctual. People crowd cheerfully in, packages and string bags filled with food and bargains. They eat and drink with gusto. Some passengers have no interest in talking to an American in the same carriage; others ply him with questions.

After the 1917 Revolution, the Bolsheviks made a brief effort to eliminate class distinctions on trains.[2] In tsarist times, Russians could choose between luxurious saloons, or two "soft" and two "hard" classes (benches set up in freight wagons). In December 1918, all classes were abolished and the former third class was declared to be standard. But even then, old habits and even newer rules conspired to perpetuate *klass*. "For the convenience of the passengers" special fast trains could still run at night. Extra payment could ensure numbered seats and bunks on night and long-distance trains. From September 1918, special carriages were reserved for the All-Russian Central Executive Committee, the Council of People's Commissars, and the Commissariats of War, Communications, and Foreign Affairs. By April 1920, officials and anyone else traveling on business had the right to the former "soft" class.

As with Aeroflot, internal train travel remains below the general standard of Western Europe and the United States. The best train the Russian elite can take, the overnight from Moscow to Helsinki, is given special *klass* attention because foreigners use it, but it is hardly a reincarnation of the Orient Express. There was no restaurant car in our time. Beds were hard and even the "soft" class *vagon* was filled with the smell of coal burning in a small furnace in the entryway, sizzling with the remains of conductors' meals tossed on top. An hour after departure, we could order a glass of weak tea and perhaps some thick Soviet cookies. If we had forgotten a book, all we could read were diatribes against the West in the propaganda rack, or about how the Party defeated the Nazis, or how Soviet steel production was surpassing the targets of the current Five-Year Plan.

One of the worst trains Margaret and I rode was from Moscow north to Petrozavodsk. The trip itself was well worth the inconvenience: it led to a swift hydrofoil ride to the spectacular eighteenth-century wooden churches on the island of Kizhi which were made without nails but lavished with artistry and devotion. However, our dining car was filthy, the tablecloth unspeakable, and the choice of food either a single, questionable cut of meat, or eggs. The waitresses were uninterested. Our carriage had not been cleaned in months and the toilets at each end stank.

At the other end of Soviet travel is usually a hotel. At the top level are the newer, Western-built establishments designed to imitate deluxe hotels in the United States and Europe. To construct anything of quality intended for use by the Soviet Top Class the Soviet Union must import skills, and so Finns built the excellent Viru Hotel in Estonia; a French company provided the Kosmos Hotel in Moscow; a Swedish company built a new hotel in Leningrad.

In the summer of 1982 I walked into one of the newest of them all, the International Center on the northern embankment of the Moscow River opposite the Stalin-Gothic towers of the Ukraine Hotel. A combination hotel-conference center, it was under construction almost all of the years I spent in Moscow as a correspondent. I had talked at length to American supervisors in charge of electrical, fireproofing, plumbing, and other work. Now I saw the size of the project on which they had labored. From the outside, it looked like two unpainted concrete blocks. Inside, a giant, enclosed lobby was filled with greenery. Glass-walled elevators climbed up on one side. Carpets, shops, a food store, and a health club complete with saunas gave a Western air, as did the prices, about $150 a day to keep out all but Western and Japanese businessmen.

One of the best hotels was the Viru in Tallinn, the capital of Estonia. I shall not soon forget the feeling I experienced when I first walked into my room after my first few months in Moscow. I had learned to accept bathroom tiles that seldom met and hotel rooms lit by a single twenty-five-watt bulb; but the Viru room had bright lighting, the floor was carpeted, and none of the bathroom tiles lay in shards on the floor. The bath itself was clean and, yes, there was an electrical socket.

Other, more ordinary hotels that have rooms-with-bath were assigned to Western tourists: the Intourist, the Ukraine, and the old Metropol in Moscow; the Leningrad and the Moskva in Leningrad. Yalta had a relatively new Western hotel. So did some other resorts. On a lesser level were such establishments as the Rossiya in Smolensk, the Intourist in Brest on the Polish Border, which looked modern but was relentlessly Soviet underneath; and the battered Lena in Yakutsk, in eastern Siberia, whose odors, dirt, and discomforts were extreme.

Below those levels were hotels into which lesser-*klass* East European travelers were thrown: the Belgrad and the Ostankino in Moscow, for example, and the Baltiiskaya in Leningrad. For Russians with little *klass*, hundreds of shabby, poorly maintained structures lay in wait.

High-ranking Soviet officials use *klass* advantages to ensure good hotel rooms when they travel. Oleg, a senior engineer in the metallurgy ministry in Moscow, was ordered to travel to Voronezh, south of Moscow, to inspect a factory, and because of his rank, and his ministry, the Party itself smoothed his way. The factory director personally telephoned the Party Committee in his city district; the committee immediately ordered a room in the best local hotel. An engineer of lesser rank might traipse from hotel to hotel for hours, even days, trying to find a room. His travel document, proving that he was on an official business trip, was powerless against the overcrowding and the network of bribery by which travelers buy their way into rooms.

It is illegal for Soviet citizens to stay in a hotel in the city in which they live. "If we allowed that," said one hotel receptionist, "even fewer rooms would be available than there are now. One of my jobs is to go around the lobby each night and order all the people sleeping here to get out and go to the train station or somewhere else."

Even Soviet officials find hotels uncomfortable. Why, asked a reporter for the newspaper of the Young Communist League, did hotels lock their doors at midnight?[3] It was inconvenient for guests. Why were Soviet guests awakened at 7:30 A.M. to pay their bills, instead of being allowed to come downstairs to the lobby on their last day? Why must the woman on duty on each floor burst into your room and count all sheets, towels, and drinking glasses, and peer into your bathroom to see if you have stolen the mirror? The answer: it suited hotel staff schedules, and complied with red tape. In most Soviet hotels, the guest came last.

The points made by the newspaper indicated why *klass* is so precious. "While traveling in the Soviet I stayed in the Tsentralnaya [Central] Hotel in Leninsk [in Kazakhstan] regularly for ten years," the reporter complained, "during which time I never saw the elevator in working order. To my inquiries the hotel manager replied, 'So what? Our people are young, they can climb up on foot. . . .'

"Inoperative hotel elevators are more the rule than the exception. I have seen them in . . . the Hotel Ukraina in

Feodosia, the Chuvashia in Cheboksary, and the brand new, very comfortable Druzhba [Friendship] Hotel in Pushkinskiye Gory. At the Hotel Volga in Kostroma, only people staying in the hotel are permitted to use the elevator. If an acquaintance wants to visit you he has to walk up twelve floors.

"You'll always find in your room an advertising leaflet describing the types of services supposedly available to you: reserving train tickets, calling a taxi, room service, long-distance telephone calls, etc. But most of the time this is all 'just for show'. . . . The Hotel Riga [in Latvia] suspended its room service some years ago after an Italian who had waited two hours for his dinner grabbed the tray out of the waiter's hand when he finally arrived, and, screaming '*Madonna Mia!*' threw it out of the fourth-floor window. . . .

"That same Intourist Hotel in Novgorod has telephones in the rooms but it is forbidden to use them, and there are excellent color television sets in the halls, but they work poorly, because they aren't attached to an outside antenna. . . . In the Hotel Onar [in Ioshkar-Ola] I would have been pleased to exchange [an inoperative] television set [in the room] for an ordinary nightstand, a table lamp, and a bar of soap, none of which the room had." The reporter called for more training of hotel staff. He singled out for approval the special courses for administrators, waiters, maids, and elevator operators run by the Hilton chain in the United States.

In Smolensk in the western USSR on the classic Napoleon and Hitler invasion route, Margaret and I appeared to be the only Westerners at the Hotel Rossiya. We arrived by car at 10 P.M. to be told that the restaurant, filled with people, and displaying a notice saying that it stayed open until 11 P.M., was closed. Eventually we were given some soup and meat, but no coffee. "None left," the waitress said. The doors by which we had entered were locked before we finished our meal. Because we had complained, the staff would no longer help us. The supervisor studiously refused to unlock the door as she continued to count the day's takings.

Eventually, back on our floor, we told the *dezhurnaya* by the elevator—women sit on almost every floor of every big hotel, holding room keys and checking to see who comes and goes—that we thought the behavior of the restaurant staff was *nyekulturny* (uncultured). There is no greater insult to a contemporary Russian than to suggest that he has not progressed beyond his rural past. Within half an hour, the waitress was at our door, offering a teapot half full of black liquid and saying she had "misunderstood" our request. The pot had no lid, and it was the worst coffee we had ever tasted; but she had made a gesture of apology, and we thanked her.

The quickest way to obtain good service was to ask for the complaint book that all hotels and restaurants are required to keep. Staff would do almost anything to avoid entries, which could reduce their salary bonuses. Inattentive waiters and cold food were transformed into smiles and warmth even at the hint that the book might be requested. Not even the complaint book, however, could remedy toilets that would not flush without ten minutes of tinkering with the float in the tank, or cracks in the walls, or miniature bathroom mirrors, or a chronic lack of hot water.

The Hotel Iveria in Tbilisi, Georgia, run by the state travel agency Intourist, was a catalogue of poor management, especially in winter. Rooms were dirty, carpets worn, the key ladies on each floor complacent, and the restaurant without fresh fruit in a republic that earns millions by growing fresh food and smuggling it to the north. The room charge for Westerners was $60 a night, more than ten times the price charged to Soviet citizens.

But *klass* found its ways. The best service in the Iveria was found behind an unmarked wooden door in the outside wall to the right of the official entrance. A local resident told me to push it open if ever I felt really hungry. I discovered the kitchen staff doing a thriving private business selling tea and pastries, both of which were delicious; it was a typical use of state property for unofficial private gain.

The Top and Rising Class status of Soviet officials, scientists, creative artists, and top athletes shields them from some of the hardships of travel, but even for them services lag well behind those of the West. Yet, "you can find every type of scenery in the world right here in the Soviet Union," Muscovite friends would tell us proudly. They were right, from the expanse of the prairies to the slopes of the Urals with their pine trees and steeply pitched wooden roofs, to the blue of Lake Baikal, the sun of the Black Sea and the Latvian coastline, the heat of Central Asia, and the mountains of Tadzhikstan. Landing at Alma-Ata airport in Kazakhstan was an experience in itself: the plane glided in between snow-topped peaks brilliant against a blue sky.

But the natural beauty was marred by a system of travel that punishes everyone, except those armed for the journey with the most valuable of all Soviet commodities—a substantial quotient of *klass*.

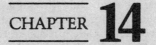

KLASS AND COUTURE: DRESSING UP IN THE SOVIET UNION

My wife and I went to a party to celebrate Russian New Year's Eve (January 13) at the home of veteran American correspondent Edmund Stevens and his Russian-born wife, Nina, on Ryleev Street in Moscow. What we saw was Soviet-style couture.

Members of privileged Moscow society, flamboyantly dressed, stamped about the room to loud disco music. The women wore Western dresses, or their own versions of French designer fashions. Sasha Zaitsev, then head of the designer team at Moscow's Dom Modelei, or House of Fashions, wore a sequined jacket of peacock blue and white that Liberace might have envied, over dark trousers and a pair of heavy, ultrafashionable American cowboy boots with pointed toes. One of his two sons almost shook the record player's needle from its groove as he banged down tall leather boots worn with a khaki safari suit. The other son sported a bright red and white football jersey and a matching scarf long enough to wind around his neck and still reach the floor.

When midnight struck, this microcosm of Soviet *klass* toasted itself with champagne. The women took flecks of gold makeup from their faces and scattered them on their men. Bolshoi ballet superstar Maris Liepa snapped his fingers to the music, wearing a dark suit without a tie. A dozen chic members of the Soviet film world clustered around the tall figure of Hollywood actor Curt Jurgens, in town to star in a Soviet film about World War II. The evening was a Soviet attempt, not wholly unsuccessful, to follow the fashionable mores of the West.

The fashion rule in the Soviet Union is simple: imported clothes from Western Europe and the United States signify *klass*. They show *klass* when worn; and they require *klass* to obtain. Increasingly, Soviet elites are learning to experiment with Western fashions and to add a dash of non-Soviet color and panache to their outfits. The process is slow; still Soviet society remains remote from many European and American styles and modes. For the Urban Class, change is glacial. For the Rising Class it is faster. For the Top Class it is faster still.

For the Rising and Top Classes, clothing that is Russian-made is déclassé. Rising Class women envy anything new from abroad that a friend might wear. The Western adage is that you cannot judge a book by its cover, and the Russians say the same thing in rhyme: *po odyozhke vstrechayut, po umu provozhayut*, a sentiment that literally means that on the "second look" you judge a man by his brains, but on "first glance" you judge by the clothes. Unlike the situation in the West, where middle-class people often dress as well as the rich (in Britain they dress better), you can identify the social class of a Soviet woman, or man, by clothes. Hats, coats, suits, dresses, gloves, shoes—even underwear—are a clue to status and access to privilege.

The dowdiness of Urban and Rural Class Soviet women is legendary, but competition to dress well among Rising Class women is intense. "My impression," says a recent Soviet émigré in London, "is that Russian [Rising Class] women worry more about their appearance than many women do in the West. Here it is often fashionable to be casual, but there it is necessary for women of rank to show themselves off as much as they can. Women will give literally their last rubles for a pair of fashionable winter boots or a good dress."

For Anna, one of our Rising Class acquaintances, it was going to be a splendid evening out. The occasion was an office party, with plenty to eat and drink, held on the decks of a motor launch as it sailed into the sunset between the green banks of the Moscow River. For a few hours, at least, the cares of *klass* and life in the world's first socialist state could be put aside. Anna had been looking forward to the party and the chance to dress up.

Anna, a professional woman, was a member of the lower rungs of the Rising Class. Her husband worked for a government agency that did business with the West, and had already achieved a trip abroad. She did not have access to special clothing stores, but she knew her way around. She belonged to a growing group of Soviet women determined to express their femininity, and their social status, through their clothes.

Unlike American or West European women at her social level, Anna did not have the opportunity to follow fashion or to own many stylish clothes. Her high school graduation, her twenty-first birthday, even her marriage, had been straightforward affairs at which she had worn what was available. Now, however, she was determined to show herself to advantage on the motor launch. She had leafed through West German and French fashion magazines that her husband had brought home, and she set out to devise a stunning party outfit.

The first challenge was the blouse. She met it by calling on her husband's contacts. Anna borrowed a satiny, open-necked, puff-sleeved model from a West German woman who worked in his office. She used her friendship with a department-store clerk to secure a bolt of lightweight material for a long skirt, which she sewed herself on her East German sewing machine. She sought out a sales assistant in a shoe store whom she had been bribing for months; from her she extracted a pair of imported leather shoes that the assistant had been saving under the counter. They cost many rubles, plus the promise of extra favors.

On the day of the outing, Anna took time off from work to have her regular girl at the local beauty shop cut, wash, and set her hair. She gave herself a careful manicure, using a brilliant nail varnish her husband had bought abroad. Before setting out with her husband in their small car, she slipped on a silver bracelet bought at the jeweler's for the occasion, at a cost of twenty rubles, or 10 percent of her monthly salary. As she stepped onto the deck of the motor launch she uttered a sigh of relief. She had made it, well dressed.

Most Soviet clothing, while improving in quality, remained drab in design and poor in construction during our years in Moscow. The concept of fashion, in a Western sense, hardly existed. Where it did, it did not necessarily mean good taste. In the Soviet Union, "fashion" was anything unusual, or better than average in quality.

Russian women were not experienced at coordinating their clothes. They tended to wear items whose colors and style clashed with the rest of their outfit. Soon after we arrived in Moscow, state shops sold a consignment of canary-yellow plastic clogs from Scandinavia, touches of color in a drab world. Women wore them all that summer, regardless of whether they conflicted with other colors they might have had on.

"Fashion" could be a fuzzy, knitted mohair hat; a stiff vinyl belted jacket; a colorful pair of shoes; a belt with an unusual buckle. There were no rules or guidelines as in the West: fashion was made up as you went along. Television did not spread ideas about fashion, nor did newspapers carry regular features on clothes. The surest way to dress fashionably was

to travel to, or have contacts with, the United Sta
ern Europe. Elderly bureaucrats returned from a   ....ιπ
English suits for themselves and French fashions for their
wives; young people thirsted for the status symbols of Levis
and Wrangler jeans and jackets.

Supplies of clothes in state shops were so erratic that it was
usually impossible to create complete outfits or to find
matching accessories. Yet for those with *klass*, a new world
of fashion opens. When we saw Russian women wearing coor-
dinated clothes, it was obvious that they had had access to
Western ideas through magazines such as *Vogue, Elle*, or the
West German *Burda*.

Early in my Moscow days, my eye still attuned to Western
cut and fit, I walked down to Red Square on a late Saturday
afternoon in August, a favorite time for weddings. Taxis (for
the Urban Class) and Volga and Chaika limousines (for the
Rising and Top Classes) fluttered with white streamers. Dolls
or teddy bears were fixed to radiator grilles for good fortune. I
stood at the dark pink marble pile of the Lenin Mausoleum as
couple after couple came from the civil registry to pay their
respects to the founder of the Soviet State by laying flowers in
front of the main door (shut at the time and guarded by two
Kremlin military cadets motionless with fixed bayonets). The
Communist Party encourages this ceremony (and also laying
flowers a short distance away at the grave of the Unknown
Soldier and its eternal flame commemorating the war against
Hitler). The couples I saw were Urban Class and Rising Class,
though many intellectual families tend to ignore the Party's
wishes and have nothing to do with Lenin on their wedding
days.

It was an interesting sight. Wedding parties had done their
best. Many accumulated *klass* credits had been used to buy,
beg, or borrow suits and sports jackets, and short skirts for the
brides. Best men had white sashes across their chests. Brides-
maids carried flowers and giggled. One groom wore a light
blue suit; his bride was all in white down to the ground. The

next groom (couples followed on each other's heels, seconds apart, at the mausoleum) was in a black suit, and the next appeared in a brown sports coat and gray trousers, with the bride followed by a tiny flower girl in a dark blue velvet dress, light blue knee socks, and a huge blue-and-white ribbon in her hair. In many wedding parties the small flower girls were the best-dressed of all, symbols of the care Russian mothers lavish on their children.

Along came another groom, this time with a daring ruffled shirt front. Instead of a tie he wore a large blue brooch; his shirt front kept escaping from the lapels of his coat and he clutched at it nervously. Another bride wore a gown of blue silk. Behind her was a bride in a short bright-red dress. The most attractive bridesmaid I saw wore a gold blouse, long brown skirt, and white sling-back shoes, with her blond hair pulled back into a smooth chignon.

It is the contrasts I chiefly remember—the unevenness of the *klass* of couture. There were our intellectual semidissi-dent friends who dressed carelessly and not well—and the hauteur of the Zaitsev sons with their cowboy boots and long scarves. I think of the typical drab Urban Class male with his round-toed shoes and shapeless winter coats; and of *Pravda* columnist Vselevod Ovchinnikov standing in a corner at the journalists' club, Dom Zhurnalista, one winter night in 1980: his words were pure Party line but his clothes were Oxford Street in London, where he had just spent four years as *Pravda* correspondent. His blazer was double-breasted, dark blue with brass buttons; his shirt was a crisp white; his tie dark; his gray trousers properly creased; his shoes good, brown, and English. Such quiet, well-tailored clothing might go unnoticed on the East Coast of the United States or in a dozen European capitals. In Moscow, capital city of a super-power, sixty-three years after Lenin sounded in the name of Marx the death knell of social class, it stood out like a beacon, signaling that its wearer had reached some of the highest levels of social *klass*.

Welcoming a group of American correspondents to his office in 1980, the son-in-law of former premier Alexei Kosygin announced his status with the most impressive suit I saw on any Soviet official. Djerman Gvishiani, a deputy chairman of the State Committee on Science and Technology, appeared in a well-cut, fine-quality dark gray wool suit, its white pinstripes just far enough apart to show a knowledge of the latest Western styling. Gvishiani had either bought the suit in Western Europe or had used his Top Class *klass* to have it made in a Moscow *atelye* (custom tailoring shop) that catered only to senior Soviet diplomats. The *atelye* fitted its clients in secluded comfort, and charged between fifty and seventy rubles for a finished suit, which is less than a crudely tailored suit available to the Urban Class would cost at the GUM department store on Red Square.

The Party is so sensitive about its Soviet-made clothes that members of delegations due to travel abroad receive passes entitling them to a set of good clothes from skilled *atelyes* or special clothing stores. State shops might be inadequately stocked for the average citizens, but prestige abroad must be maintained.

On their return, travelers rush to convert their foreign currency into "certificate rubles" and to use them in unmarked, special shops in the larger cities. They choose Western suits and coats, Polish or Hungarian shoes, and other items, and wear them for years as marks of status.

Western clothes not only look and feel better than Soviet ones; they also have other uses. Friends in one large Soviet city received an occasional well-cut *dublyonka*, or sheepskin coat, from visiting relatives from Western Europe. In bitter Russian winters such coats are virtual necessities, yet if one is not in the police, the military, or in the upper ranks of the Party or government, there is little chance of owning one.

"The coats must be a gift from heaven in the middle of the Russian winter," I remarked.

"Oh, we don't wear them," was the amused reply. "A for-

s worth at least 700 rubles on the black
is more than four months' salary. No,
e the coats because we can sell them or trade
things."

enterprising young Muscovite who spent much of his li n the fringes of the black market, once asked me for a dozen pairs of American jeans. He suggested I could buy them on my next trip West. When I said that jeans were selling on London's Oxford Street for about £12 (at the time, $20), he was pleased. "Good," he said. "I will keep one or two pairs for myself, and I'll sell the others for 100 rubles each." Had I cooperated, he would have earned about 800 rubles, or five months' salary, in one transaction. Jeans are almost a fashion obsession in the Soviet Union. In the Black Sea port of Odessa, seamen bring in American jeans and sell them on street corners. In the early 1980s, a denim top and trousers, complete with American label, commanded 300 rubles, twice the average monthly wage.

An excellent way for a woman to have a quality dress made is first to acquire a popular item such as a small, collapsible umbrella with matching cover on a trip abroad. Marina, a travel guide, did exactly that. "Before I had the idea, I did what all of us do in this country," she told me. "I tried to find the best *atelye* I could. It's easy to get an appointment in a poor-quality one, but good *atelyes* always have long lines. You have to give the women something as a gift or a bribe. Otherwise, they are rushed, and your fittings are brief, and you have to wait weeks or even months for the finished item.

"But after I came back from a brief trip to England with one of those folding umbrellas, I had no more trouble. I gave it to the director of a good *atelye*. She found out that I went abroad now and then, and there was nothing she would not do for me. I had the best service, the best seamstress, the best materials she had to offer. All because of an umbrella so small she could slip it into her bag."

Maids who worked for Westerners can be splendidly well

dressed. Until 1981, they had the right to receive an extra month of salary each year in hard-currency coupons obtainable from the Bank of Foreign Trade. The money often went for imported clothes sold in certificate ruble Beriozka stores. Maids—and translators and drivers—kept sharp watch on colleagues to see what was available. When our own maid came to work in the morning, she took off a well-cut Finnish sheepskin coat, hung it up with her stylish imported fur hat, placed an elegant pair of gloves beside the hat, unzipped knee-high leather boots from Austria, then put on her apron and began emptying wastepaper baskets. My wife once wryly remarked that her ambition was to dress as well.

All Western contacts are treasured by the fashion-minded in the USSR. An attractive Leningrad girl I knew was sitting one day with her boyfriend in the restaurant of the Evropeiskaya Hotel when she struck up a conversation with some American men at the next table. She flirted mildly, but swears she did not encourage any serious advances. A few weeks later, a letter from New York came from one of the Americans. He enclosed a number of jazz magazines and asked if there was anything she wanted from the U.S. A second letter asked for her shoe size. She drew the outline of her foot on a piece of paper and mailed it off, not really expecting a response.

In due time a large parcel arrived, the steep customs duty prepaid in New York. Inside were *klass* riches beyond compare: four pairs of high leather boots, almost unbelievable touches of luxury in a Russian winter. She kept one pair and sold the others, and later wished she had kept them all. When eventually she emigrated she met her American friend again, and he was touched at her delight. "I felt like Santa Claus when I sent them," he said. "It was something I could do to help, and I enjoyed doing it." Meanwhile, the young man to whom she had given the magazines used them to begin a profitable sideline as a jazz expert and critic.

Many a young woman in Moscow and Leningrad willingly

spends a month's wages, 150 rubles or more, for a pair of imported winter boots. They wear them on special occasions and try to make them last for years, despite shortages of shoe polish and the rigors of the winter months.

The search for clothes of quality is unending. Unofficial "shops" can be set up anywhere by the ingenious. One young woman found it necessary to make daily trips to the women's bathroom at Leningrad State University when she was a student because foreign clothes, particularly underwear, were on sale there. A lack of attractive, feminine underwear is one of the banes of Soviet life for women. Soviet styles include brassieres that look like Viking shields and slips that are large and clumsy enough to double as tents. European students at the University are under constant pressure to sell what they do not need; the ladies' bathroom is a lively center for the swapping and buying of not just underclothes, but of cardigans, tights, boots, and handbags as well.

Even hotels can be used to set up impromptu shops for ladies' clothes. Lyuba, a plump and determined woman who worked in a small urban hotel that catered to East European tourists, remembers the electric thrill of hearing on the staff grapevine, "Quick, the Poles are selling in Room 34." In frantic haste, she and others would paw through slips, skirts, dresses, and blouses far superior to the items sold in Soviet stores.

Klass opens otherwise unobtainable fashions to Rising Class Russians. Margaret joined several Russian friends on a visit to a small, exclusive showing of fashions by Sasha Zaitsev not far from the Detsky Mir children's department store. The audience of forty people included prominent writers, officials, and actresses. The mood, and the clothes, was more Western than Russian. The styles were designed for figures of un-Slavic slenderness. They were patterned after high Western fashion but, inevitably, they were already dated. The ideas were interesting and at times striking, but small touches were lacking. Neither were the clothes helped by frowning models, some of whom seemed to have come straight from behind the department-store counters. Prices were in the 300-ruble range, which put the clothes far beyond the reach of the average Russian.

The fashion shows emphasize the gap between the clothes worn by average citizens and those available to the elite. One showing I saw in the late seventies began with faintly military, no-nonsense coats and pants suits in greens, browns, beiges, and grays. Late afternoon and evening wear went from orange to yellow, and sometimes combined both colors in the same dress, with mixed results. The shoulders were padded and square in Joan Crawford style. Sports clothes were full, loose, and blousy. The most attractive styles were based on the head scarves, full skirts, colorful bodices, and embroidery of traditional folk styles. I would have been even more impressed had I ever seen similar clothes in average department stores.

Sergei, the lone male model, appeared from time to time in pale-colored suits, always with vests and scuffed brown shoes. These men's clothes were also absent from the stores I visited. The whole showing was remote from the Urban Class people on the streets outside.

A Western friend once ventured into a small center of *klass* fashion for men simply by going up a flight of private stairs in that vast gray bazaar called the GUM department store which forms one side of Red Square. He noticed that the crowds had vanished, and that there were more hovering sales assistants than usual. Lighting was subdued, carpeting covered the floor, and display cases glittered. The atmosphere was more like the Stockmann Department store in Helsinki where many of the resident Western community do their clothes shopping. He sensed that something was amiss when the sales assistants began staring at him. He realized that he had stumbled into the clothes section of GUM reserved for senior Soviet officials.

One way to obtain quality clothing is to join a profession that provides a uniform. The reason is obvious: uniforms are made of better material than ordinary clothes. I also discovered another reason: if the head of a family happens to be a senior army or navy officer, the women in his family are able to divert part of the bolts of thick khaki or dark blue cloth issued to him twice a year, ostensibly to be made into uniforms and greatcoats.

"It was wonderful," remembers the émigré daughter of a Colonel. "Father would get this magnificent cloth. He'd have his uniforms made from it, and he'd have no need of any more cloth for years. The military is the military, and he received his bolts of cloth every six months whether he needed them or not. My mother was an excellent dressmaker, and she made the cloth up into clothes for us and for herself. She still wears one of the overcoats she made. You cannot get such fine material from the civilian shops, you see. How we looked forward to father's cloth!"

Lacking the obvious benefits of military *klass*, ordinary Soviet citizens rely on ingenuity in their quest for fashion. "I am serious," one attractive Soviet wife told me, "very serious in saying that when you are about twenty years old, good clothes are important to make men notice you. Even an unusual pair of spectacle frames can make a girl stand out from the crowd."

The attraction of fashionable spectacles in the Soviet Union became clear one bitterly cold Sunday morning in Yakutsk, thousands of miles from Moscow in eastern Siberia, as I wandered through a bazaar held on the local farmers' market. A group of smiling young women began studying me intently, whispering and smiling to each other, but my male vanity collapsed when I made out the word *ochki*. The object of their scrutiny were my silver eyeglass frames, made in Italy.

A sharp eye is always required to obtain quality fashions. A translator friend of mine was walking on a Leningrad street one August when he noticed a short line of people outside a shop. He asked, as shoppers usually do, "*Chto oni dayut!*" (not, "What's on sale?" but "What are they giving out?").

"Winter hats, good fur ones," was the reply.

Such hats usually cannot be found in winter; only in summertime are the lines short. Without hesitating, he joined the line and waited for about fifteen minutes. As many Russians do, he carried wads of ruble notes for just such a shopping emergency. Happily he paid out almost two weeks' wages for a thick fur hat with earpieces tied across the top. Soviet shops do not wrap goods, so he carried the hat home in his hand. Several people rushed up to him, asking where the hats were on sale, then sprinted away to get to the store before the stock was sold out.

Ingenuity is always essential, especially if a person is too large or too small for standard sizes. Shops for the tall and the short do not exist in the USSR. One Leningrad woman we knew was small enough to be able to buy boy's trousers at eight rubles a pair, but they were always an inch or two too short, even for her small frame. She knitted cuffs from wool and sewed them onto the trouser bottoms, pretending she had created a new fashion.

Sewing is a cherished skill. It makes good dressing possible for many who could not otherwise afford it. Russians speak fondly of ancient Singer sewing machines that have been in their families for generations, and of a newer East German model, Veritas. Many a Soviet wife and mother makes her children's clothes on an old, treadle-operated machine. A man whose wife is a skilled seamstress spreads the word quickly so that the wife can earn favors and rubles on the side in almost unlimited amounts.

Because it is easier in the Soviet Union to buy bolts of material than finished clothes, a common way to shop for clothing is to look for paper patterns, then to have the clothes made, either at home or at an *atelye*. At a fashion show at

Dom Modelei in Moscow, I found that although elite Soviet women were upstairs watching the models, the typical Urban Class women were downstairs studying paper patterns in glass cases, choosing carefully between them. Each pattern cost twenty-nine kopeks, about forty-two cents.

Some Soviet women are so skilled at sewing that they can make clothes even without patterns. Margaret's women friends liked to pore over her Western fashion magazines and choose styles they could copy with sewing machine or knitting needles. Names like Dior and Givenchy were from, and for, another world. Her friends were more interested in a dress in an advertisement or illustration that could be adapted for an office night out. The West German *Burda* magazine, seen in a Moscow office, can bring it to a standstill as women study its patterns.

To the casual observer, Soviet fashion seems quite reasonable and available. At the Vyesna (Spring) shop on the showcase Kalinin Prospect in Moscow, it even looks attractive from a distance. Well-dressed mannequins in the windows entice shoppers inside. Once there, however, the picture changes rapidly. There are constant complaints from women shoppers that the dresses displayed on the mannequins are not on the racks; nor is it possible to browse through the racks at will. So many women are perpetually hunting for something of quality that crowds are often held back by ropes. Shop assistants permit only a few people at a time to enter the area where the racks are kept.

Rarely do women bother with changing rooms. They hold up a dress against themselves or a friend, glance in a mirror, and decide. Others waiting in line often call out advice: "No, no, too big . . ." "One of the seams is coming unstitched . . ." "Yes, that's pretty . . ." Size is important but not crucial; if the fabric is good and the style passable, women buy first and plan later. If a dress or a blouse does not fit or cannot be altered, there is always a friend or relative who needs something new.

One day Margaret found herself in the Vyesna shop, the ground floor jammed with elbowing Central Asians and other out-of-towners who had come to Moscow to find clothes rarely available in their own remote areas. But it was the scene upstairs that caught her eye. Hundreds of women were lined up around the walls, trying to draw closer to a crowd at the top of the stairs. Two girls were selling machine-knitted wool cardigans, beige in color, with panels of brown suede set into either side of a central row of buttons down the front. In a Western store, such East European merchandise would sit on shelves for weeks. In one of the largest clothing stores in the Soviet superpower, the sight of them was enough to draw crowds. They were hardly bargains: the cardigans cost seventy-four rubles each, half of an average monthly wage.

"Buy one for me," called a woman to someone at the head of the line. Others behind shouted angrily that it was one to a customer. "Well, it doesn't fit," said another as she walked away with her prize, "but it doesn't matter. I know plenty of people who'll want it."

We saw similar scenes all over the country. Two thousand miles to the southeast, in Alma-Ata, the capital of Kazakhstan, men formed hasty lines when Polish shirts appeared on the second floor of a department store. The shirts were poor quality, highly colored in wide and unattractive stripes and checks, but the men bought them as if they were Cardin fashions.

The *atelye*, or custom tailor shop, is widely used in all Soviet cities. It is divided into *klass* categories, from those reserved for the Kremlin elite to the humblest room on the side street of a remote city in Moldavia. "We have never really solved the problem of clothes," recalled a Leningrad émigré. "Oh, yes, there was the *atelye*, but if you didn't know someone there, you waited for hours before you had your two fittings and, eventually, your dress or your suit. Mostly it was badly sewn. Well, you offered tips and bribes, and sometimes they worked, but it was hard to obtain a good dress. More than once I took in a roll of good material, and the *atelye* women stole half of it and skimped on the rest."

The Soviet comedian Arkady Raikin capitalized on the problem in a skit about a hand-tailored suit that emerged with one sleeve too long and the other too short. Soviet audiences were convulsed.

Women can wait between two weeks and a month for their hand-sewn dresses, and pay from twenty to thirty rubles or more for the work. "What fashions do the women who work in *atelyes* actually know?" asked one Soviet woman. "What fashion or home magazines do they see? Their wages are small, very small. They depend on gifts or bribes. If they make something you don't like, you can reject it. They will repay you the cost of the material, and then turn around and sell the dress to someone else. There's always someone else."

The European Baltic states, especially Lithuania and Latvia, have the reputation for the best *atelyes*. One shop run by a Baltic tailor in Leningrad was so good that it was nicknamed *smert' muzham*—"death to husbands," a reference to the ruinously high prices it charged. But most of the state-run *atelyes* can be such a problem in quality that many turn elsewhere. "We had our own 'little woman,'" says one Russian woman who lived in Leningrad before emigrating to London, "and we used her almost as a Western family might use its medical G.P. We were friends with her. She would come to the apartment, take tea with us, and fit us. It was a good arrangement all around."

Dressing well can cost a great deal in the Soviet Union. For all but those with the highest Top or Rising Class *klass* it takes a higher percentage of income than in the West. On Smolenskaya Square, across the main ring road from the Stalin-Gothic spire of the Foreign Ministry tower, was a men's store called Ruslan. I stopped and checked the prices in the way a Soviet citizen might do.

A black-and-white checked sports coat, produced at the Bolshevichka factory, was priced at fifty-five rubles. That was about $85, the price I would have expected to pay back home. Then I remembered that fifty-five rubles is one third of a standard monthly salary; and that made the cost equivalent to about $550 for an American earning $20,000 a year. It was not a deluxe model from a master tailor, but an ordinary jacket, for everyday use. Beside the Bolshevichka hung a smartly styled Hungarian coat in wool and synthetics, which seemed a much better buy at twenty-eight rubles (at the time, $42). Prices rose rapidly for overcoats, which are absolute necessities for most of the year. The models I saw ranged from 95 to 155 rubles, the higher figure a month's salary for millions of Urban Class people, the equivalent of more than $1,000 for an average American.

Prices for women were just as high. Even a lightweight overcoat suitable only for spring and summer was 146 rubles in downtown Moscow. Everyday dresses were 50 rubles. Tall leather boots for winter were 150 rubles, a full month's wages for a typical working woman. Stockings were 7.90 rubles a pair. The prices were almost punitive. Only those with substantial incomes could afford them.

Increasingly visitors to Moscow have been saying in recent years, "I didn't realize people dressed so well!" They mentally compare what they see today with newsreel images of the days just after World War II. Certainly, clothes have improved, and even people without *klass* manage somehow. Many an *atelye* does a serviceable job. Soviet shoppers are as determined as any I have encountered. Yet clothes have improved more slowly than in Eastern Europe, let alone the West. Rarely did we see an outfit on a Moscow street that rated a second look.

One other aspect of fashion in the Soviet Union is a continual challenge: laundry and dry cleaning. Many of the washing machines in Moscow apartments are small and not automatic. Dryers are almost unknown for the average family. Finding space to dry the washing is a problem. Dry cleaning, like many other daily Soviet activities, is an ordeal that requires endless ingenuity and patience.

Dry cleaning *punkty* (collection points) advise customers to remove all buttons in advance. Service is erratic and can take weeks. Several times we encountered mix-ups between *punkty* and the distant premises on which cleaning was actually done. While much of the cleaning was adequate, items accepted without question one month would be rejected by a different employee the next. Fortunately, perhaps, Russians wear their clothes almost into the ground. Jeans and overcoats become ingrained with grime but no one seems to mind: it is part of the price to be paid for trying to look stylish in a country where style is hard to obtain.

The desire for better clothes and fashions will grow as more people become aware of the standards even next door in Eastern Europe, and see and hear more of fashions further West. The generation now in its twenties, already searching for American jeans and Italian boots, will retain and expand its taste for Western couture. The Party makes plans to manufacture better-quality blue jeans by importing production methods and skills. No Soviet youngster is holding his breath.

Expectations for more Western-styled and Western-produced clothes by the Rising Class and the Urban Class is a consumer trend with which the Party must deal. The Kremlin is aware that the people whose loyalty it needs must be adequately rewarded by special *klass* privilege in clothes, as well as in other aspects of life. It is part of a Westernization of the Soviet Union—not in politics but in Top Class, Rising Class, and in some Urban Class ways of living.

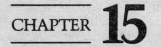
NOMENKLATURA: THE HIERARCHY OF PRIVILEGE

Across the vast white plain of Russia just below the Arctic Circle east of Arkhangelsk, blizzards sweep down onto land permanently frozen a mile deep. From a droning Aeroflot plane 10,000 feet above, it does not seem possible for a landscape to be so drained of color. The whiteness reaches away to the horizon, marked only by blurred dark lines beneath the surface showing the twisting, turning courses of the bed of the River Pechora.

Temperatures drop to minus seventy and eighty degrees Fahrenheit. Life is as bleak as the land, but hard as the winters are, Siberians prefer them to the few brief weeks of summer. Then, the top six feet or so of the permafrost begins to melt; wooden houses lean crazily a few more inches to left or right as the topsoil shifts beneath them. Rivers whose surface sheets of ice serve as highways all winter long dissolve into torrents; people must travel by boat. Docks and piers and landing stages are few and far between.

Some of the blurred lines beneath the whiteness are the edges of bogs and swamps, which trucks cannot traverse in the warmer weather. Squadrons of dive-bombing mosquitoes make work outdoors a misery. Improperly laid roads and airfields have been known to disappear into the ooze in a single summer. Workers escape to the south and the west on summer vacations, returning only when ice and permafrost have regained their grip. "The winter," Siberians say firmly, "is our friend."

In this upside-down world, far from Moscow, something else also seems, at first glance, to be wrong side up. An outsider might imagine that power lies in the hands of the local Communist Party committee and its leaders. He would discover, to his surprise, that it does not. The regional Party committee does have some authority, but genuine power belongs elsewhere: to teams of geological surveyors dispatched by central Party to headquarters to look for traces of oil and gas. Sent from Moscow and from Leningrad, they are the lords of the earth around the Pechora River.

They bring with them their own long, narrow, round-nosed exploring vehicles looking like a cross between a hydrofoil and a tank; their own supplies of food and vodka; and reserves of cash with which to hire local workers. They come and go as they please, regardless of what the local Party chief might say. He is a small cog in the countrywide machinery of the Communist Party who must answer to higher levels in his *oblast* (region) or *respublika* (republic). He lacks personal contacts in Leningrad, let alone in the shimmering, all-powerful remoteness of Moscow itself.

The survey teams are different. They report directly to Moscow, through their own separate communications lines. The chief of their Ministry, sitting on the Party Central Committee, is superior to officials at lesser Republican and *oblast* levels. The Pechora Party chief knows what that means: power, patronage, and speed of decision making. "It was a remarkable thing," recalls Vladimir Bukovsky, the dissident now living in the West. He spent some time with geological expeditions in an attempt to escape the tentacles of the Moscow KGB. "Those survey teams didn't pay much attention to the local Party men at all. In fact, it was quite the reverse. The local men would seek out the team's leader and ask him for favors—vodka, for instance, which is better than money in places like that."[1]

The scene on the Pechora River illustrates one of the important ways rank, status, and privilege—*klass*—are organized in the Soviet Union. In the West, there are many avenues through which to earn rank and status; in the land of the Kremlin, now as before 1917, only one way really counts. It used to be the favor of the tsar; now it is the patronage of the Party. The men from Moscow outranked the local Pechora men because their Party jobs were of a higher rank, closer to the capital. The very word *Moscow* means power in remoter areas of the vast Soviet Union. The framework on which the Party dispenses jobs and privileges is known as *nomenklatura*.

Nomenclature, to use the English word, is a list of names used to classify knowledge in any particular field. But in the Soviet Union, Party *nomenklatura* is three separate and secret lists of names that control the destiny of the Soviet elite. The first contains names of the positions that the Party has the sole right to fill. The second is the *osnovnoi*, or basic, list of candidates by whom the jobs can be filled. The third is the *uchetnyi*, or registered, list of candidates in reserve, being watched by senior Party officials to see whether they are loyal and hardworking enough to be promoted one day to the *osnovnoi* list.

On the face of it, *nomenklatura* is a dull word, describing a dull process. In fact, it is alive with human passion and ambition. It is part of the fabric of everyday life for any member of any social class who wants power and significant privilege. That includes all 23 million people in all three layers of the Rising Class, upper, medium, and low. To have a *nomenklatura* job means to rise above many of the shortages, lines, dirt, and frustration that make life onerous for Urban and Rural Classes. Men and women compete for *nomenklatura* status. They fight hard to hold on to it.

For a Westerner to begin to grasp what Soviet citizens know intuitively, a word is needed here about the Communist Party itself and the organization it uses to bestride one-sixth of the world's land surface from Poland to Japan.

Starting at the bottom, the basic Party unit is called a primary Party organization. It is better known to outsiders, perhaps, by its original name of "cell." It exists wherever people work, and ranges in size from fewer than fifteen members in a small office to many more in large factories. Big ones divide into subunits. In 1977, the Soviet Union contained 394,014 primary organizations and 414,000 subunits, as well as 550,000 even smaller groups. Primary organizations have the right to supervise the management of office, factory, or plant. They are not supposed to interfere directly, but may appeal to higher Party organs to step in.

Above the primary organization is the Party committee in the microdistrict of the city in which factory or office is located. In a smaller urban center, it will be a district committee. To be a Party official at this level is to begin to feel the bottom layers of real privilege in a society of general shortage and want: a black chauffeured car; an apartment in a good area; access (though limited) to good food and superior clothing in special shops; guaranteed seats on perennially overcrowded trains and planes; health-care clinics a cut above local ones where lesser mortals stand in line; some theater tickets; the ability to choose a prestigious institute or university for son or daughter.

Next comes the city Party hierarchy. In a big city such as Moscow, it is enormously powerful. The chief of the Moscow Party apparatus, Viktor Grishin, has sat for many years on the Politburo, which governs the entire country. In Moscow and in Kiev, capital of the Ukraine, city government organizations are held to be so important in themselves that they don't even report to the regional (*oblast*, roughly equivalent to a county or province in the West) Party committee nominally above them. Instead, they are under the Party committees of the Russian and Ukrainian republics respectively. The USSR has fifteen republics in all; Moscow is capital of the Russian Federation as well as of the USSR as a whole. The republic covers the width of northern Russia. The heart of the empire of the tsars, it is as big as the forty-eight contiguous American states and Canada combined.

Four other important cities break the usual hierarchical rules. Leningrad's city government reports to the Russian Federation in which it is located, although the city's Party officials (government and Party are separate in the Soviet Union) reports to the Leningrad *oblast*. The same situation applies to Minsk, capital of Belorussia; to Tashkent, the Uzbek capital, the largest city in Soviet Central Asia and a showcase of Soviet planning for Asian and other third-world visitors; and to Sebastopol, a major naval base in the Crimea, closed to Westerners.

In more normal cases, city Party groups report to *oblast* organizations. *Oblast*s report to Republic capitals. Moscow *oblast* chiefs have the extra authority and *klass* of a seat on the Central Committee of the Soviet Party, which meets in Moscow twice a year.

In theory, all power in the country resides in the Soviet Party Congress, which meets once every five years to approve the next five-year economic plan and to review the previous one. The Central Committee is supposed to run the country between Congress sessions.

In fact, real power is held in the Party Politburo in the Kremlin. Under Leonid Brezhnev it met once a week, often on Thursdays, in sessions lasting for several hours. Between meetings, decisions were taken by a select committee of the Central Committee known as the Secretariat, a small but immensely powerful group on which the most influential members of the Politburo also sit.

When the 280 or so members of the Central Committee do go to Moscow, they meet in secret for a day. All has been stage-managed in advance. The following day the 1,500 deputies of the Supreme Soviet meet. "*Soviet*" in Russian means "council," and so the Supreme Soviet is the country's nominal legislature. Never in seven decades has it rejected a recommendation by the Central Committee. Deputies are said to be elected, but in fact they are preselected by Party committees in secret and ratified by enforced and virtually unanimous "voting" in public. Any Soviet group that meets in public is sure to take only decisions previously thrashed out, decided on, and handed down in private.

Nomenklatura is not only a Party affair. Sets of *nomenklatura* lists are kept by non-Party bodies as well, including the Council of Ministers, the KGB, the Young Communist League (the Komsomol), the trade-union movement, and the Academy of Sciences. The most important lists, however, covering the jobs with the most privilege, are maintained by Communist Party committees in cities, towns, and villages. The most significant lists are the preserve of Party headquarters in Moscow.

Officially, Party headquarters uses its lists to fill Party jobs only. The Supreme Soviet is supposed to appoint government ministers and ambassadors. Formally, the Academy of Sciences, the Komsomol, and the trade unions are all able to appoint men and women to their own top, middle, and lesser positions. As is the case in so many other aspects of Soviet life, the outward show masks a different reality.

The fact is that the ruling Politburo and the Party Central Committee uses its all-powerful set of *nomenklatura* lists as the mechanism by which to keep ultimate power in its own hands. Party headquarters defines the jobs, candidates, and reserve candidates who will be included on its lists. It goes further and allocates levels of privilege to each job and grade of appointment. It has the final word on exactly what kind of jobs may be included in all non-Party *nomenklatura* lists as well.

This adds up to massive power over personnel. It is the unseen means of maintaining day-to-day Party control of virtually every important job in the Soviet Union. It works this way: only the Politburo itself can appoint or approve the appointment of Central Committee Secretariat members and those who run the KGB, police, heavy industry, the armed forces, education, science, culture, trade unions, youth affairs, and senior levels of the Academy of Sciences in Moscow, in the republic capitals, in other large cities, and in *oblast*s as well. National bodies and the Supreme Soviet in fact rubber-stamp what the Party has already decided. In reality, the Politburo selects or approves ambassadors and government ministers; it also exercises strict, though hidden, control over one other national organization with a following estimated as large as 30 million: the Russian Orthodox Church. The Patriarch and high-ranking clergy are approved by the Politburo and must conform to Party dogma in all public utterances.

On the next level down, the Central Committee Secretariat appoints officials of the rank of deputy minister in Moscow and other large cities. Through its relevant committees it appoints directors to Academy of Science institutes and senior-to middle-level Komsomol, education, youth, and cultural officials. In *oblasts*, cities, towns, and even villages, local committees of Party, government, trade union, KGB, and other branches select workers on lower levels.

Out on the Pechora River, the team leader's job was on a Central Committee list in Moscow, while the local Party man's job was inscribed only on a regional Party list. The local man could not win any test of strength.

The rank and privilege of any *nomenklatura* job depend on two things: the prestige and infighting skills of the organization that controls the position, and its location. On paper, one man can rank higher than a colleague but receive fewer benefits because he lives in Georgia while his colleague is posted to Moscow. A man in a republic capital can seem inferior to the man sitting at the desk beside him yet receive a larger apartment, a better car, and a more exclusive vacation because his job listing is controlled from Moscow. His appointment might be by the KGB or the Komsomol; the other man may have been appointed by a non-Party body.

The deputy director of an Academy of Sciences institute is supposed to be senior to the number-three man below him. But if the number-three man is a Moscow appointee and the deputy director owes his job to a regional Academy listing, the Moscow man with a Central Committee *nomenklatura* will carry more weight.

Before he emigrated to the West, Professor Alexander Zinoviev confirmed in a long talk with me and with the former Moscow bureau chief for the Reuters news agency, Robert Evans, that Central Committee listings were the most valuable. They even included, he said, "trainers, Olympic coaches, and sportsmen, as well as directors of large institutes and ranking professors at Moscow State University."

Rank was not always obvious in the Soviet Union. "You always have to remember," said the professor, "that in the Soviet Union people are not ranked by their official duties. Our society is more complicated than that. You in the West will never really understand it." He made a distinction between privilege and advantage. He defined advantage as those *klass* benefits an individual could extract from his job. The director of an Institute had his Academy of Sciences ranking; his deputy fared better because of his Central Committee listing, but the institute's deputy director for finance might well extract even more day-to-day advantage than the other two because his *otdel*, or department, controlled the car pool and he himself authorized the use of each car. That brought him a stream of return favors that made his life one of socialist privilege.

When a Westerner meets a group of Soviet officials, it is often difficult or impossible for him to tell who holds the most power. The man who speaks for the group may in fact report to the faceless individual in the corner. The captain of a ship, for example, is under the ultimate control of the senior Party official among his officers. Outsiders cannot tell the Party man because he wears a naval officer's uniform like the others, but every Russian on the ship knows who he is, just as they know the identity of the KGB man on board. Since the Party and the KGB men are responsible to Moscow for anything that happens on the voyage, theirs is the final power to decide to stay in port, to set sail, or to turn back. The captain is in charge only of navigation and practical details. He is subject to superior *nomenklatura*.

Nomenklatura is a maze of vertical and horizontal lines of power. To rise to a *nomenklatura* job, even a non-Party one, is considered a major achievement in the Soviet Union today, as it was to reach the lowest of the fourteen grades of rank, or *chin*, on the Table of Ranks under the tsars between 1722, when Peter the Great established it, and 1917, when the Revolution replaced it.

Deep within the crisscrossing network is the thread of political surveillance. One false step and *klass* can be forfeited. Always watching is the committee for state security, better known by its three transliterated initials, KGB. The Party Politburo in Moscow appoints the KGB chief, who until 1982 was Yuri Andropov and is now Viktor Chebrikov. It also names his senior deputies, as well as the top rank of the ministry of internal Affairs, or MVD. Both the KGB and MVD possess their own *nomenklatura* lists, radiating outward from KGB headquarters in Lubyanka and MVD offices on Granovsky Street. The KGB is the country's personnel agency at home and abroad. The MVD is the domestic police force, operating in public and in secret.

Nomenklatura complications arise in the fifteen capital cities of the Soviet republics where party leaders (First Secretaries) have been native ethnic figures since 1953: a Russian in the Russian Federation, a Ukrainian in the Ukraine, a Georgian in Georgia. The Second Secretary is usually a Russian, and always so in sensitive, not fully trusted areas such as the three Baltic states. The Second Secretary is Moscow's man. He runs the local KGB and personally reports on the work of the First Secretary above him. The standard procedure is to have a First Secretary in a republic appointed by the Politburo, and the Second Secretary appointed or confirmed by the Politburo in consultation with the KGB, whose own *nomenklatura* is subject to Party confirmation. When Stalin died, the Central Committee strengthened its own authority to make sure that there were no more Lavrenti Berias, the KGB chief who tried to seize power after Stalin.

The principle of KGB surveillance is expressed in the euphemism *doveryai, no proveryai*—"trust, but check." When

Eduard Shevardnadze became First Secretary of his republic, Georgia, he knew that his Second Secretary would begin sending a stream of reports back to the KGB in Moscow on his behavior. Shevardnadze was in a good position to counteract those reports because of his status as a nonvoting member of the Politburo and his personal ties at the time to Brezhnev and other senior figures, yet he still had to reckon with his number two's reports as facts of life.

Shevardnadze's case was more complex than most. Like the First Secretary of Azerbaijan, Geydar Aliev, he was a senior officer in the KGB before reaching the Politburo. Shevardnadze had extensive experience inside the Soviet Union, while Aliev was a senior agent in Latin America. It might seem unnecessary for such graduates of inner KGB councils to be subjected to KGB reports, but that is the *nomenklatura* way. No one in the hierarchy is exempt. There is always the possibility that the KGB will dominate, but so far the Politburo seems to have balanced its need for KGB surveillance with its own requirement to hold the agency in check.

Power shifts and flows among the balance of Party, the KGB, and the military leadership. Muscovites say they can feel changes in the power balance as instinctively as Westerners might sense changes in atmospheric pressure, "through our very skins," as émigré Vladimir Solovyov puts it. Power moves according to individual issues and personalities. Such changes have included alternate hard-line and soft-line approaches to Jews and hesitation and delay in punishing some of the compilers of semidissident prose and poetry, including the *Metropol* anthology in the late 1970s. Conventional wisdom is that the KGB at one time in the 1970s advocated a tougher line against Jews and dissidents than the Brezhnev faction, which was working with "détente" and felt too much open pressure would alienate world opinion.

The Party could have chosen other, less complex ways of retaining power and apportioning privilege than *nomenkla-*

tura. In 1917, Lenin could have decided upon a strict chain-of-command structure. The Moscow Central Committee of the Party could have appointed the fifteen republican committees; these could have controlled the regional Party committees (*obkoms*) in their own territories; the *obkoms* could have been responsible for filling city Party committees (*gorkoms*) and the cities could have handled *raion* committees and state-farm directors. This was not the method Lenin chose. Nor does today's system resemble the conception commonly held in the West: a Party organization running parallel to the government apparatus at every point, controlling it by having a regional Party man supervise a regional government official, a city Party man a city official, and so on.

Instead, the Central Committee in Moscow holds all real power in its own hands. It appoints all significant Party and government posts throughout the country, from republic Central Committees to the heads of the more important *obkoms* comparable in importance to American states.[2] Moscow appoints the senior Party officials in the larger cities. The aim is a flow of information and accountability from the field back to the Center, and channels of command from Moscow to wherever they are needed. It is a system that ensures that power is shared and divided at local levels rather than dominated by one man. The first two goals have been largely achieved; the third has given Moscow more trouble.

An *obkom* Party secretary is a powerful figure,[3] the ruler of his territory, usually appointed by Moscow. If he is ambitious and unscrupulous, he can do a lot on his own, provided he keeps his industrial production up to standards set by the Plan. But his senior staff—Party instructors, organizers, lecturers, administrators—are not directly appointed by him. They answer to the Central Committee of his republic. The chief cannot fire or move them outright but must play politics, for Moscow retains ultimate authority. The same basic system is found at lower levels: city and district Party chiefs are appointed by the next highest Party levels (republican or regional) while the senior workers "beneath" them are appointed locally.

So important are larger groups of factories in Moscow, Leningrad, Minsk, and Baku, that they are supervised directly by the Central Committee in Moscow. When it comes to directing factories, *obkom* Party chiefs can jump in without even consulting city or district Party men below them. One way to measure the low priority and status the Party gives to the average consumer and his retail shops, eating places, hospitals, polyclinics, courts, secondary schools, and kindergartens is to see who appoints the heads of these establishments. The answer is the government, usually the executive committees of the local *oblasts*; but the posts are not important enough for the Party to intervene directly. The *obkoms* spend their time on Party affairs, particularly on ensuring that regional factories meet industrial targets set in Moscow. Unless he performs well, an *obkom* chief might be demoted to a lesser *nomenklatura*, a step that would be nothing short of a *klass* disaster.

About forty minutes' drive through snowy birch forests from Novosibirsk, the biggest city in Siberia, lies another example of how *nomenklatura* works. The chief of the Novosibirsk *gorkom* is a figure of some stature, with contacts in Moscow, but one man in the city is free to obey him or not, as he chooses. He is the director of a discreetly placed collection of well-built apartment houses and laboratories known as Akademgorodok, literally, "the little Academy town."

The director derives his independence from the *nomenklatura* system because he is also a deputy director of the USSR Academy of Sciences in Moscow and takes his orders directly from the Academy's chief director. The director during my days in Moscow, Anatoly Alexandrov, was in turn a full member of the Central Committee and one of the most powerful men in the intellectual and military-industrial communities.

The Academy is a remarkable institution. The Party depends on it for the scientific and technical skills that underpin its superpower status. It is almost a private empire of privilege within the USSR. The Academy has its own links to scientists and institutions abroad, and its own *nomenklatura* at home, which extends to 246 Academy Institutes, including Akademgorodok. In 1980 it employed 41,836 of the brightest minds in the country, more than half of them with a doctoral degree or higher. Its *nomenklatura* was strong and sought-after, especially for the 241 elected Academicians and 437 nonvoting members. It provided its senior members with handsome apartments in choice locations, elite food and clothing shops, an Academy limousine for traveling to meetings and on other Academy business, and a measure of intellectual freedom from the daily supervision of Party hacks.

Nikita Khrushchev established Akademgorodok in 1957 as a place where prominent scientists could work in peace and seclusion. He showered it with privilege. By the early 1960s, reports were filtering back to Moscow of parties with Western jazz music, Western movies, and exhibitions of modern art that were still taboo in Moscow and Leningrad. When I visited it, some 25,000 scientists were working in the birch forests, establishing worldwide reputations in such fields as petroleum and chemical catalysts (G. K. Boreskov); economics (Abel Gazevich Aganbegyan, and Nobel Prize-winner Leonid Kantorovich); computers (Yuri Ivanovich Marchuk); and geological research (Andrei Trofimyuk).

An order from the Novosibirsk *gorkom* to the head of Akademgorodok need not necessarily be obeyed. Instead of implementing the *gorkom*'s order to have more Party lectures on Soviet triumphs in foreign policy for example, Akademgorodok scientists might go skiing. In case of a dispute between the scientists and the politicians, the city chief could appeal to the Novosibirsk *oblast* Party chief, who is a member of the Central Committee. Whether the *oblast* chief would prevail would depend on the issue and the moment.

Except at the top, the system safeguards against excessive individual power. One safety measure is to have a person controlled by more than one *nomenklatura* list. Senior Akademgorodok officials are appointed by the Academy, confirmed by the sciences department of the Central Committee, and may be on the Central Committee's reserve *(uchetnyi)* list for future promotion as well.

In an important factory in the Ukraine, the director would be approved by the local *obkom* or *gorkom*, and lower-ranking officials by lesser Party organs. The ministry in charge of production in the field would have a *nomenklatura* covering some of the senior posts on the shop floor. Many managers would be on both a Party and ministry list. Some would be on a ministry list only and their privileges would depend on the weight their ministry carried in Moscow. Steel workers, coal miners, oil and gas drillers, and skilled construction specialists tend to have the best apartments, vacations, and access to health care and private cars. Statisticians, librarians, shop assistants, psychiatrists, and philologists—so-called nonproductive workers—receive less.

Late one Moscow afternoon I came face-to-face with some of the intricacies of *nomenklatura* and Soviet power when I talked with three members of the Young Communist League, or Komsomol. The League organizes 38 million young people between the ages of fifteen and twenty-eight. I asked to meet some delegates to the congress of the Komsomol in Moscow, an event held once every five years.

Across a long table from me in a Komsomol headquarters conference room sat three young men, carefully selected for their Communist zeal. Nikolai Sudarikov, smiling and neat in an open-necked shirt and brown jacket, entered the giant Moskvich auto plant when he was sixteen, had joined the

Komsomol at the same time, and had done well in both. Now twenty-eight, he was a tool maker and designer earning twice the salary of an average worker, and secretary (leader) of a cell of fifteen Komsomol members. He was deeply involved in a range of Komsomol work including propaganda, sports, and social events. His Komsomol duties kept him running in his lunch break and filled his hours before and after work and on weekends. He had been selected as a deputy to the Supreme Soviet of the Russian Federation.

Nikolai's *nomenklatura* was complex. Friends explained later that he would have been on the prestigious list of the Moscow party, and so under the eye of Politburo member Viktor Grishin, the Moscow Party chief, and of a department of the Central Committee. He would also have been on the reserve list of the Russian Federation's Party. As a worker in the Moskvich plant, he was subject to general supervision by the automobile ministry, although he took his main direction, and privileges, from the Moscow Party and Komsomol. Many eyes were on him; many reports written about him. Ahead lay great possibilities, and dangers.

Slumped into a chair beside him was Nikolai Minin, who looked drawn as he twisted an ornate leather watchstrap and talked about his nonstop life. He had not joined the Komsomol until he was eighteen and in the navy for his national service. He felt he was drifting, he said, until he fell in with a group of friends who were Komsomol members. Also twenty-eight, he was studying for a graduate degree from Moscow Teachers' Institute. The Institute was a big Komsomol center, with 8,000 members among its enrollment of 11,000. Nikolai led a local Party group. He worked through lunch and on weekends; appointed to the Moscow Committee for the Komsomol, he toured the city supervising branch work and hearing complaints and suggestions.

Minin was also a deputy to the Supreme Soviet of the Russian Federation and a full member of the Communist Party. He would have been on the *nomenklatura* of the Moscow Party or of the Russian Federation's Central Committee, and on an *uchetnyi* reserve list as well. For part of the day he would have been under the supervision of the Institute; because of his various posts, he would have had a larger degree of privilege than other Komsomol members.

The third man at the table was a scientist with a black beard, Vladimir Ochkin, a physicist whose work in plasma and laser research had already earned him a trip to lecture at Oxford and Cambridge. He was thirty-three (showing that Komsomol work does not always end at twenty-eight). Scientists tend to have less time for, and interest in, ideological affairs, and only 800 out of the 4,000 scientists at his Academy of Sciences Moscow Institute of Physics belonged to the Komsomol. Dr. Ochkin had joined at the age of fifteen. He was now a full Party member and also sat on the Moscow Komsomol Committee. He would have been on the *nomenklatura* of the Russian Federation's Central Committee, on a Party *uchetnyi* list, and also on the *nomenklatura* of the powerful Academy of Sciences.

Government officials and bodies in the Soviet Union are far from independent: they exist to execute Party decisions. The Party appoints their senior levels, but from the Council of Ministers down to city executive committees, they too have their own *nomenklatura* lists. The Moscow Central Committee appoints senior ("All-Union") ministers and supervises most others.

The Central Committee also controls the Soviet military at all levels, with the aim of nullifying the possibility of armed threat. The Committee works through its Chief Political Administration, which appoints political officers throughout the officer corps. The KGB is heavily involved as well, reporting to itself and to the Politburo.

Just before his unit moved into Czechoslovakia in 1968, a former armed forces company commander saw a group of officers and sergeants being briefed in the open by the KGB.[4] Briefings were usually held in private to keep secret the identity of the KGB informers, but the situation was so urgent that there was no time to hide. The commander strained to identify the faces of the *stukachi* (informers). "Familiar faces—oh, hell, that dark guy! I never would have thought . . ." the commander, who emigrated to the West, wrote later. He was certain that the informers had been told to shoot any Soviet soldier or officer who tried to defect to the Czech side. The commander also saw the "legal *stukachi*," or Party workers in uniform.

"In every platoon consisting of thirty soldiers and sergeants there is a Komsomol secretary and his two assistants, plus a platoon agitator, plus an editor of the *Boevoi Listok* (military newspaper). Indeed, every detachment of seven soldiers has its own *Boevoi Listok* correspondent," the commander wrote.[5] When his vehicle moved into Czechoslovakia, the officer who sat beside him was a candidate member of the Communist Party. He suspected that his signals officer was a KGB *stukach*; his machine-gunner was definitely a KGB man; and in front of him was a Party representative. Ideological control over the Soviet military is obviously not taken for granted.

Officers are integrated carefully into Party life. Ninety percent are members of the Party or Komsomol. A Party card is obligatory for majors and above. Political officers control the daily armed-forces newspaper published from Moscow, *Krasnaya Zvezda (Red Star)* and other publications. To avoid commanders becoming too closely identified with local Party leaders, the boundaries of the sixteen Soviet military districts are drawn so that they do not coincide with republic or regional borders.

The trade-union movement, with a membership of 121 million, is held under equally tight rein by the Moscow Central Committee. Unlike unions in the West, the Soviet variety do not fight for the economic interests of the workers. They are conveyor belts for Party instructions, carrying punishments and rewards to industrial and collective farm employees. Soviet trade unions work with their employer, the government, and not against it. They have their own *nomenklatura* for relatively minor posts, but the union movement as a whole carries little of the *klass* of senior Party, government, or military posts.

Nomenklatura lists created by the Party even determine who is "elected" to office. The Kremlin presents the system as "democratic." It insists that one level of authority elects the next one up the ladder, from districts to cities to *oblasts* to republics to Moscow. Regions send delegates to the Party Congress every five years, and in theory they elect the Central Committee. The same process is said to operate within the Party in the republics, trade unions, and the Komsomol. Secretaries of local Party branches are supposed to be elected. So are the chairmen of executive committees at all levels of government, even collective farm committees.

In reality, everyone is appointed, basically from the top down; it is the opposite of democratic rule. The Party has its own lists of approved candidates for every "elected" post. The number of candidates rarely exceeds the number of posts to be filled. Elections to the two chambers of the country's Supreme Soviet, 1,500 deputies in all, are well rehearsed, in secret, although after much effort, some foreign correspondents did manage to attend a long meeting at the end of the 1970s at which a candidate was presented to the Supreme Soviet. It was, as Robin Knight of *U.S. News and World Report* recalled, "excruciatingly dull, so much so that at least one of the officials on the platform nodded off as the speeches continued."[6] One after another, seven officials representing Party, government, Komsomol, trade unions, and three other organizations rose to their feet and made precisely the same speech down to the last detail of the candidate's life history. The audience sat impassively, rousing itself only to clap at the right moments.

Far more interesting would have been the Party meeting at which the candidate was selected and his actual qualifications discussed. Our requests to attend such meetings were denied.

To vote for a candidate, all the voter has to do is collect the ballot paper and place it in the box, with no mark required.

To vote *against* the Party candidate, a Soviet citizen must cross the floor of the hall, in full view of the officials present, and enter a special curtained booth where he may, if he is brave enough, delete a name, and even write in a new one. He must then emerge from the booth and drop his ballot paper in the box. It is less conspicuous, and safer, to vote for someone.

As with other *nomenklatura* jobs, accession to elected office carries privileges. Deputies to the Supreme Soviet receive two paid trips to Moscow each year to attend sessions; they shop in elite *klass* stores and have preference in obtaining apartments and private cars. One special advantage is being able to bypass the dense crowds in all Soviet train stations and airports and to use secluded waiting rooms reserved for officials. A special staff takes luggage and clips tickets in an atmosphere of *klass*. In Central Asian Republics, such waiting rooms are air-conditioned.

In return for their privileges, deputies applaud speeches in both the Council of Nationalities and the Council of the Union, and sit on various commissions. Their actual duties are light. Year after year I saw Deputies chatting or leafing through newspapers as Politburo members and ministers read long speeches from the dais. When called upon, 1,500 hands went into the air as one to approve whatever Party decision had been put before them.

Only the scientific community is somewhat freer from the Party yoke. Elections in the Academy of Sciences are more difficult to fix. The Politburo appoints the head of the Academy and the KGB watches the apparatus immediately below him, but the 241 Academicians and the 437 nonvoting members are elected by the scientific community in which the Party's room for maneuvering is somewhat more limited than usual.

Even when the Party has exerted strong pressure, as in the case of dissident Andrei Dmitrievich Sakharov, the Academy held out as long as it could. The tall, cerebral Sakharov developed the Soviet hydrogen bomb, turned against the Party, and went on to win the 1975 Nobel Peace Prize for his defense of individual freedoms. He remained the most prominent dissident of all, yet, until he was abruptly exiled to the city of Gorky in January 1980, he retained the use of an official Academy car and the right to submit scientific papers even after years of dissident defiance.

The Party attacked him publicly and in private, as Stalin had the brilliant physicist, the late Pyotr Kapitsa, when Kapitsa refused to work on the atomic program in the 1930s. Kapitsa was forbidden to travel abroad for thirty-one years, from 1934 to 1965, but he was not arrested. Even Stalin realized he could not execute a world-renowned scientist without risking the refusal of other Soviet scientists to work on new military and industrial projects. Besides, Stalin needed Kapitsa's skills in other fields, and eventually built him his own institute complete with luxury apartments for senior staff.[7] Scientists can be a puzzle for the Politburo. They may be forced to work, but they cannot be intimidated to create on demand.

Nomenklatura is designed to retain power and the dispensing of privilege in the hands of Party headquarters in Moscow; the Party might benefit from the system, but the country does not. *Nomenklatura* not only rules the USSR, it chokes it. It leads to a conservative, play-it-safe approach, and encourages the survival of the most mediocre politicians. It leaves the country open to patronage and personal power, with all the opportunities for self-aggrandizement patronage brings. The Party tries to prevent it, but it is endemic in the way Soviet society is set up.

The system encourages more and more central control, whether it be from Moscow or a republic or *oblast* capital. The Party is tempted to solve problems, such as when factories do not meet production targets, by pulling key posts including chief engineers and skilled workers from a lower *nomenklatura* to a higher one to achieve tighter supervision, as well as more privilege, for the man being promoted: stick and carrot. Too often the procedure squelches what the country needs most—local initiative and imagination.

Those who have achieved Party *nomenklatura* enjoy the vacation passes, food, clothing, and extra apartment space it brings. They may or may not believe in Party ideology, but they know that the red Party card is necessary for further success. One Soviet friend referred to his card as his *khlebnaya knizhka*, or "bread book," something he needed to garner more *klass*.

Being a member of the Party provides other privileges. A Party member is usually immune from prosecution unless his local party organ has given prosecuting authorities the green light. A Party member may appeal to his local branch to have an investigation halted. In addition, he can use his local Party office like a labor exchange, asking it to find him a better job. Party committees can tell him where his skills are needed elsewhere in the city or in the country, perhaps at a higher salary and with more attractive privileges. A member's local Party branch keeps his name on a card index and he may not be moved from his job—promoted, demoted, transferred—unless the local branch agrees. Approval can often be routine, but circumstances vary.[8]

The Party protects its own. When the first secretary of the Azerbaijan central committee, Akhundov, was forced to resign for accepting systematic bribes for making appointments to the state and Party apparatuses, he was elected vice president of the Azerbaijan Academy of Sciences a few months later.

That investigation of Akhundov was carried out by Geydar Aliev, and it helped propel him into the top Party post in Azerbaijan. In Georgia, Eduard Shevardnadze was minister of internal affairs when he exposed his Party chief Vasily Mzhavanadze, who was a friend of Khrushchev's. Mzhavanadze was not expelled from the Party; instead, he received a personal pension five times higher than usual. His second secretary, Churkin, was expelled, but was picked up by another Party *nomenklatura* and appointed to a Party post in the Russian Federation. In 1976–77, a series of trials in Uzbekistan implicated a woman who had just been appointed to the post of chairman of the Supreme Soviet Council of Nationalities in Moscow. She was not expelled, but was appointed a deputy minister for industry instead.[9]

High office is often a passport to riches in the three republics of the Caucasus and the five in Central Asia. Large bribes have been reported given to Party officials to extract important *nomenklatura* appointments: the job of Party leader of a district committee had been secured by the payment of between 150,000 and 200,000 rubles to a republican Central Committee functionary in Georgia and Azerbaijan. The position of minister for social security in the two republics has cost 100,000 rubles, and the job of minister for trade, who controls all retail shops, went for 250,000 rubles.

The Marquis de Custine traveled through imperial Russia 150 years ago looking for evidence to support a return of the monarchy to France. He was struck by Peter the Great's 1722 Table of Ranks, established with fourteen grades of *chin*, or rank, for the civil servants, nobles, and the military. He commented that:

> It is solely the will of the tsar which brings about advancement of the individual ... the favor of advancement is never asked for, but always maneuvered ... there is in this an immense power of fermentation which is put at the disposal of the chief of state. ....
>
> Such a social organization produced a fever of envy ... a straining of minds towards ambition.[10]

This is still an accurate description of *nomenklatura* today. It is a mechanism of control and favor operated by the tsar's heirs, the Communists. It keeps millions of people scheming for the advantages of promotion, and toward avoiding its opposite. It rewards the obedient with consumer goods and privilege, and encourages mediocrity through fear of losing these rewards.

It remains to be seen whether the roots of *klass* will in time grow so deep that they will cause the political earth above them to shift, or whether Party *nomenklatura* will continue to dictate the behavior and ambition of the Soviet Urban, Rising, and Top social classes.

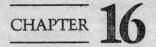

CAN *KLASS* CHANGE THE SOVIET UNION?

> Do you need an explanation
> What the Russian God can be?
> Here's a rough approximation
> As the thing appears to me. . . .
>
> God of medals and of millions,
> God of yard-sweepers unshod,
> Lords in sleighs with two postilions,
> That's him, that's your Russian God.
>
> Fools with grace, wise men be wary,
> There he never spares the rod,
> God of everything contrary,
> That's him, that's your Russian god.
> —Prince P. A. Vyazemsky, 1828.[1]

As Russia was yesterday, so is the Soviet Union today: a country of medals and millions, of poor yard-sweepers and a hierarchy of privilege, of great gaps between social ranks and subranks.

The Kremlin, of course, would have us think otherwise. It favors pronouncements of Utopian possibilities: "Today all sectors of our society have accepted the ideological and political positions of the working class, and the collective farm peasantry and intellectuals are jointly (with it) building a communist classless society where there will be no social distinctions at all."[2]

That is no more true than this sign, spotted on a collective farm building: "Liquidation of differences in social, economic, cultural, and living standards between city and country is one of the greatest achievements of the building of communism." However, almost 16 million people fled the boredom, isolation, and primitive conditions of village and farm to Soviet cities in the 1970s alone.

The "classless" society of the Soviet Union is in fact filled with sharply differentiated rank, status, and access to privilege. Urban and Rural Classes endure cramped apartments, cabbage-and-potato meals, long lines, chronic shortages, and monotonous lives, while above them stretch ladders of privilege, each rung carrying its own prized portion of *klass*. Collectively the rungs reach up through section chiefs, foremen, and supervisors to local, regional, and central Party and government officials; to military officers, scientists, and police; to intelligentsia, performing artists, and many more elites as well.

Politically speaking, the Soviet Union may be a one-party, centralized state, but socially its expanding Rising Class has begun to mirror the middle classes of the West rather than blaze a unique ideological path of its own. In the names of Marx, Engels, Lenin, and Stalin, the Party has tried to leapfrog the bourgeois stage that began under the tsars. It attempted to catapult society from a near-feudal state in 1917 directly into advanced socialism. It continues to promise full communism as the next and final step. Yet the effort to avoid the ascendancy of the social class known to the West as the bourgeoisie has failed. The Rising Class has come alive in the USSR. It seeks prestige and status. It is growing. Restlessly and insistently, it searches for larger apartments, foreign travel, better food, more stylish clothes, improved and less impersonal health care, more comfortable and convenient vacations, private cars, and university places for its children. This materialism helps fill a vacuum in individual lives caused by the failure of state Marxist atheism to provide compelling alternative causes or ideals.

Today almost one in every five Soviet citizens has access to some significant form of *klass*.[3] Throughout history, bourgeois and upper-bourgeois classes everywhere have been ambitious and creative; they have created great cities and filled them with the symbols of status and self-expression: homes, shops, consumer goods, architecture, music, literature, theaters, museums, churches. In America, the rise of the middle classes helped create more wealth and military power than the world had ever before seen, all accomplished with a set of unique political institutions based originally on religious conviction. With a surging, frontier-style energy, the profit motive, private enterprise, and a dominant world position after World War II, America has helped to change the West. Its own vigorous middle classes have served as examples for striving bourgeoisies elsewhere, particularly in Western Europe.

In the Soviet Union, the process has been very different. The middle class has been much smaller. For centuries, trade was largely barter. Cities were small, and the central authority of the tsar was not significantly weakened. Accustomed to strong central rule; knowing little of decentralized, democratic ways; cut off in remote areas by snow in winter and mud in the spring; taught by the Russian Orthodox Church that the tsar ruled by divine right and that secular authority was to be obeyed; all this has meant that the average citizen is more submissive, more long-suffering, more fatalistic than in the West.

Remoteness means ignorance and distorted ideas about the outside world. Russians were, and are, both too pessimistic and too optimistic about themselves. They swing between excessive criticism of the West and adulation of it. Two decades ago, many Russians said *"u nas luchshe"* ("we have it better here"). Today many of the new Soviet bourgeoisie say *"u vas luchshe"* ("you have it better there"); some shake their heads and add, *"u nas khuzhe"* ("here it's worse").

Russia resembles Winston Churchill's famous description of October 1, 1939, "a riddle wrapped in a mystery inside an enigma." It is a paradox as well. Its people combine a superiority complex—with an equally deep inferiority complex. By definition almost any Western product is deemed by many of the Rising Class to be better than a Soviet one. In 1982, to give an example, Soviet factories were turning out an insecticide that worked well against the armies of cockroaches that have long occupied city buildings; but the Rising Class still sought out cans of bug spray from Helsinki. One Russian listened carefully to my praise of the Soviet brand, and shook his head. "I'm sure," he said with finality, "that the Finnish spray is better." The same holds true for cars and cosmetics, for clothes and shoes, for stereos and digital watches, for movies and pop music.

The Rising Class is continually and increasingly aware of the outside world. In Moscow, Leningrad, Kiev, Minsk, and the Baltic capitals, it sees more foreign tourists than ever before. It scrutinizes background scenes in news and documentary films on television for clues to Western life. It reads between the lines in *Pravda* and *Izvestia*. It lives better than its parents did, and it knows it; but it wants more.

Consumer expectations are rising rapidly. *Izvestia* correspondent Melor Sturua was perhaps more accurate than he meant to be when, soon after I arrived in Moscow, he told me in his office that the Soviet Union was no longer immune to the Yellow Submarine of the Beatles' song, the common craft on which the whole world had to live together. He was trying to say that the Soviet Union was as sophisticated as the West; he boasted that his own children wore jeans and listened to rock music. Indeed they did: Sturua had served several terms as *Izvestia* correspondent in New York.[4]

In private, however, and for most of its citizens, the Party tries to hold Western influences in check. Sometimes, in non-political areas, its strategy is to co-opt Western ways and control their spread (much as it did in 1984, for instance, with classes of Jane Fonda–type aerobic exercises; it announced "official" classes to pop music but failed to produce the leotards, tights, and sweat bands that help create the aerobics image in the West).[5]

Sturua himself represented the topmost rungs of the Rising Class. He had come a long way from the heady days of the 1917 Revolution, when his parents chose his first name, Melor, because the first five letters in it stood for Marx, Engels, Lenin, October, and Revolution. Another name popular in those years was Vladlen, for Vladimir Lenin. It would be rare indeed for the current generation to bestow such names on its children. The fervor has gone. It has been largely replaced by the search for *klass*.

The search tends to be more concentrated than in the West, and less distracted by other channels for middle-class energies, such as involvement or interest in public affairs, or the individual's right to have his voice heard in government or foreign policy, no matter how small that voice might be. The new Soviet bourgeoisie cannot take up politics or develop admired antiestablishment ideas. The Party sets itself as the judge of permissible political expression. It maintains the monopoly on political power. At the same time, the Rising Class does not wrestle with large mortgages or complex money management. Rents are low. Basic health and education are free. Salaries are also poor by Western standards, but the Rising Class has the time and the rubles to devote itself to the search for *klass* with single-minded drive.

The result is, in part, a new Soviet middle class turned in upon itself, often simply ignoring government and public issues, and bored by its officially controlled media. It concentrates its energies on its families and friends. It spends endless hours cultivating contacts on the job, among relatives and friends, and anywhere else it can, to extract status and privilege from a system which perpetuates civilian shortage and want.

In 1920, young people crowded into the second congress of the Communist Youth League and listened as Lenin told them, in his high-pitched, intense voice, that those aged fifteen would live and work under full communism in their own lifetimes. Of that audience, those who have survived purge, collectivization of farm land, and war are approaching eighty today. They have long since discovered that Lenin was much too optimistic. They are by no means living under an egalitarian communism. Nor did they outstrip the United States in living standards by 1980, as Nikita Khrushchev once boasted they would.

According to the late Mikhail Suslov, they are living under something called "developed socialism," or "the state of the whole people." Individuals are still rewarded unequally. Only at some future time are they to be rewarded according to their needs. Marx and Engels, it seems, did not envision a large and growing Rising Class grasping for bourgeois ways with greater energy than that with which it advances the cause of socialism. The relentless pursuit of *klass* refutes the ultimate theory of Marxism–Leninism.

What might this refutation mean for the Soviet people? For the Kremlin? For the West? Could it be a long-sought key to open the Russian soul to wider Western influence, perhaps even to some form of greater acceptance of Western states? Might the leaven of *klass* and privilege eventually reduce the threat of a suspicious, isolated, often medieval Soviet outlook, one which has used its socialist ideology to justify expansionism abroad and one-party rule at home?

Well, perhaps. But not soon, and certainly not now.

The changes taking place are comparatively recent. Lenin himself appeared little interested in personal ostentation, but privileges for the Party, and for Top and Rising and Military Officer Classes, have existed since 1918. One veteran émigré recalls that in the Moscow of 1918, while people were starving in the streets, cooks would not serve soup to Party leaders inside buildings on Gorky Street unless it was so thick with meat and vegetables that a spoon could stand upright in it unaided.

Stalin codified privilege as he established industry and millions flocked from countryside to city. In the poorest major industrial society on earth, traditionally one of the least rich countries of Europe, the roots of a Rising Class began to spread: senior and middle-ranking Party and government officials, office managers, factory directors, Jews who filled gaps left by exiled or flown Russians, the best of the new workers in steel, oil, and natural gas, army officers, intellectuals, scientists, artists and performers, senior lawyers, medical specialists. Stalin widened the circle to include the cultural figures; the growth of industry and the outbreak of World War II meant new *klass* rewards for scientists and the military.

Stalin died on March 5, 1953. By 1957 Nikita Khrushchev felt firm enough in power to allow a World Youth Congress to spill tens of thousands of young outsiders over central Moscow, playing guitars in the streets and opening the eyes of young Soviet intellectuals to the manners, clothes, and ideas of other societies. It was Khrushchev who encouraged special high schools teaching English, math, and other subjects, helping to give official sanction to the notion that some children were more gifted, more sophisticated, and therefore more deserving of *klass,* than others.

It was Leonid Brezhnev who presided over almost two decades without major purges or Party upheavals, allowing the concept of *klass* to take deeper hold. Détente with the U.S. in the first half of the 1970s opened up Party, professional, and creative elites to Western ideas and to travel; even after détente had iced over, by 1980, the exposure continued to nourish the increasing sophistication of the Rising Class.

The search for *klass* is not necessarily a dissident political movement. So far, in fact, it has taken place without an overt political dimension. The various strands of the dissident movement—nationalistic and religious—have acted under the banner of human rights rather than consumerism. The bulk of Soviet citizens with *klass* privileges want more of them; they are unlikely to support dissidents who could upset their desires. Much of *klass* acts as a conservative rather than a radical force. To speak out against the status quo leads to a loss of privilege, as Andrei Sakharov, Anatoly Shcharansky, Volodya and Maria Slepak, Yuri Orlov, and a host of other dissidents can attest.

So far the Party is firmly in control. It governs an empire without hint that it might take its own advice to the West and decolonize. Imperial Russia marched its troops into south Azerbaijan at about the same time that Britain seized Ceylon. It moved into Uzbekistan when London claimed Nigeria. It took what is now Turkmenia when the Raj began in Ghana. All three British possessions have long since become independent, but the tsars' conquests remain integral parts of the USSR.[6] Since then, the Kremlin has added parts of Poland and the three Baltic states, a slice of Finland (Vyborg), political control of Eastern Europe, and dominance in Mongolia.

The empire is held together by force, fear, and by a degree of self-interest among the ruled: Christian Armenia is free from encroachment by Moslem Turkey as long as it stays a part of the Soviet Union.

The Kremlin feels it cannot allow any doubt to linger about its ability to rule it. Having moved into Afghanistan, the bear must keep control there, or perceived weakness might encourage the Poles, or the rest of Eastern Europe, to test its grip. The challenge of Solidarity in Poland in the summer of 1980 made the Kremlin even more determined to stand firm.

Soviet fears will not quickly dissipate. The USSR possesses the longest borders of any country in the world, 37,000 miles, surrounding an area three times as big as the United States and twice as large as China. Most of its population lives west of the Ural mountains, leaving only a few million in Siberia directly north of the one billion people of China. No mountains or rivers prevent invasion from the West; for centuries invaders have included: Livonians, Poles, Swedes, Teutons, Frenchmen, Nazis, Turks. The first and most brutal invasion, the Mongol Golden Horde from the east, left scars still visible today. It subdued the city states around Moscow and to the south for two centuries. It taught the Russian tsars who followed it to be equally domineering and hard. As in the past, so it is today; the Kremlin feels it must concentrate on armaments to a degree that the West finds excessive, expansionist, and threatening.

It is tempting to believe that the search for *klass* could loosen the Soviet system; however, *klass* will remain for the moment just one more control mechanism in the Party's hands. If change in the Russians had in the past ever come from beneath, from the grass roots, it would be more plausible to say that *klass* might force the Party to be more responsive to its people and to the West. While this cannot be entirely ruled out, it seems more likely that the Party will continue to dole out *klass* privileges for the rest of this century much as it does today.

Certainly, *klass* pushes individuals further and further away from the official ideology of the Soviet State, but most Russians are more pragmatists than theoreticians. They are accustomed to a single central authority (once the tsar, now the Party), to endless red tape, to imposed order. Authority moves from top to bottom, from center to edge.

Most of the Rising Class, for all its fascination with the West, is not watching breathlessly for the day of political liberation, or to emigrate. The average family wants the better things of Western life, but still believes to some extent at least in the negative aspects of the West presented by the official media: crime, pornography, drug addiction, exploitation. Most Soviet people, the Rising Class included, are accustomed to others making decisions for them and to the government's providing job security, cheap housing, and free education. The notion of taking democratic responsibility for their own lives—apart from searching for greater privilege—is beyond their experience.

Except in the very early years of the Revolution, in the minds of activists like Lenin and Trotsky, "Marxism" has remained abstract to most Russians. It hardly exists as a living force today, except as something requiring lip service and formal, perfunctory study before any significant Party, military, or police promotion can be achieved or any academic or cultural achievement officially recognized.

Skillfully, the Party has identified itself with patriotism. Russians have never known any system other than their own. They cannot travel or make their own comparisons with other systems. They can see the shortcomings in their own system, and they wield the weapons of *klass* to overcome them, but still they are proud of their country, and they love it with a deep, mystical fervor as their "Motherland." The average Russian (if indeed there is such a person) may find Marxism and Leninism distant and abstract, but he finds his own country and its position in the world to be, on the whole, a source of pride. He accepts his own system, with all its faults, as normal. He does not know, for he is not allowed to know, any other in detail. "We defeated Hitler," you hear people say, "and we can do more things, and achieve more . . ."

For the moment, the Party doesn't fear *klass*. It uses it. If the Party can no longer limit its access to a few, as it did up to World War II, then it can (and does) ensure that its growth remains slower than in any other industrial country in the world. If the Party cannot blot out all the Western world's ideas, it does its best to filter them. It succeeds so well that the USSR today remains (as it has always been) remote from the mainstream of European (and American) thought.

The Party is helped by the fact that in many ways the Soviet Union today remains what Russia was before 1917: not only a land bridge between Europe and Asia, but a collection of peoples who often display cultural traits and economic behavior that are more common in Asia than in Europe. Russians are more communal by nature, more family-centered, more ready to barter than to buy, slower to change in social affairs, than most Europeans. Their hygiene (or lack thereof), their penchant for open bribery, their preference for dealing with family and friends rather than with strangers, their emotion and openness within family–friend circles, and their hostility to those outside them . . . all this smacks of Asian, and often Middle Eastern, ways rather than Western European ones.

Klass is one way millions upon millions of Russians and Ukranians and Uzbeks and others clamber over, around, and under the ill-planned, badly made, coughing and spluttering engine of the Soviet economic system. The engine doesn't work properly. *Klass* is the lubrication that keeps at least some of its cogs and pistons ticking over.

Nor should it be forgotten that, although the West has focused on the aspects of purge, famine, war, and dictatorship in the Soviet Union since 1917, the Party has a number of achievements to which it can point, and for which it takes credit.

Since 1917 an illiterate, mostly Asian and rural people has seen its country become a military superpower preoccupying the strategic thinking of the mighty United States itself, though the human cost of achieving that superpower status has been awesome. The Party wraps itself skillfully in the flag. It identifies itself with a semimystical patriotism. It claims credit for the defeat of Hitler's armies and hardly mentions Allied aid.

Soviet citizens today believe that they eat and live better

than their parents. Stalin's buildup of heavy industry created millions of new urban blue-collar and white-collar jobs, vastly expanding upward mobility in the Urban Class and sowing the seeds of the urban phenomenon of the Rising Class.[7]

The Party continues to stress the growth of heavy industry and to take the high ground of glory for the "Motherland." Despite the obvious flaws in the system, and the sometimes wishful thinking of Western conservatives, the country offers little support for the view that it is on the verge of a second Russian Revolution. The barricades are unmanned. The cannon is silent.

One of the best images to describe what is happening in the Soviet Union today comes from historian and semidissident Roy Medvedev. He saw Soviet society under Stalin as a huge lake frozen down to its bed. The lake is still covered with ice today, he believes, and it looks as though little has changed. Beneath the surface, however, the ice is no longer solid. New currents have caused some of it to yield. Using the same analogy, the surface ice of the Party control is not about to melt. It is still firm. But it does not reach down as deep.

The process of seeking and retaining *klass* is one of the new currents, moving gradually faster, eating away at the ice above.

One result may be to create pressure on future Soviet rulers to divert more economic resources to consumer areas. Light industry could benefit. The military and heavy industry might have to make do with less, though they will remain high-priority areas. Even with Party discipline, more people will become dissatisfied with lines and shortages. They will be less willing to sacrifice new standards of living in the name of old ideas. Shortages of meat and other foods could become less tolerable, forcing the Party either to produce more grain or to spend even more hard currency abroad to buy it. As more and more people join the Rising Class, the Party will have to use more resources to feed, clothe, and house them in better style. Expectations keep rising.

* * *

Major shifts did not come from the layer oi rulers once led by Konstantin U. Chernenko and now in their sixties and seventies. More likely to seek change is the next layer down—men of the age of the new General Secretary of the Communist Party, Mikhail Gorbachev, born in 1931, or of Leningrad Party boss Grigorii Romanov, born in 1923. Men like these have more formal education than their elders. Having grown up with *klass*, they take it for granted. They are less likely to believe that it can be suddenly restricted or abolished without risking social upheaval. They will continue to give priority to the military and to heavy industry, but they will have to devote more resources to the demand for a middle-class existence. Will that make the new leaders more willing to negotiate and deal with the West, or less? Much depends on the answer.[8]

It seems to me that Washington would do well to keep in mind the search for *klass*, and to do what it can to nurture and reward it. Little can be achieved overnight. Nothing can be done by constantly talking down to the Kremlin, by calling it a cheat and a liar and the center of an evil empire. Such words reinforce the Party's own claim that the United States does not take the Soviet Union seriously or accord it the respect for which the Kremlin longs. They hardly induce the Kremlin to consider, let alone to offer, real concessions in any field. The big verbal stick just doesn't work. It is counterproductive.

The West should keep its military defenses strong. That is vital. Anything less would be treated not as conciliation but as weakness by the Kremlin. The West could also patiently and persistently shape its trade and cultural exports (détente permitting) so as to make high-profile consumer goods more available. Yes, many of them would trickle down no further than the top layers of *klass*. No, their influence will not unleash a grassroots passion for democracy. Yet actual Western influence on Soviet behavior is now, as it has always been, extremely limited—much more limited than many American politicians seem to believe. It is right to lead from armed strength (though not always right to keep on proclaiming that fact in public) but it is also right to lead from the strength of Western ideas, and the personal comforts, style, fulfillment, dignity, efficiency, and free time achievements, they generate. Individual Russians want the fruits of Western ideas— eagerly, openly. Their Party is determined to ration those ideas to favored classes and subclasses. The West has no easy way to help people against Party—but such a goal ought to be clearly held in view.

Better for the new generation of Soviet leaders already moving to power following the death, in March 1985, of Konstantin U. Chernenko, to concentrate on preserving the *klass* system than to risk blowing up our system and their own.

Part of the power of the West is in its constant flow of ideas, new and old. The extent of that power is understood by the Kremlin, which reacts to it with ambivalent fear and respect. This was well illustrated during one of the most fascinating periods I spent in Moscow: the months leading up to, and including, the Summer Olympic Games of July and August 1980.

On the one hand, the Kremlin wanted the Games as a prestige symbol: as calculated propaganda to fill the television screens and living rooms of the West and the Third World with glowing, color, moving pictures of Soviet achievements. On the other hand, the Kremlin understood that foreigners bring alien ideas with them. They knew that the five cities chosen to host Olympic events—Moscow, Leningrad, Tallinn, Minsk, and Kiev—would be crowded with tourists. For months, Moscow Party chief Viktor Grishin made speeches saying that the Soviet Union had been awarded the Games in the first place in recognition of the country's "principled" foreign policy. (When I asked a Soviet official why Los Angeles had been awarded the Summer Games for 1984, he looked surprised and professed not to see the point of the question.) Grishin added that all Muscovites must beware of foreign spies smuggling in dangerous and inflammatory propaganda in false-bottomed suitcases and even in special pockets in their underwear.

Thousands of out-of-town police were brought in to patrol the central city area for three weeks. Trucks that normally came into or through the city were stopped and turned back at the outer ring road. Sidewalks were cleared of all but a handful of local residents. Traffic all but disappeared. So did the spontaneity and good humor of Olympics Games in the past. A number of known dissidents were told they could not leave their apartments, in case they tried to stage incidents for foreign television crews.

The Kremlin wants the prestige of being part of the wider world, but without fresh currents of thought circulating through its intellectually isolated population. Yet it cannot have one without the other. Part of the challenge to the West is to keep those currents flowing, to stimulate the growing awareness that life is better "out there." It can only be a long-range hope.

Can we encourage the Soviet Rising Class to expand and rise even further? Can we gradually increase its appetite for Western goods, living standards, ideas, aspirations?

For, taking a long, long view, the search for *klass*, as materialistic and grasping and self-centered as it may be, focuses attention on human beings rather than on the formalisms of state and ideology. Ultimately, then, it works not to strengthen Party control, but to undermine it.

In 1982 I flew back to Moscow for a few days with my wife, Margaret. She was gathering material on Russian ballet and folk-dance tradition, which she admires. I was curious to see how the city had changed.

Outwardly, the city lay gray and somber under iron clouds. Its larger-than-life Soviet scale of twelve-lane highways and angular modern buildings surrounded the ancient Russian glories of Kremlin domes and the Byzantine beauty of St. Basil's Cathedral. Moscow wore the unfinished air I remembered so well: untended lots between buildings, walls crying out for a coat of paint, buildings still under construction years after they were begun.

Our Russian friends were also almost unchanged: emotional, warm, voluble, stoic, showy, proud, vulnerable, grasping, all at the same time. Avidly they drank in details about how we lived, but flushed with pride in their own country every now and then. Envy mingled with patriotism. The struggle between the two lent their attitudes, their lives, their thoughts, a tension and a restlessness that characterize the new Rising Class.

Men and women alike told us of new possessions with glee. Sitting once more in their shortage-plagued society, feeling my own world recede far over the horizon, I sensed once again the impact and the importance of such possessions in the Soviet context: an imported Volkswagen bus bought by a pair of Bolshoi dancers; a new silver tea strainer that hung from the teapot spout, picked up in a local jeweler's shop to celebrate a wedding anniversary; new winter coats and boots. It was reminiscent of the race to consumerism in America in the 1950s, and in Europe in the 1960s.

In one conversation, which could have been lifted directly from New York or London, we were told about the twelve-year-old daughter of a scientist who had badgered her mother unmercifully until she was allowed to have her ears pierced. Her local school forbade earrings, but so great had been the pressure from the pupils that the school now permitted its students to wear the tiniest studs. Schoolgirls, we found, were sighing over the Leningrad pop singer Mikhail Boyarsky. They still wildly coveted Western jeans.

The trappings of privilege were everywhere. A skilled dressmaker came to the apartments of certain senior officials with her own East German sewing machine to run up a flattering dress in a single day. She worked directly on the premises and charged 300 rubles, twice the monthly salary of an average worker. I drove again past the elite restaurant reserved for members of the Academy of Sciences of the USSR on Lenin Prospect—seven double, white-curtained windows stretching southward along the block that begins with Gubkin Street. There was no sign, nothing to mark it out as a place of privilege. Further along the block was a special food shop, also unmarked, with five double windows facing the street painted white up to eye-level. Cold-storage food chests visible through one window held fresh meat, fruit, and vegetables for the elite.

One set of friends told me that burglary, held by official propaganda to be purely a product of capitalism and the class divide, was increasing in Moscow. When I visited them, several militia men (police) were camped in their apartment, hoping to capture a gang of criminals thought to be from Georgia. One of its members had recently been captured with a list of potential burglary targets in his pocket. The gang had already made several hauls; our friends regaled me with details of other gangs and their modus operandi, including one group that gained access to apartments by posing as a medical team on an emergency call: told they had come to the wrong apartment, one member, dressed in the white uniform of a nurse, asked if she could come in for a moment to telephone her hospital.

While Margaret stayed on to finish her research, I left the new bourgeoisie searching out still more privileges, and drove back to Sheremetyevo Airport for the four-hour flight back to the older and more familiar class structure of Britain. The Boeing 737 took off and swung westward over forests and lakes as I strained at a window to see all I could in the grayness of the late afternoon. Much of the sky was lidded in low cloud, but through one break a shaft of sunlight poured down onto buildings and streets in central Moscow. The sun was like a theatrical spotlight, throwing a circle of light onto a huge and mostly shadowy stage. The light held steady as the

Boeing climbed higher, and I carried its image with me. It seemed for that moment a symbol of the contrasts I had observed in the Soviet Union for so long: wide areas of society gray with lack of privilege, and in the center the illuminated beginnings of a newer existence for millions of people searching for *klass*, for a better, more individual form of expression and life.

I look for no early change inside the USSR, but my mind goes back to the remarkable Marquis de Custine:

> The Customs has no power over thought; armies cannot exterminate it; ramparts cannot stop it; it goes underground; ideas are in the air; they are everywhere, and ideas change the world.[9]

ABOUT THE AUTHOR

David K. Willis was born in Melbourne, Australia. Educated in Sydney, he joined the *Sydney Morning Herald* in 1956 as a copy boy, rose to cadet (trainee) reporter, and spent a year in Melbourne as the *Herald*'s assistant interstate representative in 1958. In 1961 he was sent to the newspaper's New York bureau, and joined the *Christian Science Monitor* in New York in mid-1964. He was transferred to Washington, D.C., early in 1965, served as State Department correspondent until January 1969, and in 1967–68 appeared as a regular panelist on the first ninety programs of PBS-TV's "Washington Week in Review."

After a tour in Tokyo and Seoul as Northeast Asia correspondent, he became the *Monitor*'s National News Editor in October 1970, coordinating and editing the paper's national file from every state until July 1976, when he began a four-and-a-half year assignment as Moscow bureau chief. While in Moscow he also broadcast for CBS radio, then NBC radio (for which he covered the Moscow Summer Olympics in 1980), National Public Radio, the British Broadcasting Corporation, and the Australian Broadcasting Commission. He contributed regular articles to *MacLean's* magazine in Canada.

Mr. Willis holds a B.A. degree from the University of Sydney and an M.A. in international relations from New York University. In 1981 he won the Edward Weintal prize for diplomatic reporting from the Georgetown University Institute for the Study of Diplomacy in Washington, D.C., for a final series of five articles about the USSR. The Overseas Press Club of New York gave him its 1981 Bob Considine award for best daily newspaper or wire service interpretation of foreign affairs for his Soviet series and for another series on the spread of nuclear weapons around the world.

He is currently the *Monitor*'s Third World correspondent, traveling widely in Africa, Asia, and Latin America from his home in Surrey in the U.K., where he lives with his wife, Margaret, who studied ballet in Russia and is a dance teacher and writer. They have three children: Sarah, Alexandra, and Alastair. He currently broadcasts for the BBC from London on both domestic and World Service programs.

NOTES

Chapter 1

1. The nuances of social distinctions were as natural to imperial Russia as water and air. Everyone knew whom to address as "Excellency"; which ranks could wear white-trousered uniforms and which could not; which were able to transmit rank (*chin*) to its children; which had money, and which pretended to have it. Everyone knew that if a man gained the lowest (fourteenth) rank in the civil service (letter carrier, clerk) or in the military officer corps (cornet, or second lieutenant), he at once scrawled the figure *14* on the door of his home to show not only his imperially acknowledged status, but that he could now invoke the law to protect himself. The vast mass of population without *chin* could be beaten or cheated with virtual impunity.

When a boy was born in the sleepy river town of Simbirsk on April 22, 1870, and named Vladimir Ilyich Ulyanov, he was the grandson of a serf. But he was also the son of a man who had risen through the ranks to become an inspector of schools, eventually reaching Rank 4. The boy grew up in a large house with a cherry orchard and a court for croquet. He took the name of Lenin, and the revolution of 1917, aimed at sweeping away the world of class, was led not by a peasant, or by a worker, but by a member of the privileged elite with *chin*.

Lenin's shimmering ideal was to eliminate social class. His concept, taken from Marx, was that class divisions sprang from the state itself because the state was, by definition, an oppressor. Do away with the state, he preached, and class warfare would fade. The reverse would also be true: remove class frictions and the state must wither. The theory is elegant, but quite false. While Soviet divisions today are not "classes" in the accepted Western sense, since they are not based on the private ownership of land or on inherited wealth,

329

they do meet perhaps the most important definition of class: cleavages of economic position, power, and opportunity, and inequalities of opportunity.

2. Approximate sizes of the Rising Class and other classes mentioned are based on my own study of Soviet statistics (especially the annual *Narodnoe Khozyaistvo* since 1976), as well as such cross-references as demographer Murray Feshbach (Bureau of the Census, U.S. Commerce Department, Washington, D.C.); the helpful *Privilege in the Soviet Union* (Allen and Unwin, 1978), by Mervyn Mathews of the University of Surrey; and Herwig Kraus of Radio Free Europe/Radio Liberty in Munich.

Mathews estimates a top elite of some 227,000, using as criteria salaries above 450 rubles per month. The national average is said officially to be around 160 rubles per month. I emphasize status, rank, and access to privilege; money, at least at the higher levels of Soviet society, is a byproduct of *klass*.

The 23 million for the Rising Class is a figure for workers only and is reached by totaling Soviet figures for various substrata: 10 million of what Soviet officials call "engineers" (specialists of various kinds, together with farm directors and animal husbandry experts); 3.7 million in science and education; 1.1 million in medicine; 100,000 legal experts; 400,000 in communications; 1.5 million in trade, food, and storage; 3.8 million planners and supervisors; 2 million state and economic "administrators." I have rounded the total to the higher number and have lowered some of the figures somewhat in the hope of balancing the official Soviet practice of using figures to gild lilies.

The Soviet Union is in good company in possessing class distinctions, of course. Even such outwardly egalitarian countries as Australia and West Germany have their prestigious strata of high civil servants, doctors, surgeons, business tycoons, and others. The Japanese have their subtle distinctions; the Indians have their castes high and low.

In the U.S. itself, a recent study (Richard P. Coleman and Lee Rainwater, *Social Standing in America: New Dimensions of Class,* Basic Books, 1978), found no fewer than seven layers: the old rich with aristocratic family names; the new rich; the college-educated professional class and managers; the comfortable middle class; the middle class just getting by; the poor but working lower class; and the nonworking welfare poor.

Britain retains a strong awareness of its own ancient class divisions. The USSR is late in coming to a delineated class structure, but it is coming nonetheless.

By the last half of the nineteenth century, less than 1.5 percent of the Russian population was included in the one rank that really counted—the *dvorianye* (from the word *dvor*, or court), the Table of Ranks. Only 10 percent of them actually owned land worked by serfs; the rest were, by European standards, dirt poor. By 1979, a century later, the Top, Rising, and Military Ranks in the allegedly class-less Soviet Union totaled roughly 24 million officials, officers, and workers—almost 17 percent of the work force. The figure includes many wives, since more than 90 percent of women work, but even if the figure is only doubled to take account of other family members, it still works out to almost 18 percent of the population as a whole (46 million out of 265 million).

So the percentage of people laying claim to *klass* has gone up under communism, not down. A "victory" for the system—or a refutation of Marx and Lenin? The latter, I believe.

3. The figure for the Military Officer Class is reached by using Professor John Erickson's estimate of one officer to every five men. If we assume that each officer has a wife and one child (leaving aside aged parents), the total number of people enjoying the benefits of Military Officer Class membership is, conservatively, 2.4 million.

4. Two reasons the Rising Class is gathering momentum are an increasing knowledge of the West by those in the bigger cities, and a general desire to leave behind an era of the bleakest war, famine, death, and chains. The years 1910 to 1950 are the most terrible in Russian history. After Lenin died, Stalin vanquished his rivals and killed, jailed, or exiled the cream of the country's farmers. He told Winston Churchill in 1942 that 10 million kulaks had been involved, and that "the great bulk . . . were wiped out by their laborers." (Churchill, *The Second World War*, vol.4, Houghton Mifflin, 1950, pp.498–499.) Robert Conquest estimates (*The Great Terror*, Pelican, 1971, p.710) that those killed during the purges of the 1930s and in the postwar years totaled at least 12 million.

This is not to say that Soviet elites are all straining at the leash, ready to rush to the West the moment barriers fall. They might go and see the rest of the world, but they would then return to their beloved birch trees and open spaces, their dark bread and their vodka and collective lives. It is to say that although the Rising Class feels it lives better than its parents, it is still not satisfied. The more it gets, the more it wants, in the manner of upward-driving middle classes everywhere.

5. Alexander Galich's surprise is related by Norwegian artist Victor Sparre in his book *The Flame in the Darkness* (Grosvenor Books,

1980, p.68). Sparre is a longtime supporter of Soviet dissidents and friend of Alexander Solzhenitsyn.

Sparre also tells of Galich's falling through the bottom of his bed and onto the floor on the first night he spent alone outside of Oslo after emigrating from the USSR. Galich rang Sparre the next morning: "We must get a carpenter immediately." Sparre said he would come and fix it himself. When he did, he asked for a hammer he had already loaned Galich. The Russian brought it, "staring at it as though it was a snake which he did not know whether to take by the head or the tail. All that was needed were a couple of nails to hold the struts in place. The next morning again he rang me in delight, obviously more impressed by my carpentry than by my painting. I slept wonderfully all night,' he assured me. You are a Leonardo da Vinci.'" Sparre's comment: "The next time I go to the land of the Hammer and Sickle, I shall take my own hammer."

6. This turning away from contemporary reality is well presented and analyzed by *New York Times* correspondent David K. Shipler— whose own four years in Moscow overlapped mine—in his book *Russia: Solemn Idols, Broken Dreams* (Times Books, 1983).

7. The de Tocqueville quotation is from his *Democracy in America*, ed. P. J. Mayer, vol.I (Anchor/Doubleday, 1969), p.413.

Chapter 2

1. Some 100 million of the 136 million work force in 1978 reportedly used factory canteens (*Kommunist*, organ of the Communist Party of the Soviet Union, 1979, vol. 13, pp.34–45). The most prestigious plants provided the best food: autos, electronics, oil production. Yet the average canteen remains below Western standards; ready-processed foods are rare, and even *Kommunist* acknowledged the lack of incentive to produce cheap and well-prepared food when the sole criterion of performance remained *val*, or gross takings in rubles.

2. Information from my own Soviet sources.

3. The hunger for such delicacies by writers whose only talent was owning a union card was derided by the brilliant Mikhail Afanasievich Bulgakov, who wrote his epic novel *The Master and Margarita* between 1930 and 1938. He describes the menu of those years in chapter 5.

4. Another joke Muscovites told in 1980: a heavily publicized film

was issued by the Party about growing grain in the Virgin Lands of Kazakhstan, called *Vkus Khleba* (*The Taste of Bread*). The joke was that a sequel was being made, to be called *Zapakh Myasa*—*The Smell of Meat*.

5. Craig Whitney, the *New York Times*, reprinted in the *International Herald Tribune*, 1980.

6. Information from Soviet travelers in Tula at the time. Tula figures in another ironic Soviet story, which also refers to the way the Party honors cities for bravery against the Germans decades after the event: "Is it possible," a man asks a friend, "to travel by horse from the Hero City of Moscow to the Hero City of Kiev?"

"In principle, yes," replies the friend. "In practice, no. The horse would be eaten when it reached the Hero City of Tula."

Chapter 3

1. Examples of the new bourgeoisie's flaunting *klass* privilege and consumer goods are presented here without intention to criticize; after all, they are small compared to the snobbery and nouveau-riche attitudes of Western countries. All examples come from contacts of, or known to, my wife Margaret and myself.

2. It was about Brezhnev that one heard this joke: his mother came from the Ukraine to Moscow to visit him, and his huge ZIL limousine picked her up at the airport. Servants took her luggage. Her son showed her the treasures of the tsars, then led her to his Aeroflot plane for a flight to his palatial dacha on the Black Sea. She gazed at the swimming pool and the chandeliers, but said nothing. "What's the matter, Mamochka?" Brezhnev asked. "Don't you like it all?"

"Oh yes, Lyonya," the old woman replied nervously. "It's wonderful, but what will happen when the communists come?"

3. Prices for rugs rose 50 percent in January 1977 and another 50 percent in July 1979; gold jewelry and coins (though not, to our friends' relief, gold fillings for teeth) jumped 60 percent in 1978 and 50 percent more in 1979, partly reflecting world prices; better-bound books rose in 1977; car prices went up by 18 percent between 1977 and 1979; evening meals in restaurants rose 25 to 40 percent. Official Soviet prices are set by a special prices unit and generally fail to reflect supply and demand, though they sometimes do.

4. Custine, *La Russie en 1839*, translated by Phyllis Penn Kohler, whose work is entitled in English *Journey for Our Time*, p.58.

Chapter 4

1. *Ivankiad*, Vladimir Voinovich, Farrar, Straus and Giroux, 1977.

2. A Ukrainian factory worker told me he paid 5 rubles 90 kopeks a month, plus another 7 rubles 10 kopeks for utilities. In Moscow, a friend paid 17 rubles 62 kopeks (at the time, $26.50) a month for three rooms thirty minutes from Red Square; electricity and heating cost him four rubles a month more (steam radiators); telephones were two rubles. That came to about 14 percent of the average monthly wage. Both husband and wife worked, so the percentage of their combined income was even lower.

3. Sasha Levich is by no means alone in feeling that some origins are better than others. Many of the 290 or so members of the Party Central Committee claim to come from simple beginnings, but at the beginning of 1978, only two actually worked on a farm at the time they were appointed. When children of rural families in Novosibirsk were asked if they wanted to stay on the land, only 12 percent of graduate high schoolers said yes. *Klass* can also mean particular jobs; in the big cities, surveys show children see *klass* in physics, chemistry, math, some branches of engineering, and in medical specialists—surgeons, professors, researchers. The military itself is not popular with urban elites, especially the draft; but space scientists and cosmonauts retain a certain glamour. So do air force test pilots.

Chapter 5

1. Information about Soviet ballet in this book is based on articles by Margaret E. Willis, 1979–82, including "Bolshoi Ballet—Why There's Discontent," the *Christian Science Monitor*, international edition, February 22, 1982, and her articles in British dance magazines.

2. For some of these details I am indebted to Efim Slavinsky, an authority on Soviet and non-Soviet literary scenes who emigrated from Leningrad several years ago and who now works for the Russian Service of the British Broadcasting Corporation in London.

3. Solomon Volkov, *Testimony: The Memoirs of Dmitri Shostakovich*, Harper and Row, 1979, pp.133, 134, 156.

4. Stalin set up a vast network of movie theaters as a way of spreading the Party line. Today, knowing someone who can procure

a ticket to an exclusive showing in the raked, comfortable auditorium on an upper floor of Dom Kino, the House of Film, or film workers union club, is a definite and coveted sign of *klass* status.

I knew of more than one senior Soviet official who exulted in the *klass* of owning a videocassette player flown in from New York or brought back by a high-ranking friend. These officials sit high above Moscow streets in exclusive apartment blocks watching cassettes of *Jesus Christ, Superstar, Grease, Jaws,* and other popular Western material also brought in through private channels. Pornography was also favored on cassette.

Chapter 6

1. Marina Voikhanskaya spoke to me at length in her home in Cambridge, England. Volodya, the Russian who preferred connections to money, was another acquaintance of mine.

2. In fact, wage differentials in the Soviet Union, while not as pronounced or wide as in the U.S., compare remarkably well with those in many Western countries. According to Peter Wiles, in his *Distribution of Income, East and West* (North Holland, 1974), the top 10 percent of Soviet incomes by the mid-1960s were an estimated six times higher than the lower 10 percent. It was a narrower gap than in the United States at the time, but wider than Britain and Sweden. After Leonid Brezhnev raised the pay of collective farm workers, the Soviet wage gaps narrowed somewhat, but remained surprisingly large into the 1980s: twelve to one between a marshal of the armed forces and an average worker.

3. Peter Hann worked for *Business Week* magazine. He also found a thirty-three-year-old section chief at a polyethylene plant earning 265 rubles a month, plus an extra month's bonus each year and two weeks' vacation in a resort for a mere 8 rubles. The man owned a 1975 Moskvich sedan he bought with his father for 6,000 rubles, and his wife earned 155 rubles a month in the broadcasting industry.

4. George Feiffer, *Our Motherland,* Viking, 1974. Feiffer took 50 percent of Plisetskaya's booking fees abroad and allowed her (at the end of the 1960s) only 100 dollars a performance. Margot Fonteyn was earning $2,500 a performance in those days; Bolshoi defector Alexander Godunov was said to command $10,000 each time he danced (William Como, editor, *Dance* magazine, New York, January 1982, p.28). Nureyev, Baryshnikov, and Makarova earn much more.

5. See Mervyn Mathews, *Privilege in the Soviet Union*, Allen and Unwin, 1978.

Chapter 7

1. Mervyn Mathews, *Privilege in the Soviet Union*, p.82. Lenin himself, not given to personal flamboyance, did acquire a Rolls-Royce, which was fitted with rubber caterpillar tracks for use in heavy snow. It is on show in Leninskiye Gorky, 34 kilometers from Moscow.

2. U.S. figures from the Motor Vehicle Manufacturers' Association, Detroit.

3. Commentator Lev Belkin answered an Algerian reader of the weekly *Moscow News* about car ownership in 1978 by saying, in part, that "our main policy is the development of public transport, and not that of individuals. Using private cars for business trips in large and medium-sized cities has little effect, but it creates a number of problems and harms the environment. . . ." The Moscow Metro is clean and efficient, with trains every three minutes from 6 A.M. to 1 A.M.

4. Here is a list of car prices tacked to a notice board in the wooden trailer in the Novodevichy lot in June 1979 (one ruble equal to about $1.50):

			rubles
Volga	GAZ	24-02	18,150
	GAZ	24	15,550
Zhigul	VAZ	2102	6,636 (station wagon)
	VAZ	21014	6,666
	VAZ	21022	7,436
	VAZ	21024	7,466
	VAZ	2103	8,732
	VAZ	2106	9,232
	VAZ	21011	7,336
	VAZ	2121	10,396
	VAZ	2111	10,365
Zaphorozhets		9680	5,300
Moskvich		2138	6,717
		2140	7,417
		21046	7,279

5. Officially, rubles may not be taken out of the Soviet Union since they are a nonconvertible currency, but Geneva and Vienna listed exchange rates on airport bank boards anyway. In fact, Soviet authorities play fast and loose with rubles for political reasons. Brand-new ruble bills can be bought in Switzerland and Austria, and are brought back into the USSR by small third-world embassies whose diplomatic support Moscow is anxious to keep against the United States and China. Some embassies, including North Korea and some black African and Arab states, can buy rubles cheaply abroad and use them in Moscow, in effect receiving a subsidy on running costs. I know of no expert who can explain the presence of new rubles in Europe except through Soviet connivance. Tourists do not take them out of the Soviet Union because they cannot be used anywhere else.

6. George Feiffer, *The Sunday Times*, London, July 20, 1980.

7. Konstantin Simis, former lawyer and Ministry of Justice researcher in Moscow, in "The Machinery of Corruption in the Soviet Union," *Survey*, vol.23, no.4, Autumn 1977–78, p.51.

8. Ibid, p.40.

9. Toli Welihozkiy, "Automobiles and the Soviet Consumer," U.S. Joint Economic Committee of Congress, October 10, 1979.

Chapter 8

1. A word about maids: the *domashnaya rabotnitsa* (literally, "home woman worker") is a holdover from before 1917. When apartments were smaller than today, they lived in the kitchen or in the corner of a bed-sitting room. They were usually young rural girls in the employ of engineers, actors, scientists, and other Russians of extreme *klass.* Employing them was technically illegal—a typically Russian "gray" area known and tolerated because of the influence of the families doing the employing. Fewer and fewer girls want to work as maids today, as is also the case in the West. So the painter we knew who had a cleaning woman twice a week, the university teacher whose parents had one, the translator whose cleaning woman came in from the country once a week—these people had even greater status in the early 1980s than when maids were more freely available.

2. Goldfarb talked to me in London in February 1982.

3. Reported in the journal *Sociological Research*, January 1980.

4. Many of these details come from a talk given by Margaret E. Willis to an international women's group in Moscow in 1980, and from her articles written for the *Christian Science Monitor*. Also helpful was Dede Albers and Harlow Robinson's "Moscow Adventure" (*Ballet News*, May 1981, p.15). Miss Albers studied at the Bolshoi School for ten months.

Chapter 9

1. Ronald Hingley, *The Russian Mind*, p.187.

2. Mikhail Stern, *La Vie Sexuelle en U.R.S.S.*, Paris, 1979.

3. From the Soviet census of 1979; women outnumbered men by 17.8 million because of decades of war and purges after 1917. The gap had narrowed from 20.7 million in 1959; for people aged fifty or less, males and females are now equally divided.

4. Elizabeth Pond, *Russia Perceived*, Gollancz, 1981, p.31. Andrei Sakharov counted the number of women for her from his personal Academy membership list.

5. I talked to Viktor Perevedentsev at the Institute of International Labor Movements of the USSR Academy of Sciences in Moscow, February 12, 1979.

According to the director of the USSR Central Statistical Administration, Professor L. M. Volodarsky (*Ekonomicheskaya Gazeta*, February 1979), the 1979 census recorded 66.3 million families averaging 3.5 persons in each. The figure apparently included in-laws as well as children. It is down from 3.7 persons in 1970. The number of families with between two and four members rose, while the number with five or more members fell.

6. For comparison, the U.S. recorded 1.18 million divorces in 1979 in a smaller population (227 million vs. 265 million). The U.S. divorce rate per 1,000 population was higher at 5.4 but divorce in ratio to marriage was the same: one in two. (Source: National Center for Health Statistics, U.S. Public Health Service.)

7. Soviet doctoral dissertation cited by Ralph Boulton, Reuters, December 16, 1980.

8. Confirmed to Ralph Boulton (Reuters) by Leonid Sharikov, the official who drew up the list of restricted jobs and a specialist with the State Committee on Labor.

Chapter 10

1. Dr. William Knaus, *Inside Soviet Medicine*, Everest House, 1981. Dr. Knaus's detailed book was helpful in writing this chapter, as was a meeting I had with him in Moscow during his research. I have also used U.S. budget figures from the Office of Management and Budget, U.S. Treasury Department; *Time* magazine's special issue on the USSR, June 23, 1980; and Soviet sources, official and unofficial, in and out of the USSR.

2. Knaus, op. cit., p.357.

3. Knaus, op. cit., p.57.

4. Feshbach has analyzed Soviet figures in *The Washington Post* (June 26, 1980) and in a landmark study with Christopher Davis, *Rising Infant Mortality in the U.S.S.R. in the 1970s* (September 1980, Bureau of Census, U.S. Department of Commerce).

5. Custine, *La Russie en 1839*, p.188.

6. Panov, *To Dance*, W. H. Allen, 1978, p.234.

7. Solovyov, "The Great Russian Saloon Series," *The American Spectator*, October 1981.

8. Viktor Suvorov, *The Liberators*, p.188.

9. Knaus, op. cit., p.356.

Chapter 11

1. Konstantin Simis, researcher in the Soviet ministry of justice for a decade, writing in *Survey*, vol.23, no.4, Autumn 1977–78.

2. A staff member of the International Labor Office in Geneva, Raffaele De Grazia, told the *International Herald Tribune* early in 1981 that the ILO was convinced the "clandestine economy" was "growing rapidly and continuously in most of the industrialized market economy countries." An official of the European Economic Community said efforts were being made to reduce it, but that "twilight earnings provide workers and employers relief from recession and inflexibilities in the labor laws which outlaw such work. . . ."

3. *Vchernyaya Moskva*, June 3, 1979, p.3.

Chapter 12

1. *Sunday Times* magazine, London, 1981, "In Search of the Missing Jews of Russia," with George Feiffer.

2. Hélène Carrère d'Encausse, *Decline of an Empire*, Newsweek Books, 1981, p.32.

3. Suvorov, *The Liberators*, p.163.

Chapter 13

1. *Khrushchev Remembers*, translated by Strobe Talbott, Penguin Books, 1977, pp.550 et seq.

2. Mervyn Mathews, *Privilege in the Soviet Union*, p.82.

3. Yakov Golovanov, *Komsomolskaya Pravda*, September 22, 1980. Translated by the *Current Digest of the Soviet Press*, vol. XXXI, no.39, pp.11–12.

Chapter 14

None.

Chapter 15

1. In a four-hour talk with me in Cambridge, England, in January 1981, Bukovsky told me that he spent twelve of his first thirty-five years in prisons, labor camps, and psychiatric hospitals before being freed in December 1976 in exchange for Chilean communist Luis Corvalán. Later he was received by President Carter in the White House in a meeting intended to symbolize the administration's commitment to human rights. After graduating in biology from King's College, Cambridge, he went to Stanford University in California to do graduate work.

2. Michael Voslensky, in *La Nomenklatura*, Paris, Pierre Belfond, 1980, estimates the total number of Moscow, republic, *oblast*, city, and country *nomenklatura* members at 1.5 million, and doubles the figure to include families. Total: 3 million or just over one percent of the population. See pp.148–150.

3. In 1979, the Central Committee included 66 *obkom* first secretaries, from Lvov in the Ukraine to Tyumen in western Siberia, where professional geologist Gennadi Bogomyakov was in charge. This was slightly more than half of the country's 120 *oblasts*; they included Yakutsk in eastern Siberia, and Kursk, Gorky, and Smo-

lensk in the west. Twenty-three more *oblast* leaders, their regions considered less important, sat as nonvoting Committee members; they included the Second Party Secretary in Leningrad and a first secretary in Belorussia. Four more were members of the Committee's so-called Auditing Commission. Thus, ninety-three *obkom* chiefs in all were appointed by Moscow, covering the cream of the country's territory and resources. Others' positions were confirmed by the Committee, which meant in effect that they could not be filled until the Committee had approved them.

4. Viktor Suvorov, *The Liberators*, pp.158–159.

5. Ibid., p.160.

6. In conversation with me in Moscow; Knight was a meticulous observer of the Soviet scene.

7. Khrushchev concedes that he made a mistake in not allowing Kapitsa to travel abroad during his own years in power; he asks Kapitsa's forgiveness in his memoirs (Penguin, vol.2, p.101).

8. Bohdan Harasymiw, "Nomenklatura: The Soviet Communist Party's Leadership Recruitment System," *Canadian Journal of Political Science*, vol. 2, December 1969, pp.493–512.

9. Konstantin Simis, "The Machinery of Corruption in the Soviet Union," *Survey*, vol. 23, no. 4, Autumn 1977–78, pp.42–49.

10. Custine, *La Russie en 1839*, p.117.

Chapter 16

1. Translated by Alan Myers in the *New York Review of Books*, February 19, 1981.

2. *Moscow News*, December 24, 1977.

3. Before 1917, not more than 3 or 4 percent of the population possessed significant class privilege. Today, 23.5 million qualify for the Rising Class, and another 2.4 million for the Military Officer Class. If each of these people has one parent living, and one child, then the number of citizens with access to *klass* privilege could be as high as 76 million, or one in four of the population of 265 million. It seems reasonable to assume that a minimum figure would be around 53 million, or one in five. Exact figures are not possible to ascertain.

About 150 years ago, the Marquis de Custine of France concluded his six months' traveling through tsarist Russia by coach with the view that the monarch possessed an "immense power of fermentation." Large numbers of his subjects wanted *klass* privilege desperately: "Tsar Peter inoculated all his people with the fever of ambition in order to make them pliable and to govern them as he liked; such a social organisation produced a fever of envy. . . ." (*La Russie en 1839*, p.117.)

4. Melor Sturua, who had spent many years as *Izvestia's* correspondent in the United States, was forbidden by the State Department to return to New York from vacation in the USSR in mid-1982. The move was taken in retaliation for the expulsion from Moscow of *Newsweek's* correspondent there, Andrew Nagorski. The Department said the Soviet action was entirely without justification.

5. *The Times* of London, August 1984.

6. Ceylon (Sri Lanka) became independent in 1948, Nigeria in 1960, and Ghana in 1956. Azerbaijan, Uzbekistan, and Turkmenia remain integral parts of the Soviet state. The Kremlin brands Western nations as "colonialist" with almost every breath. No debates are heard in the United Nations, however, about the need to free tsarist colonial appendages from the colonial rule of the Soviet Union.

7. Between 1939 and 1959, the number of persons employed in skilled labor in heavy industry rose 145 percent, from 7.5 to 18.3 million, and by another 63 percent to 29.9 million by 1970. White-collar workers with lower education rose 58 percent, to 10.7 million, between 1939 and 1959, and another 51 percent to 16 million by 1970. White-collar workers with higher education jumped 67 percent, to 8.1 million, between 1939 and 1959, and soared another 82 percent to 14.8 million by 1970. Meanwhile, the number of unskilled agricultural workers fell 5 percent, to 30.4 million, between 1939 and 1959, then 38 percent to 18.7 million by 1970.

See Jerry Hough and Merle Fainsod, *How the Soviet Union is Governed*, pp.564–565, for figures on the growth of white-collar and skilled-labor jobs between 1939 and 1970.

8. We do not know enough about the Romanov-Gorbachev generation to know whether it will in fact be more liberal, in Soviet terms. It could be argued that they will feel more vulnerable as their economy worsens and *klass* pressures build, and that therefore they might be less liberal at home and less confident abroad. Perhaps. I hope that the younger men will be more responsive to the pressures beneath them, not less.

Much will depend, of course, on how the West itself behaves in the years ahead, and what China does, and Japan. A harsh tone from the United States is not helpful. A better way to start would be a more thorough effort in the United States and in its schools to learn more about Soviet geography and history. Cultural and exchange visits are not rewards to Moscow, but a two-way street. The West suffers from swings of public emotion and mood, almost from week to week. The Soviet weakness is conservative, isolated suspicion and fear.

It seems to me vital for the United States to preserve a close unity with its main Western allies in NATO. Soviet strategy is to exploit every difference that arises, especially over nuclear arms control, and trade.

The Russians have genuine defense requirements as well as others that outsiders find excessive. They have the physical force to demand serious, responsible treatment. It is the task of diplomacy to distinguish between their legitimate concerns and their propaganda.

The United States needs a greater, more European, sense of Russian history and thought. Europe needs more respect for the U.S. superpower role in defense, more realism about Soviet Party propaganda and the diplomatic uses of military potential. These issues transcend individual leaders; the hard part is keeping them in view amid the daily clamor of headlines and events.

9. de Custine, *La Russie en 1839*, as translated by Phyllis Penn Kohler, p.215. I also go back to other statements by the marquis which are still relevant today: "Russia is no more than a conquering society; its strength is not in ideas, it is in war—that is to say, in ruse and ferocity" (p.214), and this paragraph as well (p.118):

> I see the colossus close at hand, and I have difficulty persuading myself that this creation of providence has for an end only diminishing the barbarism of Asia. It seems to me that it is mainly destined to castigate the evil civilization of Europe by a new invasion; eternal oriental tyranny threatens us endlessly, and we will suffer it if our extravagances and our iniquities make us deserve such a punishment.
>
> It is said that the Russians have nothing to teach us. That may be true; but they have a great deal to make us forget. Furthermore, are they not more capable of obedience and patience than we? In policy, the resignation of the people is the strength of the government.

BIBLIOGRAPHY

Books Consulted and Recommended

Azbel, Mark Ya. *Refusenik: Trapped in the Soviet Union*. London: Hamish Hamilton, 1982.

Bonavia, David. *Fat Sasha and the Urban Guerrilla: Protest and Conformism in the Soviet Union*. London: Hamish Hamilton, 1973.

Brokhin, Yuri. *Hustling on Gorky Street*. London: W. H. Allen, 1976.

Bronfenbrenner, Uri. *Two Worlds of Childhood: U.S. and U.S.S.R.* New York: Pocket Books, 1970.

Buckle, Richard (ed.). *U and Non-U Revisited*. New York: Viking Press, 1978.

Bukovsky, Vladimir. *To Build a Castle*. London: André Deutsch, 1978.

Bulgakov, Mikhail. *The Master and Margarita*, translated by Michael Glenny. London: Harvill Press, 1967.

Carrère d'Encausse. Hélène, *Decline of an Empire: The Soviet Socialist Republics in Revolt*. New York: Newsweek Books, 1981.

Census of 1979, All-Union, of the USSR, as analysed by the research staff of Radio Liberty, Munich, 1980.

Central Statistical Administration of the USSR, Moscow, selected publications.

Churchill, Winston S. *The Hinge of Fate: The Second World War*, vol. 4. Boston: Houghton Mifflin, 1950.

Conquest, Robert. *The Great Terror*. London: Pelican Books, 1971.

de Custine, Marquis. *Custine's Eternal Russia*, edited and translated by Phyllis Penn Kohler. Miami: Center for Advanced International Studies, 1976.

Feiffer, George. *Our Motherland*. New York: Viking, 1974.

Fitzlyon, Kyril, and Browning, Tatiana. *Before the Revolution: A View of Russia Under the Last Tsars*. London: Allen Lane, 1978.

Gerhart, Genevra. *The Russian's World, Life and Language.* New York: Harcourt Brace Jovanovich, 1974.

Giddens, Anthony. *The Class Structure of the Advanced Societies.* London: Hutchinson, 1981.

Grant, Nigel. *Soviet Education.* London: Penguin Books, 1979.

Gruliow, Leo. *Moscow.* Amsterdam: Time-Life International, 1977.

Hingley, Ronald. *The Russian Mind.* New York: Scribner's, 1977.

Hough, Jerry F. *The Soviet Prefects: The Local Party Organs in Industrial Decision-Making.* Cambridge, Mass.: Harvard University Press, 1969.

Hough, Jerry F., and Fainsod, Merle. *How the Soviet Union Is Governed.* Cambridge, Mass.: Harvard University Press, 1979.

Joint Economic Committee of Congress. Reports on the USSR, 1973–79.

Knaus, Dr. William A. *Inside Russian Medicine.* New York: Everest House, 1981.

Kourdakov, Sergei. *The Persecutor.* New Jersey: Spire Books, 1973.

Khrushchev, Nikita S. *Khrushchev Remembers,* edited and translated by Strobe Talbott, vols. I and II. London: Penguin Books, 1977.

Kung, Andres. *A Dream of Freedom.* Cardiff: Boreas Publishing House, 1980.

Lee, Andrea. *Russian Journal.* New York: Random House, 1982.

Louis, Victor and Jennifer. *The Complete Guide to the Soviet Union.* London: Michael Joseph, 1980.

Lyons, Marvin. *Russia in Original Photographs 1860–1920.* New York: Scribner's, 1977.

Massie, Robert K. *Peter the Great, His Life and World.* New York: Alfred A. Knopf, 1981.

Mathews, Mervyn. *Privilege in the Soviet Union: A Study of Elite Life-styles under Communism.* London: George Allen & Unwin, 1978.

Nagel's Encyclopaedia-Guide to the U.S.S.R. Geneva: Nagel Publishers, 1973.

Panov, Valery (with George Feiffer). *To Dance.* London: W. H. Allen, 1978.

Payne, Robert. *Lenin.* New York: Simon and Schuster, 1964.

Pipes, Richard. *Russia Under the Old Regime.* London: Penguin Books, 1979.

Pond, Elizabeth. *Russia Perceived: A Trans-Siberian Journey.* London: Victor Gollancz, 1981.

Shipler, David K. *Russia: Solemn Idols, Broken Dreams.* New York: Times Books, 1983.

Shostakovich, Dmitri. *Testimony,* As related to and edited by Solomon Volkov. New York: Harper and Row, 1979.

Soviet newspapers and periodicals: *Pravda, Izvestia, Literaturnaya Gazeta, Nedelya, Sovietskaya Kultura, Kommunist, Trud, Ekonomicheskaya Gazeta, Ogonyok, Sovietskaya Rossiya, Zarya Vostoka, Krasnaya Zvezda, Komsomolskaya Pravda.*

Sparre, Victor. *The Flame in the Darkness.* London: Grosvenor Books, 1980.

Stern, Mikhail. *La Vie Sexuelle en U.R.S.S.* Paris: Albin Michel, 1979.

Suvorov, Viktor. *The Liberators.* London: Hamish Hamilton, 1981.

de Tocqueville, Alexis. *Democracy in America,* translated by George Lawrence and edited by J. P. Mayer. New York: Anchor Books, 1969.

Veblen, Thorstein. *The Theory of the Leisure Class.* London: Penguin Books, 1979.

Voinovich, Vladimir. *Ivankiad.* New York: Farrar, Straus & Giroux, 1977.

Voslensky, Michael. *La Nomenklatura: Les Privilégiés in U.R.S.S.* Paris: Pierre Belfond, 1980.

Ware, Timothy. *The Orthodox Church.* London: Penguin Books, 1976.

Westergaard, John, and Resler, Henrietta. *Class in a Capitalist Society.* London: Penguin Books, 1980.

Wiles, Peter. *Distribution of Income, East and West.* Amsterdam: North Holland, 1974.

INDEX